Bound to Cooperate –
Europe and the Middle East

Sven Behrendt
Christian-Peter Hanelt (eds.)

Bound to Cooperate –
Europe and the Middle East

Bertelsmann Foundation Publishers
Gütersloh 2000

Die Deutsche Bibliothek – CIP-Einheitsaufnahme

A data set for this title is available at
Die Deutsche Bibliothek.

© 2000 Bertelsmann Foundation Publishers, Gütersloh
Editors: Sven Behrendt, Christian-Peter Hanelt
Copy editor: Sabine Stadtfeld
Production editor: Christiane Raffel
Cover design: werkzwei, Lutz Dudek, Bielefeld
Cover photo: Photodisc
Typesetting and print: Hans Kock Buch- und Offsetdruck GmbH, Bielefeld
ISBN 3-89204-502-X

Contents

Contents

Preface

At the turn of the century, Europe and the Middle East look like an odd couple. Their common historical experiences, geographical proximity, and economic interdependencies would deem it essential to develop closer political and economic relations. Yet, the two regions have rarely developed institutionalized forms of interaction on which more intensive relations could be based. The reasons for this are manifold: colonial history, nationalism, regionalism, and identity being only some of them. However, will the two regions be able to intensify their relations in the wake of the global transformation taking place? Will they be even ready to develop some modest forms of integration in order to be better equipped to meet the challenges of globalisation?

Developing a broad strategic vision for cross-regional interaction is one thing, identifying solutions for contemporary political and economic problems quite another. The Middle East peace process has yet to achieve broad Arab-Israeli reconciliation. Economic interaction is still limited, or at least one-sided. Comparatively few European companies enter the markets of the Middle East. Only a fraction of European exports are bound to go to this region. Political systems on the state as well as regional levels differ substantially as do political value systems. Migration causes fears and suspicions, but not intercultural curiosity. The list of obstacles to intensify cross-regional affairs could be lengthened in extenso; however, on the one hand one has to identify them, but on the other, one has to develop workable options to solving them.

For that reason, the Bertelsmann Foundation and the Bertelsmann Group on Policy Research at the Center for Applied Policy Research of the University of Munich initiated the project 'Europe and the Middle East' in 1994. Since then the project has pursued several strategic objectives. It has developed options and strategies for strengthening Euro-Middle Eastern political, economic, and social relations. It has sought to overcome the structural communication and information deficits among, as well as within, the two regions and tried to serve as a political ice breaker where formal diplomacy failed. It has sought to bridge the gap between the world of academic knowledge development and the world of decision making in politics and business.

The Kronberg Talks, gathering senior decision-makers from politics, business and the academic world from Europe, the Middle East and the USA served as the center of the project partners' efforts. The Kronberg Talks have been convened for five years now and have developed into a stable informal institution and a focal point for exchanging ideas, views and perceptions. They have always reflected the mood of the time and thus have been able to serve as a diplomatic safety net when regional relations have become strained.

To bring together high ranking political and economic leaders in Kronberg has been not enough to transport the strategic mission of the project into action. The project partners rather have an interest in contributing substantially to political dialogue among Europe, the

Middle East and the USA. The project therefore has developed options and strategies of regional and cross-regional cooperation on the basis of sound academic analysis with the support of an international network of political scientists and economists. They, in numerous workshops preparing the Kronberg Talks and at various stages, have provided the project with essential insight into the ramifications of Middle Eastern, European, and American politics shedding new light on a diverse and complex political, economic, and social environment. And several times, the project succeeded to bridge the gap between the world of academic insight and the world of political decision-making contributing to more differentiated thinking on both sides.

This volume reproduces their insight in the form of a collection of selected papers produced for the project. The contributions tackle a wide field ranging from regional security relations to the Middle East peace process, from the institutional constraints of EU foreign policy-making to transatlantic coordination of policy approaches and from the transformation of political and economic structures to legitimacy in the times of change. I hope that the public will appreciate this result of our work and value it as a substantial contribution to deepen cross-regional affairs.

I would like to take this opportunity to thank the publishers, the editors, and all those involved in this project for their great work. Beyond this, my particular thanks go to Gabi Schneider, Daniel Braun and David P. Schweikard for their support and research. I hope that this publication contributes to a better understanding among Europe and the Middle East and provides a basis for further debate of the issues at stake.

Professor Dr. Dr. h.c. Werner Weidenfeld
Member of the Board of the Bertelsmann Foundation
Director of the Center for Applied Policy Research (C · A · P), Munich

Introduction*

Sven Behrendt

Trends in international politics clearly indicate that global affairs are increasingly determined by a system of world regions. Regions integrate and become more cohesive; a process which at the same time enables states to pursue global interests from a strong home base. The relations among Europe, the Middle East and North Africa (MENA) are deeply affected by these trends and processes. Consequentially, taking up the question what the strategic options for structuring the emerging relations between Europe and the MENA region are, is not only an academic exercise but an operative necessity, if the normative goal is, as this volume seeks to, to make a substantial contribution to cross-regional stability.

This question becomes all the more relevant if one takes the structural imbalances between the two regions into account. Strategic

---

* Parts of this contribution were presented to various workshops and the Kronberg Talks at the project "Europe and the Middle East".

repositioning on the regional as well as the individual state level has dominated the relations between Europe and the MENA region in the 1990s. The EU has further pursued the process of integration, strengthening its institutional framework, and further deepening economic integration, most notably by introducing a common currency, the Euro within most of its member states. It is now on the way to strengthening its common foreign and security policy instruments. In the MENA region in contrast, integration has rarely if ever been a driving force moving political and economic relations. Rather, maintaining a regional balance of power among the constituent parts of a fragmented regional structure and the tendency to strengthen international alliances to improve regional positions have been the prevailing features of regional relations. In light of the geographical proximity, economic interdependencies, and shared historical experiences, however, from a European perspective, which this book is based on, two central questions arise: What interests does Europe pursue in the Middle East and North Africa? And how, if the goal of European policies is assumably to establish stable political, economic and social relations with its neighbours, could inter-regional relations best be organised? From an academic perspective, four assumptions of a viable European long-term strategic approach can be presented, leading the way to more stable cross-regional relations thereby fostering European interests:

The first one would start from the empirical finding that democracies rarely if ever go to war with each other.[1] Turning this finding onto its head, European contributions towards comprehensive democratisation processes of the Middle Eastern and North African countries in its human and social development as well as institutional dimension would have a pacifying effect on the region. Furthermore, democratic structures have proven to be efficient instruments of conflict resolution within states. Thus, contributions towards democrati-

---

1 Russett (1993).

sation of the Middle East and North African states are a fundamental strategic approach to achieve overall domestic and international stability in the long run. To be sure, all existing democratic systems adapted themselves to respective political legacies. Neglecting the specific political realities and traditions within the Southern Mediterranean countries would thus be a wrong operational conclusion. But stressing the principle that political transformation would have to point towards the establishment of democratic structures should remain at the center of European long-term approaches.

Second, free market economies and liberalised international trade relations improve overall standards of living. Given the stagnant economic systems in many countries of the MENA region, economic transformation has to be based on two principles: on the one hand on the need for the liberalisation of the internal economic systems of MENA countries in order to increase productivity. On the other, in its international dimension, on liberalisation of trade relations, openness for foreign private investment, and the like, as this will expose economies to international competition causing adaptation processes leading towards increasing productivity and economic growth in the long run. To be sure, in order to increase the impact of economic reform strategies, they must be complemented by an overhaul of social security and fiscal systems. Underdeveloped management skills, inefficient bureaucratic structures, the ineffectiveness of the rule of law are some other issues which need urgent attention.

Third, a framework of effective regional institutions provide mechanisms for peaceful conflict resolution processes. They lower the impact of international anarchy on the behaviour of states as they provide for a normative system of appropriate behaviour in interstate relations. They reduce transaction and information costs and thereby reduce the risk of misperception and misinterpretation causing irrational action. But as it is the case with regard to the first two points, theory is one side of the coin, political realities within and among the regions another. In a space as diverse as the Euro-

MENA region, international institutions will only succeed to display their intended function if they are established according to the principle of appropriateness, that is to provide an institutional problem solving framework where really needed.

Fourth, democratisation, economic development and integration, and international institution building must be supplemented by broader cultural dialogue. During the European integration process, Europeans realised that their relations were strained by different interpretations of political symbols and misunderstandings related to language and culture. What is essential for the creation of a common European identity, a broad cultural dialogue underpinning all levels of political, economic and social interaction, is a necessity for building a Mediterranean identity on which more stable cross-regional relations can be based.

These four principles are elements on which a more differentiated European strategic approaches towards the MENA region could be based. In order to achieve its goals, however, the European Union also needs to reconsider its own strengths and weaknesses and match interests with capabilities to fine-tune policies which it has developed in the past decades to structure cross-regional relations. In doing so, the EU can rely on four major assets. It is the dominant regional political and economic power, it has developed a culture of peaceful conflict resolution and negotiation, it maintains considerable military strength based on the collective potential of the EU member states, and it maintains strong cultural ties with the societies of the MENA region. On the other hand, Europe is still not a cohesive geopolitical unit. It has yet to define its political and social identity, and, consequentially, its global political interests. Furthermore, it will be preoccupied with Eastern European enlargement and reform of its own institutional framework in the coming years. Military integration and the development of a European defence identity have only just begun to be considered seriously.

Based on these strengths and weaknesses, it is in the interest of the EU to develop good neighbourly political, economic, social, and cultural relations with the individual countries of the MENA region and the region as a whole, based on mutual respect for respective identities. These goals can be realised by establishing appropriate fora of cross-regional conflict resolution, contributions to the ability of the respective political systems to adapt to international and domestic political changes and support efforts to gradually integrate into the world economy.

By addressing these aspects, this book takes a normative and an analytical perspective at the same time. It is normative, because it tries to contribute to developing appropriate strategies to achieve Europe's general aim of establishing good neighbourly relations with its Southern neighbourhood. It is at the same time analytic, because it uses past experiences to provide the reader with ideas of workable strategic concepts aimed at strengthening cross-regional relations. The book looks at the multilayered political, social and security relations from different perspectives: it identifies actors, their interests, strategies and normative preferences. It analyses outcomes, decomposes decision-making processes and institutions. It also analyses the overall structures within which actors of the Euro-MENA relations as well as within the MENA region itself interact. It would be a Sisyphean task to order the different cross cutting causal relationships into one cohesive whole. Obviously this is not the aim of this book. It rather reflects the multiplicity of issues on the table of the cross-regional debate.

Europe and Regional Security

The volume turns first to regional interstate relations. How can the anarchic regional system of states be transformed into a system governed by international norms guiding the behaviour of its constituent parts? The regional system of the MENA region in the past has proven to be highly resistant against efforts to develop functional international institutions. Most efforts to establish an appropriate institu-

tional framework for peaceful conflict resolution ended in the nir-
vana of endless debates on regional cooperation or produced harm-
lessly superficial and loosely organised international constructs.
Although some readers might argue that this book adds another
layer to that debate, some of the thoughts given by Said Aly, Wæver/
Buzan, and Hollis might contribute to identifying the obstacles to
international cooperation more appropriately than was done before.

The key argument of the book is presented by Abdel Monem Said
Aly, who reminds us of two streams of thought fighting with each
other over conceptual predominance not only in the mind sets of
Middle Eastern decision-makers but also in the discursive cross-
regional debates[2] on the future of Euro-MENA relations. The one is
the "geopolitical" agenda, which assumes that states compete with
their rivals for power and influence in order to insure their very survival or to sustain regional hegemony. Changing the region's relative
balance of power towards one's favour then becomes the ultimate
goal of states. In contrast to this approach based on neo-realist
assumptions,[3] the "geo-economic" agenda locates the threat to the
survival of the state not in the domain of traditional international,
that is: state-to-state relations, but in the inability of these states to
provide for an adequate institutional framework that would allow
economic growth. The threat to the state's survival stems from
within – the crisis of the state being unable to legitimise itself,
because it neither provides adequate material provision, political
participation or ideological power; and it stems from the outside
environment of the state as globalisation and economic competition
have a direct impact on the states' ranking within the international
system.

While taking a note of his argument to be used again in other
parts of the book, the first section turns to the preconditions of inter-

---

2   Risse (2000).
3   Waltz (1979).

national institution building. In their contribution Ole Wæver and Barry Buzan argue that the most appropriate way to conceptualise regional conflicts and security relations is by introducing the notion of "regional security complexes". The first, still principal, and in many ways defining core security-complex in the MENA region, as Wæver/Buzan argue, is the conflict centred in the Levant between the Palestinians and Israel. This local struggle sets up a much wider hostility between Israel and the Arab world, and to a lesser extent, between Israel and the even wider Islamic world (particularly, after 1979, Iran). The Arab-Israeli conflict, and the strong transnational qualities of Arab nationalism and Islamic politics which it amplified, is what gave the Middle East its overall coherence as a security complex. The second core complex in the MENA region, centred on the Gulf, is based on a triangular rivalry amongst Iran, Iraq, and the Gulf Arab states led by Saudi Arabia, though there is also a peripheral rivalry between Saudi Arabia and Yemen. This complex also influences security relations in the Eastern Mediterranean region, and in particular Israel has developed a clear sense for security threats emanating from the Gulf region. The third, weaker complex in MENA region's security concerns is that in the Maghreb. It is basically about a shifting and uneasy set of relationships among Libya, Tunisia, Algeria and Morocco, also extending into Chad and Western Sahara. Each of these regional complexes has a distinct dynamic at its core, only their geographical proximity helps to knit the whole MENA complex together.

Facing perceived security threats emanating from the MENA region but not realising the multifaceted regional security relations, several Western agencies have tried to engage in structuring security relations with and within these security complexes, Rosemary Hollis argues. In the 1990s, there were four prominent organisations with a remit to address certain aspects of security in the Mediterranean: the North Atlantic Treaty Organisation (NATO), the Organisation for Security and Cooperation in Europe (OSCE), the Western European

Union (WEU), and, within the Middle East peace process, the multilateral group on arms control and regional security (ACRS). NATO, WEU and OSCE were developed in the context of East-West confrontation, but have changed in their focus and outreach since the end of the Cold War. All three organisations have developed a dialogue with non-member Mediterranean countries: NATO's Mediterranean initiative of 1995 launched a dialogue with six countries: Egypt, Israel, Jordan, Mauritania, Morocco and Tunisia. As of the end of 1998, the WEU was engaged in dialogue with the same six, plus Algeria, Cyprus and Malta. The OSCE started a dialogue in 1994 and has granted observer status to Morocco, Tunisia, Algeria, Egypt and Israel.

But these initiatives are burdened by several obstacles, of which Hollis identifies two to be the most important ones: NATO and the WEU incorporate in their history and identity responsibility for the defence of Europe. When organisations tasked with the collective defence of their members enter dialogue with non-members, who are perceived as a potential source of threat, they risk reinforcing rather than ameliorating suspicions between them. Second comes the overlap between the frameworks of the different agencies. The existence of multiple initiatives represents a problem in so far as this means duplication and dissipation of effort. Of even greater concern is the potential for competition and even contradiction between the various endeavours.

What becomes clear from these assessments is that the Mediterranean region is not a cohesive "security complex". Security concerns in the Western Mediterranean differ fundamentally from security concerns in the Eastern Mediterranean. And none of the above mentioned initiatives include those countries, which play an important role in structuring security relations in the Eastern Mediterranean, notably Iran, Iraq, and the countries of the Gulf region. In addition, the slow pace of the Middle East peace process has limited the effectiveness of the dialogue frameworks.

How can that huge "melange" of security complexes, initiatives, concepts, and ideas be brought into a cohesive and comprehensive whole? If one takes the notion of security complexes seriously, that is, one assumes that security threats in this part of the world do not travel long distances, then thinking small but efficient might be an appropriate way to deal with the problems. In consequence, that would mean to establish regional security regimes in the Western and in the Eastern part of the Mediterranean and in the long run identify a way to integrate the states of the Gulf region into the latter one. Still, there might be a function for an all encompassing Mediterranean institution, but this would have to restrict itself to rather general confidence building measures.

Europe and the Peace Process

Turning towards the Eastern Mediterranean, the Arab-Israeli conflict has been the dominating cause for the retardation of regional integration processes, if they existed at all. And for decades the Middle East peace process has been a fundamental component of international politics. Most of the time the term "peace process" was not the appropriate one to describe Arab-Israeli interaction, however. More efforts were spent on digging into positions than on moving the process forward to a mutually beneficial end. At some stage, one might even argue, the survival of the indefinite Arab-Israeli antagonism was more in the interest for some of the regional leaders than the successful conclusion of the conflict. During the Cold War indeed the Arab-Israeli orbit was well connected to East-West antagonism, enabling the parties to extract essential material or political resources depending on whose side they were allying with. The end of the Cold War changed the rules and the structure of the peace process game. Outplaying East against West and vice versa was not a feasible option anymore. The only thing to offer to the international community now was talking peace. Peace rhetoric flourished tremendously; and talking peace became a multibillion dollar business. But making peace was something different. Some moves were made here and there, even some breakthroughs on the way, but no end has been put to the conflict yet. Thus, a decade or so after the end of the Cold War and the new rules of the peace process game in place, it is time for stocktaking and looking into the future.

The first lesson drawn from the experiences with the peace process is that economic cooperation cannot compensate for a political settlement. One of the conceptual assumptions of the peace process from 1991 to 1995 was that the economic vision of a New Middle East would be able to produce an atmosphere on which a political settlement could be based. Though the economic vision laid the ground for the first breakthrough among the PLO and Israel in the secret Oslo talks in 1993 and gave reason for the European Union to contribute massive financial resources to the peace process, the economic agenda has been pushed to the sidelines since 1995. Since then the vision of a New Middle East has not been able to create new impetus in the process.

The second lesson to be learnt is that implementing agreements is no less difficult than negotiating them. Indeed, what has been one of the basic principles of the process, namely the concept of gradualism in the negotiation as well as the implementation process on the Israeli-Palestinian track, developed into a stumbling block for the overall process. The concept of gradualism stipulated that those issues of the Israeli-Palestinian negotiation process which would be difficult to agree on at the beginning of the process would be kept for the final status negotiations: the future of Jerusalem, settlements, security arrangements, borders, refugees. This arrangement enabled the two sides to gradually transfer some authority to the Palestinians and to implement agreements reached on less contested issues in the meantime. This step-wise implementation process, however, caused pitfalls and stumbling blocks, as it gave both sides the opportunity to cheat on some aspects of the implementation process or accuse the other side of cheating and consequently slowing down the pace of the implementation process.

Third, all involved actors in the peace process, within the region as well as external ones, have developed a sense of what cooperative and what non-cooperative behaviour constitutes in the peace process. The international community defined the principles by which constructive behaviour could be assessed. By using positive and negative sanctions, including declaratory diplomacy, in many cases it was able to down-grading demands of the negotiating sides in the peace process.

Fourth, in the post-Cold War era uncooperative behaviour in the peace process weakened existing alliances and will eventually lead to regional and international isolation. This in turn will disable regional actors from gathering support or building new alliances against broader security threats. Cooperative behaviour, on the other hand, strengthened existing alliances and will open the possibility to develop new ones. What is valid with regard to unilateral action is also valid in relations between the region and its broader international environment. The more the Arab-Israeli orbit will prove to be unable to produce any meaningful results in the peace process, the less political attention and material contribution it will be able to attract. The international community would then gradually dissociate itself from what would be considered a helpless case, and engage in contingency planning.

Fifth, the structure of the peace process matters as much as its substance. The lines of communication among Israel and the leaders of the Arab sides could not be taken for granted. The political implications of merely talking to each other disrupted the free flow of information among the sides and led to collectively irrational behaviour. The understanding that talking to each other was an act of normalisation, a position taken in particular by some Arab governments in recent years, caused a structural and profound information deficit on which misunderstanding and misperception was based.

Sixth, the EU massively strengthened its position as a player in the Middle East peace process. It was the main actor emphasising the relevance of regional economic integration when the peace process gained new momentum after the second Gulf War. Although few steps have been taken until now to implement regional integration schemes, it was vital for the development of a positive-sum mentality that was necessary to overcome zero-sum-perceptions. In particular its work in the Regional Economic Development Working Group was a crucial contribution to the success of the Oslo secret talks. After signing the Oslo agreements, the EU massively supported the Palestinian Authority. When – in consequence of strained Arab-Israeli relations – all other initiatives such as the Middle East North Africa economic summits, the multilateral working groups and other fora of Arab-Israeli reconciliation degenerated in the period from 1995–1999, the Barcelona process initiated in 1995 to develop an Euro-Mediterranean Partnership provided a diplomatic safety net. This is not to overvalue the impact of the Barcelona process during this period, but it was the only regional forum preventing the peace process from "spilling back". The Special Envoy to the Middle East Peace Process of the EU, Ambassador Miguel Moratinos, contributed to a number of initiatives. He worked with the parties to signing the Hebron Protocol, proposed a "Code of Conduct", initiated EU/Palestinian cooperation on security issues, was active in implementing an EU-Israeli Joint Dialogue including five working groups, contributed to people-to-people programmes, and to the Palestinian agreement to the Wye Memorandum.

The lessons of the peace process and the strategic environment of the regional parties indicate that, assuming a positive scenario, the peace process will go through three phases in the coming years. In the first phase, negotiations among Israel and its Arab neighbours will result in a peace settlement. Implementation of the agreements will have to be secured in the second phase. The following third phase will witness normalisation among the regional actors and the normalisation of relations within the region and with the international community.

Based on the lessons of the peace process, now the European Union needs to define its role in the final phases and various tracks. The EU's role in the peace process will have to correspond with these phases if it is to be effective. It will change from that of a mediator or facilitator in the short run, to that of a party to the implementation process in the medium run. As political relations within the region normalise, so will regional relations between the Middle East and Europe. Eberhard Rhein and Joel Peters describe thoroughly how the EU can make an impact on the Middle East peace process. Riad al Khouri takes another look at the economic potentials after peace is achieved.

Institutions, Strategies and Preferences

Conventional studies on international relations assume nation states to be the fundamental actor in world affairs. But this assumption is insufficient if one acknowledges the empirical observation that the EU played a relevant role in the MENA region. It is not yet a state, but its actions have decisive impact on regional and cross-regional affairs. How then can the behaviour of the power in the making be explained? A closer look into the EU emphasising on the institutional design of the EU might contribute to the understanding about why the EU is behaving in a certain way. The EU is far from being a coherent geopolitical actor, reacting to changes in international relations, such as Arab-Israeli relations, in a rational strategic way. It is rather an institutionalised decision-making process in which different groups, institutions, and individuals try to pursue their own interests. The result of that process does not necessarily have to correspond with what would be a rational choice to deal with the one or the other problem in international affairs, but it is the result of an internal process producing a certain outcome. Jörg Monar's contribution thoroughly describes how the EU structures its foreign relations taking into account its institutional design.

If Monar's contribution takes an inside-out perspective, Joseph Alpher describes how the EU's policies are perceived by addressees of these policies. One of the fundamental problems of the EU in the Middle East peace process and among the regional actors is that from an outsider's perspective it is hard to understand why the EU is behaving in a certain way. This problem becomes all the more relevant if the EU's policies are addressed to make a difference in a policy field in which other actors act to defend their perceived vital interests. The imbalance between limited attention and capability and defence of vital security interests causes fundamental misunderstanding. This might be one main approach to explain why the Israeli political elite and public have been so hesitant in endorsing a more pronounced role of the EU in the Middle East peace process.

The section turns yet to another aspect of Europe's regional approach, which at the same time sheds light on the differences in terms of the conceptual foundations of foreign policy making in Europe and its transatlantic partner, the USA. At the time of publishing, transatlantic tensions over appropriate Western strategies to cope with states perceived as destabilising their regional environment, most notably Iran, decreased. But in the mid-nineties, transatlantic relations were tested by disagreement over what were appropriate approaches towards dealing with Iran. Trevor Taylor, Phebe Marr and Anoushiravan Ehteshami use this phenomenon as an instructive case study to show how a different institutional set-up and political culture affects foreign policy-making. They discuss the different strategic approaches of the US and the European Union towards Iran in the 1990s with reference to actual developments and policies, thereby also illustrating how the different strategic approaches of the Trans-Atlantic partners stood in sharp contrast to each other.

Sven Behrendt

Transformation and Legitimacy

After having covered the international dimension of Euro-MENA relations, the volume turns yet to another aspect of cross-regional relations: that of domestic political and economic transformation. Since fundamentalism, terrorism, socio-economic underdevelopment, and the like have been identified as threatening Europe's security interests in various ways, Europe believes it is legitimate to take a position on domestic politics of MENA states with a focus on economic and political transformation.

This book argues that one of the keys to successful transformation rests with the question of the future role of the state in the MENA region. Two aspects make the question of the future role of the state in the Middle East and North Africa a valid one: First are the overall global evolutionary processes of the new international political system, which will in the future be structured mainly along economic lines. These processes encompass all regions of the world and it is for each one of them to decide whether to remain in the backseat or join in. The flow of capital and goods pressure all countries to compete against each other on the global market for market shares and investment, and to adjust their political, economic and administrative institutions accordingly. Although the slow pace of reform processes in many Arab states suggests otherwise, there will be no escape to adapt to the demands of globalisation.

A second, and more immediate cause for embarking on comprehensive modernisation, is the Barcelona process as initiated by the member states of the European Union and the Southern Mediterranean countries. In their statement of November 1995 the signatories of the declaration agreed to the "acceleration of the pace of sustainable socio-economic development; improvement of the living conditions of their populations, increase in the employment level and reduction in the development gap in the Euro-Mediterranean region, encouragement of regional cooperation and integration."[4] The economic relationship between the EU and the states of the Southern Mediterranean region was to be based on new contractual grounds, and the implementation of the principles set in Barcelona to be realised through the conclusion of bilateral association agreements. Until now such agreements have been concluded with Tunisia, Morocco, Jordan, and Israel, an Interim Association Agreement with the PLO in favour of the Palestinian National Authority, and negotiations finalised with Egypt. Only Algeria, for its long domestic political problems, Lebanon and Syria which only slowly decided to embark on negotiations with the EU, are left behind. Libya for political reasons has been completely left out of the process as of now although moves in the spring of 2000 indicated that the Libyan government understands the necessity to connect to the process.

Only few observers doubt that the future role of the state necessarily has to be redefined if the goals of the Barcelona process are finally to be realised. The World Bank in its World Development Report of 1997 stated that the "last fifty years have shown clearly both the benefits and the limitations of state action"[5]. In particular it is the limitations of state action in a modern global economy that will be of relevance for the future political, economic, and social development among and within countries. Analysts identify in particular the incumbent political regimes as constituting the greatest obstacle to both political and economic reform.[6]

However, transformation of state institutions to achieve more efficiency and to improve performance shake the very foundations of the political systems in the Middle East and North Africa themselves. The state in the MENA region has been used by various interest

---

4 Euro Mediterranean Partenariat, Euro-Mediterranean Partnership, Barcelona 27–28 November 1995: 4.
5 The World Bank 1997: World Development Report. The State in a Changing World, Summary, Washington: 1.
6 Barkey (1995).

groups to realise their political interests, while at the same time providing them with the opportunity to acquire political rents from their positions. Policy-makers in state institutions thus are moved by mixed motives and "a desire to pursue the public good and the desire to advance their personal interests." This phenomenon is by no means unique to the MENA region. However, given weak institutional provisions for "checks and balances", the "deep distributional conflicts and constraints embedded in state institutions are at the heart of the explanation for so many countries' failure to reform."[7] As the MENA countries have been slow in implementing steps towards transformation, it has led some to argue that the overall economic decline of the MENA region during times of rapid globalisation is the major fourth crisis of the Arab world, following the Six Day War of 1967, the Iranian revolution, and Saddam Hussein's hegemonic posture in 1990.[8]

Given that the international economic environment of the MENA region will change in the future as rapidly as it has done in the last decade, what lies ahead, beyond the definition of the substantial goal of the transformation process, is the organisation of the political process by which these goals should be realised. Certainly, existing cultural, economic, political, and social institutions and relationships prevent any state emerging like a phoenix from the ashes. Given these institutions, transformation processes will only unfold according to specific path dependencies.[9] It is then the organisation of the process of modernisation which matters. Essential for that process to succeed is to acknowledge that transformation processes are inherently unstable. Measures such as deregulation and privatisation, as well as the streamlining of government, which are put forward by the "Chicago School"[10] and embraced by international development

7 World Development Report (1997: 13).
8 Ajami (1997).
9 North (1990).
10 Lane (1997).

agencies, will cause severe political problems. In fact the process of modernisation and change "breeds instability", as urbanisation, increases in literacy, education, and media exposure create expectations which, if unrealised, potentially sharpen societal, political, and economic conflict.[11]

In order to escape from this ever growing lack of legitimacy of the state, and provide for the necessary steps to create the framework in which the private sector driven market economy can develop, Emma Murphy in her contribution to this volume presents three strategies for transformation: the first emphasises restructuring the state-society bargain. A process of gradual political reform, including the introduction of political party pluralism and competitive elections would be used to substitute for the state's economic obligations. This would broaden the base of responsibility for difficult decisions, although it might be more of a tactical manoeuvre than a genuine effort to open up the political arena. Another strategy would call for a new balance in public and private provision. This strategy would target the poorest within the populace which at the same time are easily recruited by political activists, and therefore are difficult to control. A differentiated system of redistribution would ensure that some of the benefits of economic policy reform would go to the lower social strata, thus making the new policies more appealing. Third, a ruler-regime differentiation strategy would ensure that the system as such remains stable, as the ruler should have the opportunity to put on the brakes if the reform policies are implemented too quickly. At the same time, he would stay out of the public debate over structural adjustment and thus could balance political forces.

Some years ago, a book with the programmatic subtitle speaking of the renewal of politics in the Muslim world caught the attention of the public. Its aim was to take another look at the problems of democratisation, and linking them to the social changes of the last

---

11 Huntington (1976).

two or three decades.[12] One of its main arguments was that the balance sheet of democratisation was not hopelessly pessimistic. Walid Kazziha argues against that hypothesis, when he states that the ultimate results of the so-called process of political liberalisation of regional political systems have been rather disappointing. But the contribution of Anoushiravan Ehteshami seems to confirm a more positive assessment. In every year since 1989 national elections have taken place in one or more MENA states. Since 1992 in particular, a flood of election activity has been gripping the region and even sometimes countries where meaningful elections had been almost completely absent in previous decades, ranging from presidential, parliamentary and municipal elections to national referenda and plebiscites. The West has had difficulties to assess the impact of elections in the MENA countries on political life. Elections eventually also took place during times of Communist rule in Eastern Europe without really presenting choices and/or being based on an environment within which a free choice could be made. But one could be well advised to acknowledge that in the MENA region elections do indeed take place, which is a good step forward. Elections might not yet be free and fair and might not stand up to international standards, but they take place and serve as a focal point in the transnational debate about their effectiveness, thus putting pressure on the regimes for improvements.

This volume suggests that the relations between Europe and the Middle East are multilayered and that all strategies towards deepening cross-regional relations have to take into account the complexities of that relationship as well as the complex political, economic, and social structures within the two regions. The following contributions should help to analyse and thereby reduce some of these complexities.

12 Salamé (1994).

List of References

Ajami, Fouad 1997: The Arab Inheritance, in: Foreign Affairs, 76/5.

Barkey, Henri 1995: Can the Middle East Compete?, in: Journal of Democracy, 6/2.

Huntington, Samuel 1976: Political Order in Changing Societies, New Haven/London.

Keohane, Robert/Joseph Nye 1977: Power and Interdependence. World Politics in Transition, Boston.

Lane, Jan-Erik 1997: Public Sector Reform. Only Deregulation, Privatisation and Marketization?, in: Lane, Jan Erik (ed.): Public Sector Reform. Rationale, Trends and Problems, London.

North, Douglass 1990: Institutions, Institutional Change and Economic Performance. Political Economy of Institutions and Decisions, Cambridge.

Risse, Thomas 2000: Let's Argue! Communicative Action in International Relations, in: International Organization, 54/1.

Russett, Bruce 1993: Grasping the Democratic Peace. Principles for a Post-Cold War World, Princeton/New Jersey.

Salamé, Ghassan (ed.) 1994: Democracy without Democrats? The Renewal of Politics in the Muslim World, London/New York.

Waltz, Kenneth 1979: Theory of International Politics, Reading/Mass.

Security Relations

From Geopolitics to Geo-Economics: Collective Security in the Middle East and North Africa

Abdel Monem Said Aly

Classic theory of collective security has emphasized the notion that war prevention among states could be achieved by implementing the principal that a war against one nation is a war against all nations.[1] After World War I, the League of Nations created a system of collective security that rested on the collective prevention and punishment of aggression. The charter of the United Nations after World War II followed equal traditions. However, the persistence of wars and conflicts in the international and regional systems has made the classic theory a myth more than a reality. In fact, in many cases alliances that were based on the theory tended to prolong conflicts because of their overemphasis on power politics and military preparedness that usually ended in escalating the arms race and tensions.

---

1 This contribution was presented to the workshop *Preliminaries to a Conference on Security and Cooperation in the Middle East and North Africa*, Rome, November 1995.

The end of the Cold War and the integrative experience of Europe, where the classic theory of collective security was originally fashioned, have changed the theory fundamentally from being military oriented to being based on extensive political and socioeconomic cooperation. The basic notion here is that nations are not deterred from aggression by power politics only, but mainly by creating a stake for them in preserving peace and stability. Collective security has been broadened to an overall concept of cooperative security that involves different forms of cooperative interactions among nation-states on both regional and global levels.

The conceptual focus of this paper is the change in regional orders from conflict-prone regions (power politics oriented) into more cooperative ones. "Regional cooperation" is an intermediate concept which tackles cooperative interactions among states in a specific regional area. It is intermediate because it stands between cooperation on the international or global level on one hand and bilateral cooperation among state actors in the international system on the other.

The objective is to relocate the concept of regional cooperation in the Middle East region. The paper's main argument is that the Middle East region and its subregions, such as the Persian Gulf, are going through a painful transition from patterns of interactions which are characterized by power politics and geopolitical concerns to new ones which are marked by the politics of geo-economics. Geopolitics here is understood as the traditional national security threats that emanate from geography as well as history of the nation-state. The survival of the nation and the protection of its territorial integrity are the main objectives of national security policy. Power politics and the balance of power are the means to achieve these objectives. Geo-economics, on the other hand, is a much more complex concept. The survival of the state and safeguarding its territorial integrity are not the subject of external threats but rather its economic well-being, its social cohesion, and ability to withstand economic competition. Raising productivity, economic reform, integration into regional and international markets, and protecting sources of income are the means to ensure national security in geo-economic terms.

Although the "Middle East" is not a well defined region and the record of regional cooperation is much less than impressive, regional cooperation is still an important goal to facilitate cooperative collective security in the area. However, because of fundamental changes in the world as well as in the Middle Eastern regional orders, a new trend of cooperative interactions is emerging. Still a new trend, traditional power politics continues to bear heavily on the politics of the Middle East. The function of regional policy from within and from without, therefore, is to help the consolidation of this trend in order to allow the Middle East to have a more constructive role in world affairs.

This contribution, consequently, will be divided into four sections. The first two sections will monitor the changes in the world and regional orders. The third section will focus on the geopolitical agenda of the Middle East, with special emphasis on the Persian Gulf subregion. The fourth section will attempt to redefine the region and to propose policies that might help in its transformation from a conflictual mood of interactions into more cooperative ones.

The Middle East: The Geopolitical Agenda

Some positive developments in the Middle East should not overshadow the seriousness, and the gravity, of the geopolitical agenda that the region still carries on its shoulders. Indeed, it is still very premature to decide if the new trends in the region are sustainable or not. Observers of the area can not overlook the bloody history of the region. For decades, the Arabs and Israelis fought each other for affirmation of their national identities, territories, and natural resources. For the Israelis, the fight was for a self-recognized sense of nationhood that would gather all the Jews of the world in the holy land of Palestine. For the Arabs, the fight was for rectifying the "original sin" of uprooting the Palestinians from their historical homeland, thus their deprivation of the right of self-determination. Over almost one-half a century, the conflict between the two sides continued without abatement in the international forums and in the battlefield. Six wars, to count only the major ones (1948, 1956, 1967, 1969–1970, 1973, 1982) between them have created bitter memories for all the parties. For almost forty-five years, the two parties were involved in a deadly arms race, mobilizing world resources and constantly preparing for another, even more devastating war. Over time, the conflict which was about the partition of Palestine was protracted to a host of increasingly complicated issues such as the occupied Arab territories since June 1967, arms race, water supplies, refugees, economic boycott, settlement and settlers, terrorism, and others.

And, for sure, the Arab-Israeli conflict was not the only conflict in the region during the same period. In fact, the Middle East, with only eight per cent of world population, has had 25 per cent of all the world's armed conflicts since 1945. The Middle East has witnessed all sorts of conflicts during the same period such as regional wars, wars of intervention, civil wars, intra-Arab rivalries and conflicts with devastating consequences to the human and material resources of the region. Most notably in the past two decades alone, the region witnessed two major wars in the Persian Gulf, civil wars in Lebanon, Yemen, Somalia, and the Sudan, and waves of violence and terrorism. Table 1 below shows the devastating impacts of these conflicts on the resources of the region. Still, these estimates exclude the opportunity cost for the area if these resources had been put to better use than for armed conflicts. The figures also show that the Arab-Israeli conflict, though considered the principal conflict in the region, has claimed some 200,000 lives in forty years. In contrast, during the same period ethnic conflicts have claimed several times as many lives. The Lebanese civil war alone matched the same number of casualties as all Arab-Israeli wars together. The Sudanese civil war has claimed at least five times as many lives as all Arab-Israeli wars. The same relative costs apply in terms of population displacement, material devastation, and financial expenditure.

Table 1: The Cost of Armed Conflicts in the Middle East and North Africa (MENA) Region 1948–1993

Type of Conflict	Period	No. of Casualties	Estimated Cost in Billions of US$ (1991 value)	Estimated Population Displacement
A) Interstate				
Arab-Israeli	1948–1990	200,000	300	3,000,000
Iran-Iraq	1980–1988	600,000	300	1,000,000
Gulf War	1990–1991	120,000	650	1,000,000
Other Interstate	1945–1991	70,000	50	1,000,000
Subtotal		990,000	1,300	6,000,000
B) Intra-State				
Sudan	1956–1991	900,000	30	4,500,000
Iraq	1960–1991	400,000	30	1,200,000
Lebanon	1958–1990	180,000	50	1,000,000
North Yemen	1962–1972	100,000	5	500,000
Syria	1975–1985	30,000	0.5	150,000
Morocco	1976–1991	20,000	3	100,000
South Yemen	1986–1987	10,000	0.2	50,000
Somalia	1989–1991	20,000	0.3	200,000
Other Intra-state	1945–1991	30,000	1	300,000
Subtotal		1,690,000	120	8,000,000
Grand Total (All Armed Conflicts)		2,680,000	1,420	14,000,000

Source: Various files of the Arab Data Unit (ADU), Ibn Khaldoun Center for Developmental Studies, Cairo, 1993.

Reasons behind this propensity for interstate and intra-state violence in the Middle East are abundant: the nation-state building process with what it entails in terms of the legitimacy of political regimes, the colonial heritage of borders, superpower and great powers' contestations in the region, transnational ideologies of Pan-Arabism, Pan-Islamism and Zionism, sharp differences in wealth and resources among states, and others. All these reasons have made power politics and geopolitical concerns the dominant factors in influencing state behavior.

A case in point could be demonstrated by having a close look at the conflict in the Persian Gulf subregion of the Middle East. The nine countries of the Persian Gulf and the Arabian Peninsula, i.e. the member-states of the Gulf Cooperation Council (GCC) plus Iraq, Yemen, and Iran share a similar status as being Third World countries with all the pains and ills that go along with it. They are all basically consumers of powers depending on outside countries for military supplies. All are oil and gas producers (about 60 per cent of world reserves) and their economies are highly dependent on that one source of income. Yet the states of the region differ in everything else: size, population, wealth, levels of economic development and modernization, and, of course, military power. The uneven distribution of material resources creates a certain imbalance that enhances ambitions and hegemonic tendencies on one hand, and apprehensions, suspicions, and fears on the other. Historical legacies from the ancient times of the Persian empire to the more recent Gulf wars are seldom forgotten in the mindset of old and new nations across the Gulf. Islam, the dominant religion across the waterway, seems to have divided peoples along the Sunni – Shi'a dichotomy.

However, imbalance of power, historical legacies, and religious divisions are not by themselves enough for conflict, though they may pave the road to it. Other forces have to come into play in order to threaten the security of a given region. Most notably in the Gulf and the Arabian Peninsula are the following:

First, there is a large imbalance between the wealth of GCC states individually and collectively and the small number of their population. At the time of writing, the GCC countries had a total population (including expatriates) of 23 million compared with 56 million for Iran, 18 million for Iraq and 13.5 million for Yemen. And while the GCC states are surplus money countries, Iran had US$ 30 billion foreign debt, Iraq had US$ 84 billion (plus reparation for the Gulf War), and Yemen had US$ 8.5 billion.

Second, the citizens of each GCC country are a minority in their own country with the exception of Bahrain, Oman, and Saudi Arabia. Furthermore, the ethnic and religious compositions of the populations on the two sides of the Gulf are quite diversified. While Iran, a Persian Shi'a dominant country, has considerable Arab Shi'a and Sunni minorities, the other eight Arab countries have Shi'a and Iranian minorities, with the exception of Bahrain.

The Shi'a minorities in the GCC states have been under a cloud of suspicion from the late 1970s and throughout the 1980s. This was mainly because of the Islamic revolution in Iran, the first Gulf War (Iran-Iraq war), and the Shi'a subversion in Bahrain, Kuwait, and Saudi Arabia. The Second Gulf War in 1990–91 helped to lift this cloud by showing Shi'a patriotism, like Sunnis, in opposing Iraq's occupation of Kuwait and led to a rapprochement between the Gulf states and Iran, causing the fear of Iranian-sponsored activities to decline. This, however, did not end the Shi'a grievances. One part of the problem is secular, especially in Saudi Arabia where the Shi'a were seen as heretics. Another problem is that of human rights in Bahrain and Saudi Arabia where any sign of Shi'a activism is harshly suppressed. Finally, the Shi'a communities in all Gulf states suffer, in one way or another, from various forms of discrimination. They, for example, are often barred from high military and civilian positions.

As a result of this situation, the Shi'a in the Gulf states remain susceptible to external influences, especially from Iran. The dispute between Iran and the United Arab Emirates over the islands of Abu

Musa, Lesser Tumb, and Greater Tumb is a good example, especially since mid-1992 when Iran decided to take full control of the Abu Musa island. Since 1971, Abu Musa has been subject to a mutual agreement between Sharjah and Tehran. The Iranian step would add more fuel to the fire and would affect the domestic position of the Shi'a communities in the Gulf states.

Third, like most third world countries, the states of the region are new states in the modern sense of statehood. They face the problems of undefined borders, which was inherited from the time of the colonial powers. These undefined borders played a major role in the armed conflicts which the Gulf region has witnessed. The Buraimi conflict of the 1950s was a direct result of a border dispute between Saudi Arabia on one side and Great Britain, representing Abu Dhabi and Oman on the other. The Iraq-Iran war of the 1980s was also caused, to a large degree, by the disagreement between the two countries over the ownership of the border area of the Shatt-al-Arab waterway. The border dispute between Iraq and Kuwait over the Rumaila oil field and the ownership of the islands of Bubian and Warbah was one of the main reasons for the Gulf crisis in 1990–1991.

Fourth, and probably most importantly, the region is divided among conservative status quo powers and radical, revolutionary powers. The GCC member states are traditional, conservative states which find its security and well-being linked to the West. Iran, Iraq, and, to some extent, Yemen are republics that also promote revolutionary visions of themselves and the regional context in which they live. This includes the Islamic revolutionary ideals of Iran, the Arab nationalist ideology of Iraq, and the mixture of both perspectives in Yemen. Iraq and Iran are clear cases. Yemen, however, is a different story. The Northern Yemeni leadership succeeded in crushing the rebellion in former South Yemen in the summer of 1994 against the wishes of the majority of the GCC member states with the exception of Qatar. The legitimacy of the state system in the area is not confirmed. For the less-fortuned, more populated, and radical Iran, Iraq, and Yemen, the GCC member states are up for grabs in the name of the Arab nation or the Islamic one or both.

These four realities constituted the basic vulnerabilities of the Persian Gulf region and led power politics and geopolitical concerns predominantly into an environment of conflict with the result that the reliance on military power is a major instrument in foreign policy behavior. All countries in the region, as well as in the rest of the Middle East, have been involved in a deadly arms race.

A World Transformed: The Victory of Geo-Economics

However, global developments toward a "New World Order" have had their impact on the region. The birth of this order came as a declaration of forces and processes that had begun since World War II and even before. In theory, any world order entails a mood of technology, a power structure, and an agenda. Technologically, the "new" in the world order has been the increasing dominance of the third industrial revolution over world affairs.

Structurally, the "new" in the world order is not really the change from a bipolar world to the much "older" unipolar or multipolar worlds, but the fundamental change in the nature of polarity itself. Traditionally, polarity was defined in terms of power distribution among nation-states or blocs of nation-states. They are engaged in an eternal pursuit of hegemony and dominance that involves the use, or the threat, of force. Now, it seems that polarity can be defined in terms of the prevalence of a whole system of socio economic-political interactions in world affairs. This system is the Western and capitalist (and also liberal) order as it dominates the world in the final years of the 20th century. It represents the powers of North America, Western Europe, and Japan plus the Pacific rim. This order is highly integrated through a large network of institutions, multinational corporations, trade, and investments.

Naturally, a change in the world structure means a new agenda and this new agenda is basically an economic one. Unemployment, inflation, exchange rates, stock markets, trade barriers, and population are the issues of the day. Global issues such as pollution, environmental safety, communication, and air trafficking are increasingly finding a place on the agenda at world summits. Transnational social problems such as drugs, refugees, and AIDS, are receiving global attention. The "Earth Summit" in 1992, followed by similar summits on human rights, population, and women have been testimonies for the change in the global agenda.

In the Third World, the socio-economic-political systems which emerged after decolonization mostly failed in dealing with their internal and external environments. Many Third World countries, particularly in Africa, became more underdeveloped than they were before independence. The third industrial revolution has led to their marginalization in the world's political and economic systems. The collapse of the Soviet bloc has deprived them of the advantages of the Cold War. The result of this development was a decline in their economic fortunes and a decay in their political institutions. However, it has to be said that some Third World countries in Southeast Asia, the Pacific, and Latin America succeeded in seizing opportunity in the need for the enlargement of the world market to associate with the rising unipolar order. They succeeded in adjusting their socio-economic, and lately political, systems to deal not only with the third industrial revolution, but also to deal with the complexities of turning the conflictual mood of interactions into more cooperative ones.

Transforming the Middle East: Towards a New Regional Order

If the world order has been transformed, the Middle East has witnessed major changes. The most important development in the region was the

Second Gulf War. The war changed the attitude of the major parties towards the Arab-Israeli conflict. Together with the effects of the end of the Cold War, a window of opportunity was opened for the whole region.

And the opportunity was not missed. Through an active American mediation effort, the Madrid peace process started in October 1991 and, by 1994, a Palestinian-Israeli agreement and an Israeli-Jordanian peace treaty were in place. What was important about the new Arab-Israeli reconciliation process is that it introduced a geo-economic dimension to its traditional geopolitical concerns of territory and security. In addition to the bilateral negotiations, another layer of negotiation was a multilateral one to discuss five issues of interest to the parties: arms control, water, refugees, economic development, and the environment. The negotiations started at the end of January 1992 in Moscow with 35 participating states, including 13 Arab countries and Israel. Syria and Lebanon declined to participate until serious progress took place in the bilateral negotiations. Unwavered by this setback, the participants agreed to form five sub-multilateral committees to discuss the five issues under consideration. Although the results of the multilateral negotiations were limited, they have inspired a host of initiatives to accelerate development and economic cooperation in the Middle East, the most notable of which was the economic summit in Morocco in the end of October 1994 and the Amman economic summit in October 1995 followed by the summits in Cairo and Doha. More elaborate vision was represented to the interlocutors of the area by Shimon Peres, the Israeli foreign minister, in his book *The New Middle East* in which he argued for a new way of thinking and moving the economy of the region "from an Economy of Strife to an Economy of Peace".

In the bilateral agreements the economic dimensions were even more concrete. Although the Palestinian-Israeli agreement entailed a gradual "political" separation between Israel and Palestine that may include the birth of a Palestinian state, it contained provisions for

consolidated linkage between the two sides. The linkage is mani-
fested in a highly complicated network of coordinating committees
in the areas of security, economics, and infrastructure. More important, Annex III of the agreement – the Protocol on Israeli-Palestinian
Cooperation and Development Programs – contains provisions not
only for legitimizing the existing linkages between Israel and the
West Bank and Gaza but also for consolidating them in the areas of
water, electricity, energy, finance, transport and communications,
trade, industry, labour and welfare issues, human resources, the environment, and communication and media. Annex IV went even further
to make the Israeli-Palestinian linkage a cornerstone in a very ambitious regional development and cooperation plan. The Jordanian-
Israeli peace treaty listed seven areas for cooperation: water, refugees, natural resources, human resources, infrastructure, economic
fields, and tourism.

Redefining the Middle East: From Geo-Politics to Geo-Economics

As we can see, new ingredients of peace in the area gave new hope
for the prospects of regional cooperation. Many of these ingredients
were motivated by global trends away from geopolitical and geostrategic interactions towards geo-economic ones.

However, for peace in the area to be completed and materialized,
it will be only through intensified and institutionalized overall cooperation among the concerned states, particularly if the political
obstacles to the Israeli-Syrian and the Israeli-Palestinian negotiations
are removed. Yet, regional cooperation is one way to facilitate negotiations and create a hospitable environment that may compensate
for the perceived loss of the parties in the bargaining process. Regional cooperation, furthermore, can facilitate the creation of a common security regime through positive security arrangements which
utilize non-military and non-territorial ways to achieve security.

Traditionally, negotiations and bargaining are perceived to be a zero-sum game. Regional cooperation, on the contrary, is a non-zero-sum game since all the parties can gain from this process. Two questions come to mind: which region should engage in cooperation? And what kind of cooperation is necessary for peace? Answering these two questions is not an easy task. What is needed is a set of criteria for the selection of states that should be involved in the process.

One possible basic criterion for the selection of states and issues could be the ones that would positively influence the thorny issues of the negotiations. The ones that should be selected are the states and issues that can overcome some of the security needs of the parties and work as a substitute for military and territorial demands of the parties with positive security measures. Another criterion is economic and spill-over viability. Parties to the conflict can be persuaded to substitute war for peace if regional cooperation can offer them rewards that narrow nationalist policies alone cannot achieve. Another criterion is that the largest possible number of states be involved in the process. This is necessary because it reduces the opposition to the peace process on the one hand and, on the other, decreases the risks that one of the parties, particularly Israel, will notice if one of the adversaries is not involved. Israeli security demands in this case would be reduced. A final criterion is flexibility and innovation in selecting types and issues of regional cooperation that draw on the different experiences for regional cooperation in the world.

Based upon this criteria, a tailored view of the Middle East region and the types of regional cooperation that is bound to achieve peace emerges. It is possible to envisage a Middle East in four interrelated parts:

- Israel, Palestine, and Jordan: the countries that are directly involved in the Palestinian question;
- Egypt, Syria, Iraq (in the future), Lebanon: the countries that participated heavily in the conflict with Israel;

- the GCC member states, Turkey (and possibly Iran when it loses
  its revolutionary fever): the countries that are involved in the conflict in different ways and that are important for regional cooperation in certain economic sectors; and
- countries in the vicinity of the above mentioned states that are
  committed to participation in regional cooperation.

These four layers, or circles, of the Middle East represent three
degrees of intensity and involvements in the issues of the Arab-Israeli
conflict. Regional cooperation among them can take five overlapping
forms:

- a common market or confederate arrangement among Israel,
  Palestine, and Jordan can be of valuable assistance in solving some
  of the problems concerning security, settlements, and refugees.
  Palestinians and Israelis have shown interest in this proposition in
  the past;
- a free trade area between the common market and the countries
  of Egypt, Syria, Lebanon, and Iraq will make war, particularly a
  surprise attack, undesirable and impossible. It will thus reduce
  Israeli military and territorial demands;
- a Middle East security regime for arms and water, involving the
  above mentioned states and the GCC member states, Turkey, and
  possibly Iran, will integrate the largest number of states in solving
  the problem of water supplies and will reduce the tensions of the
  arms race in the area. The water security regime will not only
  tackle the distribution of existing water resources, but also look
  at reducing the military forces of all states and at dismantling
  weapons of mass destruction. Verification, including sight verification, will be necessary;
- sector-specific cooperation agreements in areas such as agriculture, energy, industry, tourism, transportation, and communication among all the states of the area will be possible according to
  their developmental needs; and

– "natural" economic zones can create the linkage between the first two forms, particularly around the Gulf of Aqaba and the GCC regions.

This framework of regional cooperation should satisfy the criteria mentioned above. It is understood that many of its details need to be worked out. However, regional cooperation, as well as peace making, are difficult and complex tasks. The framework should provide the interested parties with the "Middle East" that calls for cooperation. It should also provide for the areas where cooperation may contribute to a durable peace.

The necessary conditions for the realization of this framework to be materialized are the following:

First, the completion of the agenda of the peace process, particularly in the Syrian and Palestinian fronts, must be achieved.

Second, a commitment by all the parties for geo-economic cooperation based on market forces is crucial. The multilateral negotiations in the Middle East should provide the forum for the reconstruction of a new regional order in the Middle East.

Third, a substantial strategic and geo-economic understanding among the major regional powers in the area is necessary. If the western European integration projects were built on the shoulders of France, Germany, Italy, and Britain, then Egypt, Saudi Arabia, Turkey, and Israel in the Middle East should do the same. The agenda for the four regional powers can certainly be the consolidation of peace in the area, promoting different forms of interdependence, and integrating the Middle East into the world economic system, and reincorporating the still radical states in the region into an ambitious regional economic development. Luckily, the four countries have close association with the West for different reasons and, thus, they form a bridge for the Middle East to the new emerging world order. Special attention from the West for creating this understanding among the four regional powers is needed.

Fourth, transforming the Middle East from geopolitical orientations to geo-economic ones cannot be achieved without controlling the arms race in the area. Even during the current peace process in the Middle East, countries in the region continued the race without abatement, hence fomenting suspicions and fear. Arms control efforts in conventional and non-conventional weapons, therefore, is fundamental for the transformation to occur. It will suffice here to outline the major propositions in the following pages.

Since all parties in the region agree on the establishment of a Nuclear Weapons Free Zone (NWFZ) in the Middle East, it is important to link the establishment of the zone to the peace process through the Arms Control and Regional Security (ACRS) subcommittee of the multilateral negotiations. The general principle should be the following: symmetrical and reciprocal arrangements should be the norm at the end of the road, although certain asymmetries might be acceptable to facilitate agreements. Israeli nuclear weapons should be "phased-out" over a period of time. These weapons should be reduced in number as a part of the confidence-building measures. Some of them could be eliminated as a result of international guarantees. Others should be traded with peace treaties with Arab countries. The rest should be eliminated once full normalization of relations and different types of economic and functional cooperation are installed.

The same process should be applied to chemical weapons for both sides of the conflict. The idea here is twofold. First, arms control measures should be linked with a political timetable for the overall settlement. Second, the most devastating weapons should be eliminated from the area. This could not be achieved without transparency of information about weapons of mass destruction in the inventory of both sides of the conflict. Arms control talks in Europe could not have accomplished anything without prior agreement on the arms that the talks intended to control. Transparency, then, should be the first step in the multilateral arms control negotiations in the Middle East.

Transparency also is important for negotiations on conventional weapons. Both sides should provide information about not only the existing inventory of weapons at their disposal, but also about weapons under development. A moratorium on the acquisition and development of high technology weapons should be implemented during the negotiating process. Another alternative is to apply the moratorium to the deployment of these weapons. This is particularly important for long-range (more than 150 km) ballistic missiles and anti-ballistic missiles such as the Israeli Arrow. A ban on exporting long-range ballistic and cruise missiles should be arranged among arms exporting countries. Confidence-building measures such as notification of naval movements, cooperative sea operations against drug smuggling, or against terrorist actions by regional powers could enhance both the possibilities of arms control and mutual trust necessary for peace in the Middle East. Some of these ideas have been discussed within the framework of ACRS.

If all these measures attempt to cap the existing level of arms under the command of both sides, it is worth considering the reduction of certain categories of weaponry such as tanks and artillery. In a general condition of an Arab-Israeli peace, it will be worth examining the Arab side to restructure and redeploy Arab armies in such a way as to reduce Israeli apprehensions. A shift from standing armies to mobilizing armies should be considered.

These ideas will face the major problem of Iran and Syria, which were not participants in the multilateral negotiations. Consequently, capping the Iranian and Syrian arms build-up could not be achieved without the cooperation of the supplying states, particularly the five permanent members (P-5) of the Security Council. It would strain their supplies to the area. This is not easy, however, in light of the economic difficulties in the West, the ex-Soviet bloc, and China. Arms exports will continue to be targeted to decrease deficits, create jobs, and generate hard cash. It will take a good deal of restructuring their economies and conversions from military to civil industries.

This will take a long time during which the Middle East will continue to be the largest possible market. Yet, the conditions for suppliers' efforts could not be better. The end of the Cold War, the existence of more or less stable balances in the Middle East, the dominating role of the US in the area, and the economic difficulties for the recipient countries are all conducive to new attempts to strain arm supplies to the region. Accelerating the Syrian-Israeli peace process, as mentioned above, could greatly help arms control efforts. Another idea for the P-5 is to curtail the export of new generations of weapons to the region which were developed in the 1980s. A third idea is to put an agreement in place that binds major suppliers to declare publicly every arms deal to the Middle East. A fourth one, and probably the most difficult idea to realize, is to tax all arms deals to the Middle East. The revenues developed by this taxation should be projected for economic cooperation among Middle East countries, particularly the countries involved in the Arab-Israeli conflict.

Fifth, building regional institutions could be one of the functions of the regional strategic understandings among the four major regional powers. Thus far, Middle Eastern countries belong to different regional institutions such as the Arab League, the Organization of Islamic Conference, and the Organization of African Unity. Israel is the only country that does not belong to any of these institutions. In fact, these institutions tended to take an anti-Israeli stand as a part of the Arab efforts to balance the strong Israeli association with the West. Integrating Israel into a regional institutional framework could be part of a regional effort in a new era. Once, the former Israeli foreign minister Shimon Peres suggested that Israel and Turkey should join the Arab League, provided that the League will change its name to be a Middle East regional organization. The idea was negatively received in Arab countries because it seems to replace an organization based on Arab cultural identity with a Middle Eastern one. Solving these contradictions by creating observer and association status, in addition to membership in the Arab League that allow non-Arab states to participate, should overcome this obstacle. The same principle should be allowed in all other regional arrangements. The purpose of this type of arrangement is to create the largest possible web of networking in the region.

Sixth, special attention should be given to the security of the Persian Gulf subregion. As shown before, the GCC member-states are suffering from four basic vulnerabilities. To face these threats, the Arab-Gulf states devised a security policy based on six elements:

- the Arab-Gulf states, in particular Saudi Arabia, increased their military capabilities through the acquisition of high technology weapons;
- they increased their collective security through the establishment of the GCC and a joint military force under the name of Al-Gizira Shield. The force was small (about 5,000 soldiers), but it is hoped that it will grow in the future;
- they attempted to balance regional powers by helping Iraq against Iran, Syria against Iraq and by keeping lines open with other regional powers, particularly Egypt and Turkey;
- they gave considerable economic assistance to major regional powers such as Syria, Egypt, Iraq, and Yemen. Even Iran was given assistance in the time of natural disasters;
- they created the most extensive welfare states in the world for citizens and residents alike to satisfy the population and reduce socio-economic and political tensions; and
- they consolidated their political and economic relations with the West by following a strong anti-communism and anti-radicalism policy.

These six elements of the Arab-Gulf states' security policy were not enough for the security of the Gulf. Kuwait was threatened by Iran during the Iran-Iraq war and then invaded by Iraq. Saudi Arabia was threatened directly by Iran, Iraq, and Yemen. Iraq threatened Qatar and the UAE during the Gulf crisis. Iran, from time to time, shows ambitions in Bahrain. All these threats made security in the Gulf at the top of the post Gulf War agenda.

What is needed, therefore, is to fashion the security of the Gulf in a way that reduces the short and long-term threats. For sure, every progress in moving the entire Middle East from geopolitics to geo-economics will give more security to the Arab-Gulf states. In fact, this progress will give the economic advantages of these states more opportunities in socioeconomic and probably political development. Iraq and Iran, nevertheless, will continue to pose a possible threat. Here, because of their ideological make up, their political systems and type of leadership, Iraq and Iran will continue to pose a geopolitical threat of the first order. It will be extremely difficult to seduce them to join in the geo-economic transformation in the region. Therefore, power politics and deterrence will be necessary as long as the existing regimes in both countries are still in power. A Gulf security project, as outlined by the secretary general of the GCC after the Gulf War, should offer sufficient deterrence against both countries. Security in the Gulf will be further enhanced if this power posture is complemented by strong signals to integrate the two countries into the transformation process in the Middle East if they radically change their policies and/or regimes. The strategic understanding among the four major regional powers in the Middle East mentioned above should include in their agenda the future of Iraq and Iran.

An Inter-Regional Analysis: NATO's New Strategic Concept and the Theory of Security Complexes

Ole Wæver, Barry Buzan

Judging from some very visible events of the 1990s – such as the Second Gulf War and the American involvement in the Israel-Palestinian peace process – as well as some policy statements mostly from the US but also including the 1999 new "strategic concept" of NATO, the Middle East is becoming a more systematic object of Western policy.[1] An increasing part of the defining threat image of NATO is more or less implicitly tied to the Middle East – international terrorism, proliferation of weapons of mass destruction, and rogue states – so shouldn't we expect more systematic and deliberate intervention from NATO (countries) in the Middle East? This paper intends to explore the question whether the Middle East will in the future become systematically an object of Western security policy and therefore regularly intervened in and largely externally controlled. In the

---

1   This contribution was presented to the workshop *A Future Security Structure for the Middle East and the Eastern Mediterranean*, Frankfurt, October 1999.

sections that follow we take three different approaches, concluding that the answer is no, no, and probably not.

The first answer is given by structural theory (section 1), the second through a structural analysis of regional security in Europe and the Middle East (section 2), and the third part is an analysis of the current policy of the US as well as European NATO member states as reflected in the new strategic concept of NATO. The "three nos" answer makes the case against either the expectation or the promotion of a discourse of threat between Europe and the Middle East.

With a question like the above, it is easy to get swept away by the policy of the day – today's policy statement by some President, or the crisis of yesterday and the "lessons" we allegedly learned from it. In order to get at a more general pattern, one needs theory and theoretically structured empirical analysis.

The first part of this contribution presents the theory of regional security complexes. One purpose of the section is to introduce the theory we will use throughout, but already the theory itself gives some first suggestion for the most likely answer to the question. From the abstract theory, what pattern is one to expect of two neighbouring regions like Europe and the Middle East? Part two is a more specific analysis of the complexes – their structure, main dynamics and especially the relationship between internal regional, inter-regional and global dynamics. One of the advantages of using the theory here is that it is possible to distinguish between on the one hand external ("superpower") involvement of the kind that is able to dictate or structure a region (overlay), and on the other the kind of participation which is basically pre-structured by the actors of the region, and is therefore unable to override the regional pattern (normal penetration).[2] Without the assistance of theory, single instances of external

---

2   The latter form of external involvement can at the most influence the ability of regional actors to keep or overturn specific balances but not replace one pattern with another.

involvement can easily be interpreted as signs of the former, when a more structural analysis shows the latter to be the case. In the third section, we look at current US policy as well as emerging European policy – both viewed through the April 1999 new "strategic concept" of NATO. We spell out the overall conclusions in section four.

The Theory of Regional Security Complexes

Since the ending of the Cold War, regional patterns of security have increasingly come to dominate international politics. This trend promises to construct a pattern of international relations radically different from the rigid, superpower dominated, bipolar structure that defined the Cold War. *Security complex theory* enables us to understand this process. The central argument in this theory is that security interdependence is normally patterned into regionally based clusters: security complexes. Security interdependence is more intense between the actors inside such complexes than it is between actors inside the complex and those outside it.

A global unfolding of Security Complex Theory[3] thus offers both a vision for the emerging "world order" and a method for studying specific regions. On the former score, it shares with probably the most widely known interpretation of the post-Cold War world, Huntington's *Clash of Civilizations*, a focus on a level between nation-state and "world", on the sub-systems within the global system. However, it takes something close to the opposite approach to this in-between level. Huntington emphasises how large civilizations like Islam, the West, and Asia clash, and how conflicts emerge at the fault-lines of these culturally-based macro-units. We stress that security regions form sub-systems in which most of the security interaction is internal – states fear their neighbours and ally with other regional actors, and

---

3   Buzan/Wæver in preparation.

most often the borders between regions are – often geographically determined – zones of weak interaction, or they are occupied by a buffer-state (Turkey, Burma, Afghanistan) that faces both ways, bearing the burden of this difficult position but not strong enough to unify its two worlds into one. Huntington's theory has the polemical advantage of ending up with a struggle that takes place at the system level which clearly appeals to an American audience – because the US is a global actor. But seen from most countries of the world, the relevant strategic setting is not at the system level – it is regional.

Security at the Regional Level

One of the purposes for inventing the concept "regional security complexes" was to advocate the regional level as the appropriate one for a large swath of practical security analysis. Normally, two too extreme levels dominate security analysis: on the one hand national, and on the other global security. National security – e.g. the security of France – is not in itself a meaningful level of analysis. No nation's security is self-contained: it is *about* other states and thus inherently relational. Global security on the other hand refers at best to an aspiration, not a reality. The globe is not tightly integrated in security terms, and except for superpowers, not too much can be said at this level of generality. The region, in contrast, refers to the constellation where states or other units link together sufficiently closely that their securities cannot be considered separately from each other. The regional level is where the extremes of national and global security interplay, and where most of the action occurs. The general picture is about the interplay of two levels: great power polarity at the system level, and clusters of close security interdependence (in-between which there are distinctly lower levels of security interdependence). Each region is a network of security concerns, i.e. it is ultimately made up of the fears and aspirations of the separate states (which in turn partly derive from domestic features and fractures). Both the security of the separate states and the process of great power intervention can only be grasped through understanding the regional security dynamics.[4]

The Regional Level and Global Powers

Security complex theory is useful in three steps. First it tells us something about the appropriate level of analysis in security studies, secondly it can organise empirical studies, and thirdly, theory-based scenarios can be established on the basis of the known possible forms of, and alternatives to, security complexes. First, however, we have to clarify the status of security complexes and their main analytical components.

Security complexes embody durable patterns of amity and enmity occurring within geographical patterns of security interdependence. The particular character of a local security complex will often be affected by historical factors such as longstanding enmities (Greeks and Turks, Arabs and Persians, Khmers and Vietnamese), or the common cultural embrace of a civilizational area (Arabs, Europeans, South Asians, Northeast Asians, South Americans). The formation of security complexes derives from the interplay between, on the one hand, the anarchic structure and its balance of power consequences, and on the other the pressures of local geographical proximity. Simple physical adjacency tends to generate more security interaction among neighbours than among states located in different areas. Adjacency is potent for security because many threats travel more easily over short distances than over long ones. The impact of geo-

4   It should be noted that the regions we talk about are not necessarily the regions we think of in other contexts or the ones the participants want to be in – they are the regions the world consists of when looked at in one specific way: in terms of security interaction.

graphical proximity on security interaction is strongest and most obvious in the military, political, societal and environmental sectors. The general rule that adjacency increases security interaction is much less consistent in the economic sector.[5] All the states in the system are to some extent enmeshed in a global web of security interdepend-ence. But because insecurity is often associated with proximity, this interdependence is far from uniform. Anarchy plus geographical diversity yields a pattern of regionally based clusters, where security interdependence is markedly more intense between the states inside such complexes than it is between states inside the complex and those outside it. South Asia provides a clear example, where the wars and rivalries of the subcontinent constitute a distinctive pattern that has been little affected by events in the Gulf or in Southeast Asia.[6]

One of the original purposes of the theory was to counter-act excessive emphasis on the global powers ("superpowers") – again probably a bias injected by the massive American dominance within theories of international relations. In most cases, even during the Cold War, regional patterns were not totally overruled and replaced by that of the Cold War. This only happened in East Asia and Europe and is dealt with under the rubric of "overlay". The "normal" situation is that the basic pattern of conflict and cooperation in a region is created by indigenous powers, and the global powers are only included on terms defined from within the region.

Still it is true that superpowers have such wide-ranging interests, and such massive capabilities, that they can conduct their rivalries over the whole planet. Superpowers by definition largely transcend the logic of geography and adjacency in their security relationships. The superpowers form a kind of global security complex amongst themselves, taking the whole planet as their region, and it is for this reason that neo-realist theory focuses on system polarity as its key

---

5   Buzan et al. (1998).
6   Buzan/Rizvi (1986).

structural variable. Smaller states will usually find themselves locked into a regional security complex with their neighbours.

What links the over-arching pattern of distribution of power among the global powers to the regional dynamics of security complexes, is the mechanism of penetration. Penetration occurs when outside powers make security alignments with states within a regional security complex. An indigenous regional rivalry such as that between India and Pakistan provides opportunities for the great powers to penetrate the region. Balance of power logic works naturally to encourage the local rivals to call in outside help, and by this mechanism the local patterns of rivalry become linked to the global ones. South Asia again used to give a clear example, with Pakistan linked to the United States, and China and India linked to the Soviet Union. Such linkage between the local and global security patterns is a natural feature of life in an anarchic system. One of the purposes of SCT (Security Complex Theory) is to combat the tendency to overstress the role of the great powers, and to ensure that the indigenous local factors are given their proper weight in security analysis. The classical form for a regional security complex is a pattern of rivalry, balance of power and alliance patterns among the main powers *within* the region – to this pattern can then be added penetrating external powers. Normally the pattern of conflicts stem from factors indigenous to the region – like for instance in South Asia, or in the Middle East – and outside powers (even if heavily involved) can not define, settle or reorganise the region.[7]

In the classic case, the pattern of conflict and cooperation is best understood by starting the analysis from the regional level, and extending it towards inclusion of the global actors on the one side

7   Unipolarity might in its extreme form be an exception, where the fact that both sides of a local conflict are dependent on the same power gives it a possibility to pressure conflicting parties into peace processes, cf. the Middle East (see Hansen, forthcoming) and in the case of European regional unipolarity e.g. Hungarian minorities and the Stability Pact (Wæver 1998).

and domestic factors on the other. In one other respect – to which we return – the global level "comes first": global polarity is a condition for the nature of regional dynamics,[8] but the specific pattern of who fears whom is not imported but generated internally in the region.

The Four Levels of a Regional Security Constellation

The most well-established function for SCT is as a framework organizing empirical studies of regional security. The theory specifies what to look for at four levels of analysis and how to interrelate these. The four are:

- domestically in the states of the region (particularly their domestically generated vulnerabilities),[9]
- state-to-state relations (which generate the region as such),
- the region's interaction with neighbouring regions (which is supposed to be *relatively* limited given that the complex is defined by interaction internally being more important; but if major changes in the patterns of security interdependence that define complexes are underway, this level can become significant),
- the role of global powers in the region.

Taken together, these four levels constitute the *security constellation*.[10] SCT asserts that the regional level will always be operative,

---

8 Thanks to Kenneth Waltz for reminding us of this.

9 The particular vulnerabilities of states are closely linked to domestic conditions: is the state strong due to the stability of the domestic order and correspondence between state and nation; or is it weak (Buzan 1991)? The specific vulnerability of a state defines the kind of security fears it has (Wæver 1989) – and sometimes makes another state or group of states an automatic threat even if there is no intention hereof. For instance the organizing principles of Pakistan and India mutually question each other, and the social orders of East and West during the Cold War contained implicit when not explicit threats against the other side by their very being.

10 Buzan et al. (1998: 201ff).

and sometimes dominant. It does *not* say that the regional level *must* always be dominant. The question of which level is dominant is not set by the theory, even though particular sets of circumstances (on which more later) might swing the odds one way or another. What the balance amongst the levels is rests on empirical observation of particular cases. Just as in the social world individual psychology might be most influential in explaining behaviour in one case, family structures in another, and society in another, so in the international world domestic factors might dominate some security constellations, regional ones others, and global ones yet others. The regional level may or may not dominate, but it will nearly always be in play in some significant sense, and cannot be dropped out of the analysis.

In its descriptive application SCT has been useful to area specialists and other people working empirically on specific regions. The theory has been valued for its possibility to link systematically the four levels in an integrated analysis – not forcing artificial choices between e.g. domestic and international explanations. It also provides some specific explanations, most notably the hypothesis that regional patterns of conflict shape the lines of intervention by great powers. Other things being equal, the expectation is that outside powers will be drawn into a region along the lines of rivalry existing within it. In this way regional patterns of rivalry will line up with, and be reinforced by, great power ones, even though the great power patterns may have had little or nothing to do with the formation of the regional pattern.

In studying a specific region, an important purpose of SCT is to establish a benchmark against which to identify and assess changes at the regional level. The most important forms of change are: 1) internal transformation which means that either the power polarity or the dominant patterns of amity/enmity change within the context of its existing outer boundary (because of disintegration, merger, conquest, differential growth rates, or the like); 2) external transformation which means that the outer boundary expands or contracts, transforming either or both of polarity and amity/enmity.[11]

Four Possible Forms for an Area to Exist in

An area can exist in four possible forms. The first two are situations when a region *does not form a security complex*.

Overlay is when great power interests transcend mere penetration, and come to dominate a region so heavily that the local pattern of security relations virtually ceases to operate. It usually results in the long-term stationing of great power armed forces in the region, and in the alignment of the local states according to the patterns of great power rivalry. The classic examples of overlay are European colonisation and the situation of Europe itself during the Cold War. It is not always self-evident where to draw the boundary between overlay and mere heavy penetration of a complex by great powers. The key to the distinction is that outside powers must have substantial military forces based in the region, and that the main security dynamics of the region are shaped by the rivalries of the outside powers rather than by the interests and interactions of the local states. [12]

Unstructured security regions occur where local states are so weak that their power does not project much, if at all, beyond their own boundaries, and so generates insufficient security interdependence to form the structures of a security complex. No regional secu-

11 Most probably as a result of two security complexes merging, as might happen if Israel became concerned about Pakistan's "Islamic" nuclear weapons, or a sub-complex drifting off to "independence" or into another complex – Maghreb? – or finally the grand repercussions of the disintegration of the Soviet Union which has not yet settled down in the CIS area and its neighbouring regions.

12 On the need to see overlay as not being a security complex – and reflections on the possibility of defining an overlaid region as a security complex on the basis of its distinct security dynamics within the general conflict formation imposed from the global level – see Buzan (1989) and Wæver (1990).

rity complex exists because the units do not become each other's main security concern. These states typically have domestically directed security perspectives.[13] Parts of sub-Saharan Africa after decolonisation served until recently to illustrate this condition. The image is of a security constellation dominated by the domestic level, and perhaps also the inter-regional and global levels.

The next two forms are the two main forms a *security complex* can take.

"Classical" security complexes. These are conflict formations and security regimes in which the region is defined by a pattern of rivalries, balances, alliances, and/or concerts. Within a classical complex the main element of security politics in the area is the relationship among the major powers within the region. Their shifting relations set the terms for the minor powers and for the penetration of the region by global actors. This kind of complex is clearly anarchic in structure, and polarity may vary from bi- to multipolar.

"Centred" regions where centralisation of power in a region reaches a point where its centre is primarily to be seen as a participant in the global security constellation among the greatest powers, whereas the regional dynamics no longer form a balance of power system. One example of this is North America. The region is so centred that its internal regional dynamics get suppressed. The core actor is driven much more by global than by regional security dynamics, and it is primarily global concerns that drive its security impositions on its smaller neighbours. Because the core actor is globally orientated, the security dynamics of the region are hugely distorted and suppressed. But since all other actors in the region have their concerns linked to each other, a general map of global security would still show a clear regional formation of densely knit connections compared to a lack of connections in and out of the regions for most units. This therefore can still be treated as a security complex.

13 Buzan (1991: 197f).

The potential for internal transformation can be monitored by checking material conditions for possible changes (or not) of polarity, and discursive ones for possible changes (or not) of amity/enmity relations. The potential for external transformation can be monitored by looking at the intensity of interregional security dynamics, which should act as precursors to change. Where these are sparse and low intensity, as between South and Southeast Asia, no change in the boundaries of security complexes is likely. Where interregional security dynamics are fairly thick, intense, and increasing, external transformations become more likely. The boundary between South Asia and the Middle East remains interesting in this regard, as do those between the Middle East and the Horn of Africa, and the Middle East and the Balkans.

"Deeper" conditions like global polarity or the level of technological development in a region, make usually one or more scenarios unavailable to a given region. Usually, a region is so solidly set on a self-reinforcing course that only one of the four forms seem relevant, but at crucial historical moments, two or three are possible and the underlying conditions do not fully determine which wins out – political decisions do.

Regional Security Complex Analysis of Europe, the Middle East and their Relationship

Regional security complexes are normally defined mainly by their internal dynamics, and inter-regional dynamics are as a rule among the weakest of the four levels. Often inter-regional dynamics occur in one or two of the "new" sectors of security such migration or environmental issues, but if the politico-military dynamics at the inter-regional level became dominant, we would by definition be dealing with a potential shift of boundary, i.e. a merger of or complete re-configuring of two complexes.

To answer the question with more confidence, the theory of course has to be applied and the two regions analysed so that we can decide which of the four forms the two are in, what are their major security dynamics, and thereby how important inter-regional dynamics are to them and how likely they are to become of major importance to each other.

The theory suggests that if we identify Europe and the Middle East as security complexes, we should expect the security relationship between them to be relatively marginal. What does a more empirical look suggest?

Europe

Europe has at one time or another in its history been in all of the basic forms: centred, fragmented, overlaid and being overlayer itself. But rarely has Europe been a region in the full sense, i.e. a region amongst other regions in a global system.

The earliest chapters are about empires, but an empire like the Roman Empire is not a region – most of the time it was a *world*. History from then is about the formation of two different security complexes in Europe – one in West-and-South and a North-Eastern complex around the Baltic (with Russia, Sweden and Denmark as main players). For some time in the 17th Century the two merged into one, but shortly after this, the new complex became something very special because with Europe's global expansion, Europe was no longer a region in the world – Europe became the world, or rather the power centre of the world. The European great powers became the global great powers. With the two world wars of the 20th Century, this was reversed and Europe moved rapidly from being dominant to being dominated – but again *not a security region in the world*.

For close to 45 years, Europe was overlaid by the Cold War. Now after the end of the Cold War, overlaying is no longer a possibility (because Europe is too strong in relation to any potential overlayer), nor is the unstructured form (because Europe is far too developed and too integrated to drop to that level), which left Europe with two possibilities: the centred and the "normal" complex.

The normal one would imply a return to open power balancing and mutual security concerns among the European great powers. Watching the return of wars and barbarism to Europe in the Balkan wars of the 1990s, some realists might triumphantly find their prognosis about "back to the future"[14] vindicated, but actually European developments went the wrong way for them. The conflicts in ex-Yugoslavia were neither caused by nor became the trigger for conflicting interventions by rival great powers. Instead, Europe has largely taken a very different shape: a pattern of concentric circles around an EU core. Most major issues in Europe have been of a centre-periphery nature: what is necessary to become a central – maybe "core country" – in the new Europe, and what are the advantages and disadvantages of keeping or being kept at more distance. The EU as well as NATO operate as a pole of attraction, and Europe becomes shaped by the magnetism of this Western centre. Still European integration has not progressed to the point of centralisation necessary to pronounce Europe definitely in the centred mode. The EU has not replaced the member states but co-exists with them in odd and challenging ways.

The integration scenario at first sounds like the classical idealist vision of "unify for peace" as it was professed by philosophers and irenists for centuries, but in contrast to their futile appeals, there is today a real power basis for taking integration and fragmentation as two equally realistic options: Europe is today as never before in its international history *one region amongst many*. In this situation, the main European powers are not global powers in their own right, and the vision of integration is therefore no longer an idealistic appeal to

14 Mearsheimer (1990).

the globally leading powers for surrendering their power. It is a pre-condition for re-gaining global standing and – as the other side of this coin – for repressing internal dynamics of power balancing, fear and rivalry.

Before we go into detail with the development in relation to these two scenarios, the delineation of the complex needs to be addressed, because Europe is one of the regions, where the end of the Cold War led to external transformation, i.e. a change of boundaries of the security complex. At first, the Europe that emerged seem to contain all of Europe "from the Atlantic to the Urals" – Russia was part of a generally cooperative security order based on the combination of EU, NATO and – for the Russians: not least – OSCE. Increasingly, however, the relationship between Russia and the West was strained. Russia was not taken into account and included as much as it wished, and simultaneously it built its own order with little Western influence in most of the former Soviet Union. Thus, the CIS area emerged into a security complex of its own, and a vague boundary emerged between a (West and Central) European complex on the one hand and this Russia-centred one on the other. There was no hard competition, but at worst what Yeltsin labelled "cold peace" – a gradually clearer drawing of a sphere of interest boundary, a pulling apart rather than a going up against each other. Without being spelled out, it is quite clear today who ended up in what complex: the former Warsaw Pact states from Poland to Romania in the European complex and ex-Soviet republics in the Russian one with the Baltic states as the main focus of contention.

Another boundary issue was settled the opposite way. Was the Balkans also to drift off to become a separate complex? It clearly developed a quite distinct form of security dynamics from the rest of Europe in the 1990s and much spoke for EU Europe trying to contain and isolate this (micro) complex; it intervened some but basically did not try to bring the Balkans in as part of the European complex. However, with the solutions to the two major wars being the erection of Western protectorates in Bosnia-Herzegovina and Kosovo and a large EU-financed economic programme for all of the region, it is now clear that the EU has (more or less consciously) committed itself so deeply that the only way to handle the Balkans is to bring it into Europe. A paradoxical result of the brutality of the wars has been this inclusion, which has generally speeded up an EU enlargement perspective beyond the first applicants – the EU has been reminded that only by keeping enlargement as a constantly rolling series of waves, can also the more "distant" applicants be stabilised and given a prospect necessary for security and reform. Thus, the overall structure of "wider Europe" is of two complexes – Russia-centred CIS and "EU-centred Europe" – and a sub-complex within the European one, which is not drifting off but being pulled (back) into the larger complex. The Balkan dimension reinforces core-periphery/concentric circles features of the region (to which we return below) and it ties quite a lot of EU attention and efforts into its near abroad rather than inter-regional projects. The discussion in the rest of this section of the two scenarios is with reference to EU-centred Europe including the Balkans; Russia is a separate story and not very relevant here.

In a long-term perspective, the choice between integration and fragmentation is an either/or one. Generally, states are most likely to be concerned about neighbouring states rather than far-away ones, and in a grey-zone existence between integration and fragmentation, the most likely long-term development is not to exist as semi-independent units and form ad hoc coalitions against outsiders when needed. "Nay, it is far more probable that [...] neighbouring nations, acting under the impulse of opposite interests and unfriendly passions, would frequently be found taking different sides".[15] Based on this reasoning – consonant with the basic idea of security complex theory – *The Federalist Papers* convinced Americans when they were in this in-between situations, that they had to unify more to avoid

15 Hamilton et al. (1787–89).

being pulled apart. The quote continues "considering our distance from Europe, it would be more natural for these confederacies to apprehend danger from one another than from distant nations, and therefore that each of them should be more desirous to guard against the others by the aid of foreign alliances, than to guide against foreign dangers by alliances between themselves".[16] A region with strong internal security rivalry is not able to act coherently towards the external world, and on the contrary, when you cohere enough to act together globally, this external role serves to discipline internal policy. Therefore, theory as well as history suggest that the in-between situation is unstable, and regions ultimately have their security dynamics mainly internally or a centralizing core organises the internal side while being driven itself by the external agenda.

So far the European choice between integration and fragmentation has not been decisively settled, although integration has been dominant, and fragmentation mostly operates as a worst case scenario which might actually be crucial to the success of integration, because it is a threat of what could happen if integration failed.

After the end of the Cold War, Europe has been marked by an unusual diversity of security issues. Parts of the "new" security agenda like identity and environment are prominent, and so are new "referent objects" – ethnic groups, regions, etc. Notably, there are few of the classical security issues in the form of State-A fears State-B. Increasingly, two main security issues are crystallizing out of this messy picture:

One has "Europe" as reference and the most intense and regular threat was Europe itself, the risk of Europe's past becoming also Europe's future.[17] Europe after the Cold War has generally been very reluctant to draw up new "enemy images" or build unity against some new "Other": the other is Europe's past which Europe tries to

---

16 Ibid.
17 Buzan et al. (1998), also Wæver (1996).

break free of. The security argument is that because of the risk of a return to power balancing, rivalry and thereby eventually war, we have to do this (integrate) and abstain from that (beggar-thy-neighbour, or rival intervention policies).

The other discourse is about identity ("societal security"). It links integration and fragmentation in the other direction. Together with reactions against immigrants and against globalisation, the fear of integration defines a general fearful turn towards national identity in most European countries.

These two discourses are expressions of the two underlying structural options; one is a fear of fragmentation, the other of integration. The hard choice of integration/fragmentation has so far been avoided for two reasons:

One is the complex global power structure. The post-Cold War system has a structure somewhere between multipolarity and a kind of unipolarity. The element of unipolarity – US supremacy – weakens the structural pressure and has produced a complex situation in Europe where the regional structural pressure only operates in a muted form, which explains the continued centrality of NATO.

The other is that the two scenarios drive each other because they have been discursively tied together. The two options are not only constructions on a theorist's computer screen, they are very much alive as beliefs that practitioners act upon. Therefore, integration triggers fragmentation and fragmentation triggers integration: having Germany unified and Eastern Europe freed was widely feared to contain a risk of instability, and therefore integration was speeded up, which in turn led to re-actions first in Denmark and France, which again stimulated efforts to construct a hard core, etc. It is not that the two cancel each other out because this shapes Europe in a distinct way, it strengthens a pattern of core/periphery, hard core, concentric circles, multi-speed and differentiated membership. The coherence of the core is necessary for security reasons, and if this cannot be implemented the "normal" way due to resistance, it will be constructed differently, and this drives the EU in a post-sovereign direction. The immediate future is neither a new state nor sovereign member states but EU as some kind of post-modern "empire". "Empire" because it is constructed in a radial mode around a power centre with decreasing degrees of control as one moves out through concentric circles.

In the current security architecture of Europe, the EU is the most important security institution. When one gets the contrary impression from the media, where NATO is celebrated as the key, it is because the "news" (and security experts) concentrates on actual, manifest conflicts and wars, and in that case NATO is the most potent instrument for intervention. However, it is at least as important who manages to shape a continent in a general sense and thereby pre-empts a lot of issues that never become security issues. The EU is deeper and more general than NATO and therefore it ties and shapes the West European great powers in a more effective way (both in terms of "rational choice" – it is more expensive to leave the EU than NATO – and in identity terms – the national identities have become intertwined with a vision of Europe, not of NATO). NATO is a much "thinner" organization. It can therefore not do the shaping, but it is extremely valuable to European security and thus there is an unusually widespread consensus about keeping it intact.

NATO depends on the EU, and EU on NATO. The first because the EU keeps the core West European powers (France and Germany especially) from reverting to old-style balance of power behaviour and on this basis it is possible to cooperate with the Americans in NATO. EU's dependence on NATO is partly based on the fact that integration has been easier because it could avoid the thorny issues of defence and security, and partly because the presence of the US has a stabilising function, muting mutual fears.

More concretely, the EU has three security functions, distributed according to the logic of concentric circles:

– keeping the core intact (ensuring continued cooperation and avoidance of security fears among the great powers in Europe),

- disciplining the "near abroad" (pulling applicants away from old-fashioned issues like borders and minorities towards the behaviour that is rewarded from the West: human rights, democracy, minority rights, uncontested borders, etc.),
- being a potential intervenor in actual violent conflicts.

NATO in turn is less and less of an alliance; it is not about the existential fears of the member states. Instead it has become a unique instrument for foreign policy – the world's most potent and competent military organisation. In addition, it serves to socialise "new countries" into a multinational form of military professionalism, which dampens mutual concerns about military security. NATO is therefore highly valued by its members (and applicants), but it does not have the same structural foundations as in the Cold War, and can therefore be seen as "strong but fragile".[18]

The evolving relationship between EU and NATO (ESDI, CJTF, etc.) has over ten years evolved within a basic consensus to try to both upgrade European contributions and ability to act separately and ensure that NATO is not challenged by a rival organisation. Inside this consensus there are battles at every stage about the exact balance (usually Franco-American battles), but the general impression is one of mutual adjustment and complementarity. The oddity of this organisational set-up stems from the fact that the Cold War never became hot. Thus, the organisational set-up was not redrawn from scratch after 1989. Organisations continue that could never have been invented today (NATO and maybe even the EU). Thus, the situation is not a pure reflection of underlying structure; it is path dependent. But on the other hand, there are clear advantages of building on the institutions handed over from the Cold War, and therefore the European "security architecture" is overly complex and not basically "logical", but a lot of adjustment and "interlocking" of

18 We return to NATO in more detail in section 3.

institutions takes place in a very logical way. Also the OSCE is complementary and included in the overall architecture, but clearly marginalised compared to the two other key organisations, EU and NATO. The basic triangle of those three has been supplemented by organisations like the EAPG and the WEU.

The general picture is one of a dominance of integration, but in a surprising form, partly because of global quasi unipolarity and partly because of internal opposition, which means that it does not happen directly in the normal state format but "sideways" as a post-sovereign "empire". Europe is multilayered and its politics moves between European and national layers of identity. In a sense this is the Arab story in the opposite direction: where the Arab world was previously marked by pan-Arab (and pan-Islamic) loyalties being played against national ones, and now moves in the direction of a more clear-cut sovereignty based system,[19] Europe has been the proto-typical sovereignty based region which now creates multilayered identities and politics.

How does this structure shape inter-regional and global relations? What are the international relations of this unit? Inwards, it opens Europe to some influence – from the US because of the NATO component, and to neighbouring regions (CIS and Middle East) because of unclear boundaries due to the empire gradually fading out. Outwards, the likely objects of attention for the EU also follow from this structure. The structural security agenda of the EU (not yet looking at actual policy and discourse, section 3) is, in order of priority:

- keep the core intact; the overall project of integration instead of fragmentation,
- act at the global level, compete techno-economically with the US and Japan,
- Eastern enlargement,

19 Barnett (1998).

- solve or prevent conflicts in the more distant periphery. Not least to the extent that conflict threatens, if unattended to, to escalate into problems among the core countries and thus influence the EU's first priority.

If the EU should become more interventionist in relation to the Middle East, it would have to be as a re-interpretation of its second priority, i.e. a re-definition of the nature of global competition, but there is no sign of this at all. As problems in their own right, neither the spill-overs from the Middle East, nor a European interest in shaping Middle Eastern developments figure high (or at all) on the European security agenda.

The Middle East

The Middle East is a place where the regional level of security has operated particularly strongly for several decades, despite heavy impositions from the global level both during and after the Cold War. Its security complex is a clear example of a conflict formation, albeit one that is unusually complicated, and possessing some strong and distinctive cultural features. This security complex is one in which the regional level is both strong and autonomous. The regional level is indeed the dominant one for security analysis, though this was not always understood during the Cold War, when global level superpower machinations were often credited with more influence than they actually had. The story of the Middle Eastern complex can largely be told within the state-centric, military-political framework of classical security complex theory. Hostile military-political interaction between states dominates the scene, and virtually all other security issues, whether societal (identity and migration) or environmental (water), are thoroughly enmeshed in the pervasive interstate rivalry. But as in many other places in the Third World, the insecurity of ruling elites within their domestic sphere plays a significant role in shaping the dynamics of (in)security overall.[20]

At least from 1948, the gradual process of decolonisation had produced a critical mass of independent states and a triggering issue (Israel) to start regional dynamics. Like several other regions made up mostly of former colonies, the Middle Eastern complex was born fighting. The independence of Israel moved the earlier conflict between Palestinians and Zionist migrants to the state level, and triggered the first of the many interstate wars that shaped this turbulent conflict formation. At its peak, more than twenty states formed the complex, and many of these were relatively equal in weight. This fact, plus its dispersed geography, means that this complex has more than one centre. During this period, it developed three cores or sub-complexes: two main ones centred respectively in the Levant and in the Gulf, and a considerably weaker one in the Maghreb.

It is tempting (but difficult) to try to capture the conflict dynamics of the Middle East in terms of some simple formula. The fact that the two main cores can be interpreted as Arabs versus "others" (Jews, Iranians), and that there is an earlier legacy of Arabs versus Turks from the Ottoman days (and still present in a variety of Kurdish problems), makes it tempting to look for simplifying ethno-religious explanations of the region's insecurities. Israel represents both ethnic and religious differentiation from its Arab (and mostly Islamic) neighbours, while Iran represents an ethnic differentiation and the Shi'a side of the Sunni-Shi'a split within Islam. As Chubin and Tripp note: "For Iran, a dispute with any Arab neighbour risks becoming a dispute with all its Arab neighbours [...]",[21] an observation that applies to Israel with even more force. But while this simplification captures an important element of the truth, it does not cover the whole. For as Barnett has demonstrated, the construction of

20 Ayoob (1995: 188–96), Barnett (1998: 9).
21 Chubin/Tripp (1996: 4)

Arab nationalism has generated a unique form of inter-Arab politics that has generated considerably more rivalry and conflict than cooperation and harmony.[22] The region thus also contains a distinct Arab agenda that contains rivalries over Arab leadership and interpretations of Arabism, as well as more traditional types of rivalry over water, ideology and territory. There has been quite a bit of interplay between the Arab versus non-Arab dynamics on the one hand, and the Arab versus Arab ones on the other. A case could be made that as a rule, the Arab versus non-Arab disputes take precedence over the Arab versus Arab ones, but there are important exceptions to this. Arab Syria has aligned with non-Arab Iran when Iran was at war with Arab Iraq. Both Jordan and Syria have attacked the Palestinians despite their collective Arab stand against Israel; Syria occupies a substantial chunk of Lebanon, and has on various occasions threatened force against Jordan. The patterns of amity and enmity in the Middle East are remarkable for their convoluted and crosscutting character.

The first, still principal, and in many ways defining core sub-complex was the conflict centred in the Levant between the Palestinians and Israel. This local struggle set up a much wider hostility between Israel and the Arab world,[23] and to a lesser extent between Israel and the even wider Islamic world (particularly, after 1979, Iran). This Arab-Israel conflict, and the strong transnational qualities of Arab nationalism and Islamic politics which it amplified (and indeed in some ways defined – Barnett 1998: 121-3), is what gave the Middle East its overall coherence as a security complex during this period. Without these common cultural bonds, it seems rather unlikely that a collection of small and medium-sized powers with members as geographically far apart as Morocco and Oman, would ever have cohered into a single security complex. It is the shared symbols of

22 Barnett (1998).
23 Tibi (1993: 183–4)

Arabism, and to a lesser extent Islam, and their focus on the conflict with Israel, that enabled the security dynamics of the Middle East to operate across such large distances. Without them, there would almost certainly have been no single Middle Eastern security complex. Instead, there would probably have been two or possibly three smaller complexes formed around the Gulf, the Maghreb and maybe the Levant.

The second core sub-complex in the Middle East, which centred on the Gulf, formed during the 1970s, after Britain's withdrawal from the area in 1971. This is centred on a triangular rivalry amongst Iran, Iraq, and the Gulf Arab states led by Saudi Arabia, though there is also a peripheral rivalry between Saudi Arabia and Yemen. The 1979 revolution in Iran added a sharp ideological element to its rivalry with Saudi Arabia, since both states claimed leadership of competing Islamic universalisms.[24] The hostility between Iran and Iraq stems from a variety of border disputes plus the rival power ambitions of the leaders in both states. It can also be understood as an extension of a very much older rivalry between Arabs and Persians, and the Shi'a and Sunni variants of Islam, which goes back to the eighth century. These ethnic, cultural and sectarian factors played a similarly big role in modern tensions between Iran and Iraq, and between Iran and the Gulf Arabs. The inter-Arab tensions between the Gulf Arabs and Iraq are more particular, having to do with disputes over the price of oil, a general fear amongst the Gulf Arabs of the hegemonic ambitions of Saddam Hussein, and in the case of Kuwait, the specific fear created by Iraq's repeated rejection of its claim to independence.

Although each of these sub-complexes has a distinct dynamic at its core, their close geographical proximity means that there is a lot of crossover between them which helps to knit the whole complex together.

24 Chubin/Tripp (1996: 15, 71)

The third, weaker, sub-complex in the Middle Eastern complex during this period was that in the Maghreb. It was basically about a shifting and uneasy set of relationships amongst Libya, Tunisia, Algeria and Morocco, also extending into Chad and Western Sahara. Its main focus was the Moroccan annexation of Western Sahara starting in 1975, which led to a twelve-year tension with Algeria and Libya, both of which backed the Polisario fighters against the Moroccan occupation. Morocco in turn backed Libya's opponents in Chad. The Maghreb states had enough involvement in the Arab-Israel dispute, and also in the Gulf conflicts, so that their membership in the Middle Eastern complex was not in doubt. Libya took a strong political stand against Israel, and sided with radical and opposed traditionalist regimes in the Gulf. Tunisia hosted the PLO offices for many years. In the other direction, Egypt aided the Algerians during their war of liberation against France, but in general the rest of the Arab world was not much involved in the disputes of the Maghreb sub-complex. The affairs of the core sub-complexes did however reach into the Maghreb, as when the Saudis cut off financial aid to Morocco after the latter supported the Camp David accords during the late 1970s.

If this area and its interstate (in)security dynamics define the main lines of the regional level of security in the Middle East, how did this level relate to those above and below it? What did the security constellation as a whole look like? Broadly put, both the regional and the global levels were independently strong, as well as strongly interactive, during this period. The domestic level was significant, but with only a few exceptions was largely contained within a stable state framework. The inter-regional level was of only marginal importance.

The domestic level in the Middle East bears some similarity to that in East and South Asia. Most of the states in the region are towards the weak end of the spectrum of socio-political cohesion. Democracy is rare, dictatorship common, and the use of force and repression in domestic political life endemic. But for the most part, and in contrast to Africa, this domestic turbulence does not dominate the international security agenda. Despite the whole debate about the Arab state, and the obvious centrality of Pan-Arab and Pan-Islamic ideologies (both of which create strong transnational identities and authorities that can be mobilised against the project to construct national states), the fact remains that, unlike in Africa, the state system has consolidated itself. Hurst notes the remarkably long tenure of many leaders and political systems in the Middle East.[25] Yapp argues that despite all the decades of war and turbulence, the state structures left behind by decolonisation have nearly all survived.[26] Iran and Iraq survived their long war with each other, and Iraq even survived its catastrophic defeat in the second Gulf War. Barnett also argues that the norms and values of sovereignty and national identity have steadily gained ground over Pan-Arab alternatives, notwithstanding the sustained use of Pan-Arab rhetoric by many Arab leaders to undermine each other's domestic legitimacy by appealing to the Arab "street".[27]

The global level operated powerfully in the Middle East during this period. In effect, the region became a third front in the Cold War, after Europe and Asia. This story is well known, and need not detain us long here. The United States and the Soviet Union were drawn into the regional turbulence, which was strongly active by the time they made their main appearance. Superpower interest in the region was heightened by the fact that, like Europe, the Middle East sat on the boundary between the spheres of the communist and "free" worlds. Stalin's inept policy of threatening Turkey and Iran in the years immediately following the Second World War had backfired, pushing both countries into the arms of the West. Turkey

25 Hurst (1999: 8).
26 Yapp (1991: 35–46, 411–18, 432).
27 Barnett (1998).

became a member of NATO, and was thus fixed into the main European front of the Cold War. Until the Islamic revolution in 1979, Iran fell increasingly under American sway, and became part of the rather looser alliance arrangements that connected American containment clients in Turkey, Iran and Pakistan. To counter this US success right on its borders, the Soviet Union tried to play in the Arab world behind this front line, by establishing political and military links to the radical regimes and movements that sprang up in the Middle East during the 1950s and 60s.[28]

Although drawn into the Gulf by its oil investments, and into Turkey and Iran by containment policy, the US was a reluctant entrant into the wider Middle East. It had no real interest in the numerous local disputes, but could not ignore Soviet successes during the 1950s and 60s in arming the radical Arabs behind the containment front line. Despite the waning of Soviet influence in the region after 1967, and even more so after 1973, the US became increasingly tied into the fate of Israel. Since being allied to Israel tended to put it at odds with the Arab and Islamic states, the US found itself in a bind in relation to the pursuit of its oil interests, which required good relations with the Gulf Arabs, Iran, Iraq, Libya and Algeria. These contradictory commitments, plus a basic lack of interest in the local conflicts, made it almost impossible for the US to have a coherent Middle East policy, even though it was increasingly the main outside player in the region.

In contrast with the other levels, and in line with the expectations of SCT, the inter-regional level for the Middle East is quite marginal to the overall configuration of the security constellation. There was quite a lot of activity across the frontier zone between the Middle East and Africa, but this was a largely one-way relationship with influence flowing from the Middle East into Africa, and not much coming the other way. There were also some security links between

28 Syria, PLO, Iraq, Egypt, Libya, Algeria, Yemen, see Yapp (1991: 411–18).

Pakistan, and both Iran and Saudi Arabia, reinforced by shared linkages to the US at the global level. But these links were never of such
an extent even to begin to blur the boundary between the essentially
distinct security dynamics of these two regions. The one relationship
that might have merged the security dynamics of the Middle East
and South Asia, an alliance between India and Israel against Pakistan's project for an "Islamic bomb", never amounted to more than
a rumour. On the border with Europe, Turkey remained an effective
insulator, keeping the security dynamics of Europe and the Middle
East quite distinct.

Summing up the security constellation of the Middle East during
the Cold War, we can conclude the following. The domestic level
was active but largely contained with the state system. Only in the
case of Israel and the Palestinians did the domestic level have major
upward impacts on the regional one. The regional level of security
was exceptionally strong, and deeply rooted in the character of local
politics and history. Once the decolonisation process reached critical
mass, all of the major disputes that shaped the insecurities of the
Middle East would have been there regardless of outside influence
and intervention. Because of the region's location adjacent to major
centres of world power and US-Soviet confrontation, the impact of
the global level was also strong. But the superpowers and their ideological rivalry did not, as they did in Southeast Asia, strongly shape
the regional patterns. They regularly amplified them by providing
weapons and political support to the various antagonists. Sometimes
they constrained the conflict, as in the US-sponsored peace process
after the 1973 war. But the indigenous regional conflicts were not
about Cold War issues, and it is therefore no surprise that they survived the ending of the Cold War largely unchanged.

The post-Cold War era in the Middle East can be conveniently
dated from the simultaneous dissolution of the Soviet Union and
Iraq's invasion of Kuwait in 1990 (and its subsequent defeat and
expulsion early in 1991 by a massive intervention force created and

led by the United States). The Second Gulf War, and its long historical shadow, changed some of the basic structures of the Middle Eastern complex and its component sub-complexes. Its main consequences were:

- It weakened Iraq militarily in relation to its neighbours, thus
  changing the balance of power in the Gulf sub-complex, though
  not altering the basic triangular structure of the rivalry in the Gulf.
- It strengthened the position of the Western powers, and especially
  the US, in the GCC states, making them more explicitly into protectorates, and increasing the relative weight of global factors in
  the security dynamics of the Gulf.
- It opened the way for the beginning of the peace process between
  Israel on the one hand, and the Palestinians, Jordan and Syria, as
  well as some of the more peripheral Arab states, on the other. By
  doing so it opened the possibility for normalising relations
  between Israel and the Arabs.
- More arguably, it weakened the link between the five Maghreb
  states (which supported neither Iraq nor the intervention against
  it) and the rest of the Middle Eastern complex.
- Perhaps more arguably still, Saddam's venture struck a mortal
  blow to Arabism. By using Arabist rhetoric to justify annexing
  another Arab country, Saddam added the last straw to what was
  already a compelling case that the pursuit of Arabism had been
  massively dysfunctional for both the Arab states and their people.[29]
  If this was true, then the main glue holding the wider Middle Eastern complex together (i.e. the idea that all Arab states had a right
  and a duty to be involved in the affairs of other Arab states)
  would have been dissolved.

These effects of the Second Gulf War were reinforced by the demise
of the Soviet Union and the withdrawal of Soviet military and politi-

29 Barnett (1998: 213–236).

cal support for its former clients in the region. The level of global intervention into the Middle Eastern complex did not decline, but its character changed radically. Instead of projecting a bipolar super-power rivalry into the region, reinforcing its internal lines of conflict, the post-Cold War global intervention took on a unipolar form, with a dominant US using its influence to dampen the interstate conflictual security dynamics of both core sub-complexes, though perhaps at a price in exacerbating domestic turmoil.

The prospect for the 1990s and beyond was thus shaped by two possibilities for redefining the security constellation. First was that the indigenous military-political insecurity dynamics of the region would become weaker and more moderate, perhaps to the point of changing the membership of the complex, at least around the edges. Second was that global level intervention in the region would largely cease to amplify local interstate conflict (but perhaps at some cost in amplifying intra-state ones), while playing a considerably stronger role in repressing and moderating the indigenous regional security dynamics. Taken together, these offered a serious prospect that the Middle East might move at least towards a less intense type of conflict formation. Added to these, and in some ways related to them, were two possible changes in the shape of the complex. First was the question of whether the Maghreb states would become largely detached from the Middle East core, drifting towards a more autonomous relationship with the EU and Africa. Second was the possibility that Turkey would abandon its longstanding policy by re-engaging with the Middle East.[30]

Maghreb was first of all tied into the Middle East because of inter-Arab politics, which again depended to a large extent on the Arab-Israeli conflict as unifying issue. With the Israel-Palestinian peace process and the general decline of pan-Arabism, this glue has been weakened, and only to a limited extent been replaced by the

---

30 Buzan/Diez (1999); Nachmani (1999).

inter-connections made up of a potentially cascading radical Islam.[31] The Maghreb is therefore less self-evidently part of the Middle East. In some respects it has become a part of an emerging landscape of African proto-complexes.[32] In other – and in the long run probably more decisive respects, Maghreb is a periphery of Europe. Developments relating to Maghreb are high on the list of security concerns in some (parts of) some EU states (migration, possible nearby conflicts). And in the understanding of most actors in Maghreb, Europe is a key to their own future developments.[33]

At first one might thus discern strong inter-regional dynamics between the Middle East and Europe in the western Mediterranean, but this generally happens at the same speed as Maghreb gets detached from the Middle East, and thus Europe-Middle Eastern security interaction is not growing.

Turkey has become a more independent actor these years. From being a largely passive insulator between Europe and the Middle East (and CIS), it has become more active in trying to operate its complex environment by thinking regionally in several directions.[34] One reason for this is less confidence in EU-membership (despite revitalization of the relationship after the 1999 earthquake), another cause or effect is less distaste for Middle Eastern activities (most

---

31 Gause (1999: 25f).
32 Cf. e.g. "Qaddafi says farewell, Arabia, and sets his sights on Africa", in: The Economist, 24 April 1999: 47f.
33 As a periphery to Europe, Maghreb is in interesting ways both parallel to and different from Eastern Europe. The need for EU engagement and support rests on the same kinds of (partly security based) arguments of mostly a transnational nature. And thus at one level, we witness EU bargains where France, Spain and Italy insist on similar attention and budgets for North Africa as Germany and others want for the East. But in one respect the two areas are not parallel: Eastern Europe has a membership prospect which North Africa does not. Therefore, the policy across the Mediterranean is in a sense more difficult because problems have to be solved by normal economic and political means, not by imposing self-discipline tied to the prospect of membership.
34 Kazan (1999).

importantly its strategic partnership with Israel). Furthermore, the new found interest in Caucasus and Central Asia, has led Turkey to defining a more independent, active profile. Thus, Turkey continues to be the buffer state, but its way of being so is changing and this will probably mean somewhat more inter-regional interaction, with Turkey as medium.

Generally, the Middle East moves in the direction of a more state-based, "normal" security complex with less pan-dynamics. This is *potentially* the basis for a gradual process of regime formation and more cooperative security. Still, the region is likely to remain a basically conflictual one, which means both that it remains open to some external penetration (as allies and supporters of this party or that), and that it is unlikely to be able to generate much ability to act beyond its own borders (e.g. still no Middle Eastern great power will be allowed to emerge). In relation to Europe, the most important shift might be that the Maghreb drifts off to becoming a semi-independent sub-complex tied mostly to Europe and less and less a part of the Middle East.

We have not included a discussion of the likely emergence of a different kind of connection of Levant and Gulf. It is quite a separate and complicated story, which would make this already very long chapter, much longer. But it is clearly of great importance for long-term considerations of EU policy towards the Middle East.

Inter-regional Relations Between Europe and the Middle East

The analysis shows that it is necessary to separate between Europe-Maghreb relations and the relationship between Europe and the Middle East properly. To the extent that Maghreb drifts off from the Middle East towards some African connections and primarily becoming the southern periphery of Europe. European policy towards Maghreb could become more security driven than those

towards the Middle East because on the one hand, the threats of conflict spill-over and migration are perceived as more intense in some
member countries, and on the other hand the outlook appears better
for European action actually influencing long-term developments
and thereby future threats.

In contrast, the Europe-Middle East constellation is more truly
inter-regional. What connections are we likely to see between the
two regions in the future?

Strategic interests (allies, threats, etc.)? The two regional analyses
shows that no Middle Eastern power is able to act strategically in
relation to Europe, but Europe could potentially be able to and be
interested in acting in relation to the Middle East. However, the
answer is no. There is a European interest in playing a role in the
(solution to the) Israel-Palestine conflict, but this is not enough to
generate much involvement in the region in general. General balance
of power considerations do not tie the complexes together, and Europe is neither excessively worried about the emergence of a Middle
Eastern great power (as is the US), nor close to generating a long-
range strategy for solving transnational "spill-over" threats by getting involved in the Middle East.

Other un-orthodox yet somehow military threats such as weapons of mass destruction (WMD), terrorism, rogue states? These are
not so much threats to *Europe* – more of an issue in the US. Both
because most terrorists take aim at the US, and because the US is a
more fully global actor that identifies global developments with their
agenda. Most such threats anyway reinforce the insecurity dynamics
within the Middle East complex much more than they threaten outsiders: Iraq's military capability worries Kuwait, Iran, Israel and
Saudi Arabia far more than it worries Europe.

Migration? There is clearly some securitization in Europe, but it
is not likely to lead to attempts to handle by general inter-regional
policy *in relation to the Middle East properly*, both because the main
problems today do not come from here but from Maghreb, and

because it is a daunting agenda to try to take away the sources of migration here, which implies doing quite radical things to the Middle East. Only in relation to Maghreb could concern about migration drive a potentially more active European policy.

Indirect connections? As indicated above, the two complexes can be connected occasionally because of Turkey, Central Asia and the increasingly separate Maghreb.

At the level of inter-regional relations, there is still not much that connects Europe and the Middle East.[35] Essentially the two complexes are quite distinct, and unlikely to come together in any significant way. If Europe and the Maghreb are drawing together, this is mostly not in the security sphere, and since the Maghreb is detaching itself from the Middle East complex anyway, it is of much lower relevance to this question than it would have been during the Cold War. Possibly, the key is Turkey. Even if it gets drawn into the Middle East more (by the "strategic partnership" with Israel), this will not draw the two complexes together. First, it is offset by increasing Turkish detachment from Europe, and secondly it is unlikely that Turkey will ever opt fully for a Middle Eastern route and thus the most likely scenario is that Turkey will continue to be the buffer state, but an increasingly active one.

What does this analysis tell us of the appropriateness of the various schemes for 'regional cooperation' for instance in the Mediterranean (Barcelona process)? The Mediterranean is not a security complex. Of course, it can be called a region, since that concept is incredibly flexible – the Land of Hessen is a region as is Eurasia – but according to Security Complex Theory (and we claim: according to the de facto dynamics of security), the most relevant regions for organisational efforts are those that correspond to actual security

---

35 Cf. the more extensive, but older analysis of the same issue in Buzan/Roberson (1993).

relations, and the Mediterranean does not. At best, schemes can therefore be devised that consciously reflect the nature of this area as an inter-region or a trans-region. Transfer of e.g. lessons from the OSCE process is therefore unlikely to be successful.[36] In relation to the Euro-Maghreb relationship, organisations have to reflect (if not necessarily formalise) the asymmetrical nature of the relationship. Possibly, parallels could better be drawn from the Baltic Sea Region[37] or the Stability Pacts in East-Central Europe (although these might be dependent on eventual chances of actual membership of the EU). In these cases, the institutions for the trans-region are unlikely to become strong organisations because the primary organisation remains the EU. In the case of Euro-Med 'regional' cooperation, institutions should not be thought of as projects in their own right but mainly judged in terms of their effects on the 'real regions', Europe and the Middle East.

NATO's new 'Strategic Concept': A More Interventionist NATO?

The Document

At the NATO summit in Washington on 23–24 April 1999, the Alliance agreed on a new 'strategic concept'.[38] It sets out general guidelines on a number of issues, and contains passages that could seem to indicate a more expansive agenda and a more 'flexible' approach to the question of necessary UN Security Council mandates for military action. More specifically, the Middle East can be read into it in relation to the threat definition (neighbouring regions and terrorism, rogue states and weapons of mass destruction).

---

36 Cf. Rosemary Hollis' contribution to this volume.
37 Another region with EU on the one side and states with varying relationships to the EU on the other, cf. e.g. Joenniemi (1997).
38 As in 1991, but in contrast to Cold War days: a public document.

The document is useful to focus on first because it is the currently valid status on NATO's reform and redefinition and secondly because it crystallises the current balance between American and (various) European views on future grand strategy. Therefore, we will first recall some of the central passages of the document itself (NATO 1999a), then discuss it in relation to American and European strategy in order to estimate whether NATO actually is heading for a new role definition, which includes a more active and engaged stance in relation to the Middle East.

It is programmatically stated, that NATO operates with "a broad approach to security" (par. 25). And the lists of security threats are indeed expansive:

"Any armed attack on the territory of the Allies, from whatever direction, would be covered by Articles 5 and 6 of the Washington Treaty. However, Alliance security must also take account of the global context. Alliance security interests can be affected by other risks of a wider nature, including acts of terrorism, sabotage and organised crime, and by the disruption of the flow of vital resources. The uncontrolled movement of large numbers of people, particularly as a consequence of armed conflicts, can also pose problems for security and stability affecting the Alliance." (par. 24)

Another central passage in terms of threat perception reads: "The security of the Alliance remains subject to a wide variety of military and non-military risks which are multi-directional and often difficult to predict. These risks include uncertainty and instability in and around the Euro-Atlantic area and the possibility of regional crises at the periphery of the Alliance, which could evolve rapidly" (par. 20). After this, the document lists more specifically "powerful nuclear forces" (par. 21), the proliferation of NBC weapons and their means of delivery (par. 22), the global spread of technology (par. 23) and finally the long list of 'wider' threats: terrorism, sabotage, organised crime, resources and migration (par. 24).

Seen from the Middle East, this could be worrying, both because of the 'around the Euro-Atlantic area' phrase and because the (mainly American) image of rogue states and spread of WMD is often implicitly or explicitly a reference mainly to the Middle East.

Ahead of the summit, much attention had been devoted to 'the mandate question' – whether NATO should more generally allow itself to act militarily in non-self defence situations without mandate from the UN Security Council.[39] Many observers had expected a clarification of some kind.[40]

The solution found at the Summit was more indirect than expected. The strategic concept only included the following laconic sentence: "The United Nations Security Council has the primary responsibility for the maintenance of international peace and security and, as such, plays a crucial role in contributing to security and stability in the Euro-Atlantic area" (par. 15).

By not talking mandate – and reinforced by the accompanying statements by Secretary General Solana and President Clinton[41] – NATO gave the impression (and the interpretation in the media was[42]) that NATO had decided there were no legally generated or self-imposed political limits. The criteria are whether there is a 'threat'

---

39 Being in the middle of one such operation – Kosovo – the question of course was not whether one could do it, but how to phrase this possibility; ranging from extremely rare to quite unproblematic.

40 Probably neither one extreme nor the other, i.e. neither "we only act with UN Security Council mandate", nor "we don't care", but some kind of "SC mandate is preferable but in extreme situations . . .", maybe even with a specification of what kind of situations would qualify as exceptional. A number of references could be given to newspapers from March and April 1999.

41 Cf. transcript: Clinton, Solana at NATO commemorative ceremony 4/23, United States Information Agency, 23 April 1999; <http://www.usia.gov/regional/eur/balkans/kosovo/texts/99042320.htm>.

42 Cf. e.g. "NATO asserts right to act without U.N. approval", CNN interactive, 24 April 1999.

to the Euro-Atlantic area (and security and threat is – as we saw above – defined very widely!).

In addition, the document offers a direct hint of the expansive interpretation of one's own mandate by mentioning operations in the Balkans as setting a precedence: "NATO recalls its offer, made in Brussels in 1994, to support on a case-by-case basis in accordance with its own procedures, peacekeeping and other operations under the authority of the UN Security Council or the responsibility of the OSCE, including by making available Alliance resources and expertise. In this context NATO recalls its subsequent decisions with respect to crisis response operations in the Balkans" (par. 31). It is left unclear whether this is a reference to Bosnia-Herzegovina ("operations under the authority of the UN Security Council"), or to Kosovo and thus goes beyond the mandated operations.

The NATO (non-)decision was criticised by some on the basis of the legal discussion about 'humanitarian intervention', where a specification by NATO here would have assisted in the formulation of more general rules in a possible emerging legality of humanitarian intervention in certain situations. Others, who were not too interested in this side – such as *The Economist* – still found it problematic that one did not use the opportunity for confidence building that such a specification would have offered – "to reassure a suspicious world that NATO has not given itself the right to attack sovereign nations at whim".[43] To countries like China and Russia, NATO now sent the signal, which one perceived as a right to intervene whenever one thought it morally justified.

The document contains several other issues of importance, but the above are the two most crucial for our purpose, and they were among the most controversial in the negotiations leading up to the

---

43 The Economist, 24 April 1999.

meeting.[44] It is not stated that bluntly (on this occasion), but the general trend is that NATO moves from defence of territory to defence of interests and values.

American Reading (= the concept as a component of US Grand Strategy)

In order to estimate what this 'concept' really means politically, it has to be placed in the context of overall American and European policy. NATO as such does not have a strategic vision – countries and possibly the EU have, while NATO is an instrument and its doctrine a negotiated compromise.

The issue of American grand strategy is a huge issue in itself, but for the current purpose we do not have to discuss all major competing visions for US Grand Strategy.[45] Instead we will focus on the dominant position at each of *two layers of grand strategy*:

---

44 The explicit question of area of operation could be included, but the decision was sufficiently vague that it is not of much interest. The so-called Roth report from the North Atlantic Assembly ("NATO in the 21st Century") which played a role in the debate up to the summit was explicit in stating that NATOs missions should neither be global nor 'artificially limited'. The clear impression in that report is that the Mediterranean and North Africa clearly are included, and probably the rest of the Middle East as well. The "strategic concept" did not go that far and kept repeating the un-defined "Euro-Atlantic area". However, this is probably not too important. The Americans do not want a 'global' NATO anyway and nobody expects NATO to act in East Asia, but if there is a will to act in any specific conflict, the current definition will not be a constraint. It is inevitable that NATO becomes usable beyond Europe proper. After the end of the Cold War, it is impossible domestically to justify continued American support for the defence of wealthy Europe who should now (in contrast to the Cold War) be net contributor to security. If the US continues to supply most of NATO as asset for the defence of Europe, this organization must also be made available beyond Europe. This basic bargain is inescapable. However, the specific formulations of how far such operations could be from Europe are less interesting.

45 Cf. Posen/Ross (1996/97).

One is a rationalistic, strategic discussion mainly among experts about what kind of threats to defend against, what armed forces to put up, etc. The trend has been that the Clinton administration has left its original, liberal conception of 'cooperative security' and instead has tried to uphold the same ideological vision but pursue a policy more appropriately described as a mixture of 'selective engagement' and 'primacy'.[46] Increasing emphasis seems to be placed on the interest in protecting (partial) unipolarity. And at least in the longer term, the US is likely to concentrate on serious contenders for superpower status (China?), while the absence of such candidates today makes it possible to concentrate on other kinds of threats, including 'humanitarian interventions' mostly tied to the liberal vision. Still, it is among experts clear that American policy has to be guided by an analysis of the relevant powers – regional or global – to be prevented from becoming too powerful. The problem with this kind of doctrine, however, is that it is far too cynical, geopolitical and power political to become the justificatory line of argumentation for the administration. Therefore, there is a second layer as well:

The second layer of grand strategy is that of discourse, of the foreign policy rhetoric of the President and other leading figures. The American security discourse has increasingly stabilised on a specific image of the existing order, the aspired order and the main threats. The code name for this approach is "rogue states, international terrorism and proliferation of weapons of mass destruction (WMD)".[47]

---

46 Ibid.
47 As pointed out by Stephen Zunes (1997) it has proven difficult in the US to justify action against rogue states only on their ideological and normative deviance, because this is too obviously a double standard in relation to the undemocratic nature of some of the US's own allies. "Thus, in order to mobilize public support for confrontational policies towards the so-called rogue states, American officials and their allies in the media must help develop a perceived sense of urgency and a clear case for national security interests in isolating these regimes. The issues that have been most effective in this regard have been terrorism, the attempted procurement of weapons of mass destruction, and the risk of subversion or conquest of allied nations." Therefore, the listed issues become a standard package.

The implicit image in this definition of the threat is one of a liberal, democratic, peaceful order gradually falling into place. In such a perspective, the few exceptions from the rule are allocated disproportionate attention. In one sense, it is surprising that Iran, Iraq, Libya, North Korea and Bin Laden should be that big a part of world politics, but with the optimistic picture of a liberal world order, they become central for two reasons: they are a threat to the vision itself; they are the remaining obstacles to completion, they are the ones that resist falling into line so that the liberal project can be completed. Secondly, they are the major threats if one assumes that many other problems are solved and we therefore have to move down the security agenda. The price of this vision is to downplay the more structural problems that might cause the crises of tomorrow and focus on the few extreme cases and only when they have already become manifest. Finally, it is natural that the US is more concerned about terrorism than Europe, because as the 'leader' of the world, the US is the natural target of the Bin Ladins of this world, and the US has never really accepted the idea of being exposed to others' weapons – not even the nuclear weapons of the Cold War and certainly not terrorist attacks even if numerically marginal. Thus, the dominant discourse is one that elegantly unifies an optimistic vision of a liberal world order with a quite alarmist zooming in on 'rogue states'. It has the ideological advantage of carrying over some of the discursive set-up from the Cold War: of justifying action by defining the opponent as radically different, as are now the handful of global evils: Hussein, Milosevic, Kim, Ghaddafi, Bin Laden. Therefore, this threatening image is likely to become the most powerful in public debate, because it fits much more harmoniously into the American self-conception and a promising global vision than the more cynical, geopolitical analysis.

In practice the two are probably merged in a planning that is simultaneously shaped by experts calculating in relation to global power analysis and spin-doctors estimating the public effect of various moves and arguments. American policy therefore unfolds where the two meet.

From both layers follows quite clear policy in relation to the key issues of NATO's strategic concept. The Clinton administration has departed from the original highly multilateral and UN friendly strategy but continues to seek close cooperation with its primary allies both in order to prevent new rivals and bolster the legitimacy of US actions. It is therefore natural to aim at a NATO connection for as much as possible of US security policy – in-between doubtful UN format and problematic unilateralism. Whether defined in terms of preventing dominant regional powers and new superpowers or in terms of rogue states, the US is therefore likely to seek as much European backing as often as possible for action in relation to Middle Eastern powers. NATO and the US should be free to act without UN mandate and a threat definition like the one in the strategic concept follows nicely.

There has obviously been quite some success for this US policy in recent cases: the form that action took in relation to Kosovo as well as the decisions and declarations of the Washington Summit including the strategic concept.

Still, one should not overestimate the ease of this arrangement. There are problems with this strategy. It is possible to argue – although we will not try in any way to settle this issue here – that the policy is possibly unrealistic: 1) because of resource squeeze;[48] 2) because counter coalitions are likely to emerge; 3) and it is classical realism wisdom (as well as post-structuralist) that total universalism is self-defeating, because any attempt to harmonize the world will

---

48 Generally unipolarity is not likely to prove viable in the long run and more specifically, the American defence budget and general investment in foreign affairs is both too little in relation to what experts claim is necessary only to re-fight the Gulf War, and simultaneously quite a lot to keep asking of an American public without a clear threat present.

produce its own opposition – the world is always too complicated and diverse.

Finally, before we turn to the European side, it should be noticed – as a basis for comparison – that the form of military that this US strategy calls for is unambiguously the high tech RMA (Revolution in Military Affairs) model, which promises loss-free victory in asymmetric wars.

European (Non-)Reading (= European defection and non-strategy)

Several leading European powers (notably France and Germany and to a lesser extent the UK) have had fundamental reservations about the scheme pushed by the US. Of course, they do not participate in the more geopolitical vision for keeping down challengers to US primacy. If they had calculations of this type, they would most likely reach the opposite conclusion: that the EU should be promoted as one of the new powers. Also the more ideological vision of liberalism and rogue states is resisted in Europe. It is not that Europeans do not want to participate in the fight against terrorism or proliferation, but they are reluctant to single out these issues the American way. There is a fear that this leads to a 'militarization' of third world policy and generally a too shortsighted focus on manifest deviants and not enough on the structural issues that in the future produce 'problems'.

The European NATO members therefore were not part of the grand strategy vision behind the NATO document – but nor did they arrive with much of their own strategic analysis. Thus, their stand was mostly defined as reactive in relation to American initiatives.

The general picture is one of European critical voices, actual acceptance – and likely (non)action. All decisions have to be made on concrete issues, and the scepticism that was visible up to the NATO summit will therefore reappear even more strongly in any attempt to generate joint action on the basis of the more controversial principles.

This strategy is unlikely to become European policy beyond Europe proper (and maybe a few 'easy' cases beyond) because of differences in global analysis and strategy between Europe and the US. Except for the UK, Europe is not an active participant in the guiding universalist vision with its ensuing singling out of 'rogue states' and the likes as the main threat to international peace and security. The Kosovo operation showed a willingness to define a right to 'humanitarian intervention' as preferred by the US, but Europeans are unlikely to act upon it much beyond Europe in a geography textbook sense (possibly Maghreb). As spelled out in section 2, Europe will be deeply pre-occupied with Balkan and general enlargement – plus always the underlying concern for the coherence of the core and increasing competition with the other capitalist centres – and therefore unlikely to buy into an American analysis of any Middle East issue as central to European security.

Europe is more concerned about 'failed states' such as Bosnia, Albania and Algeria; the US more about rogue states, such as Libya and Iraq. It might be added, that the Europeans to some extent have interpreted the Balkan wars according to the first model – the Americans clearly by the second.

In the abstract, it can be stated that "[. . .] no Western power has been safe without some measure of influence or control over the southern and eastern shores of the Mediterranean".[49] But the guiding mode of analysis for Europe will remain bilateral or direct: what is the direct impact on Europe, and in contrast to the US, there is so far not the classical global power logic of asking: what happens to the global order, the global system – maybe global polarity – if we do not act on this? Only the US thinks in these terms, and even the US does it only in a form which is increasingly coloured by domestic

---

49 Blackwill/Stürmer (1997: 2).

concerns, which is probably unavoidable when the degree of urgency
and 'necessity' from a threatening 'equal' is replaced by asymmetric
threats which never 'forces' any action and therefore allows for
domestic considerations.

The future European policy must be addressed in the form of two
different questions:
- The slowly emerging separate security policy of the EU: what will
  it look like?
- What kind of participation with the US will the Europeans deliver
  if there are – most likely US initiated – attempts to activate NATO
  in a more distant conflict?

In terms of concrete military policy, the Europeans spend around
half of what the US does on defence, and despite various reforms and
modernization plans, there is not the same clear-cut preference for
high-tech, RMA type defence. Assuming that most of the operations
of the future will be asymmetrical wars (peace keeping/peace enforcement), the Europeans are likely to be able to carry out these
with much smaller budgets and a lower degree of sophistication –
but with somewhat larger losses to their own forces – compared to
the American model. In the short run, this difference is a source of
tension within NATO – decreasing inter-operability – but in the long
run it could mean that it is less unrealistic than otherwise expected
for the Europeans eventually to muster the necessary military muscle
for larger operations in or in the periphery of Europe.

The Actual NATO

The question to answer is what NATO can do and is likely to be used
for – and what parts of its declarations and self-defined 'rights' seem
highly unlikely to materialise. The Europeans have gone along with
declarations signalling a more activist, unilateral and trans-regional

NATO. However, there are strong reasons to take the widely voiced European concerns from before the summit seriously. In any concrete situation they are likely to re-appear and thus limit the ability to use NATO in such more distant situations.

Is it then possible to see the US intervene more systematically and actively on its own? In principle yes, but in practice: rarely. The US is basically a 'lite power' in the sense that it wants to minimize its global power activities, and only acts reluctantly in international crises.[50] In addition to the general brakes on American 'internationalism', the US is much more likely to intervene when it can be done together with allies – preferably the Europeans.[51] Without (some of) the European NATO allies, the US is unlikely to carry out more ambitious military operations.[52]

50 Buzan/Segal (1996).
51 Cf. the Clinton doctrine where one of the "Berger conditions" for "humanitarian interventions" is that US allies participate.
52 However, all this might be too rational. One should, of course, never exclude the possibility that events run out of control. Especially not because NATO is a paradoxical thing, therefore exhibiting "irrational" features. On the one hand NATO is incredibly powerful, successful, popular and in all ways "strong", on the other hand it might be fragile now that the Cold War cement is gone. Can such a far-reaching integration in the sensitive area of military defence be maintained without an external threat? Is NATO "strong but fragile"? (Wæver 1997) Due to this underlying structural anomaly, NATO easily gets into a credibility trap. After only the smallest step into an issue, the argument will sound that NATO's own credibility is at stake. This entrapment rests on both sides of the paradox: NATO is so strong that it seems reasonable to expect a lot of it and so vulnerable that its credibility and viability can be put in question. As already seen in the case of Kosovo, the argument that now NATO's own status is at stake can propel the member states into acting on issues they basically do not give sufficient priority to legitimise intervention. But NATO itself has enough priority to justify an action.
   In the long run and as a general pattern, such mechanisms should not be expected to shape developments. The underlying structural patterns exposed by Security Complex analysis are more powerful, but singe instances – exceptions – could occur, not least for the reasons given in this note.

Conclusions: A More Interventionist NATO?

There were some signs here – in contrast to the conclusions of parts 1 and 2 – which could indicate an answer closer to yes. The April 1999 strategic concept of NATO includes definitions of threats and rights that could indicate a more active NATO also in the Middle East. However, the debate on the NATO declaration revealed that on the one hand it has an internal coherence from fitting into a strong American vision of the world, but on the other hand there were strong European doubts that are likely to materialise again in the case of any attempt to use this new NATO vision concretely. In theoretical terms, we have to deal with this by way of the relationship between the global structure (a kind of 'unipolarity') and the regional, European constellation. The European regional order cannot be analysed separately from its global context. Global unipolarity is thus *structurally* important to Europe because it is one of the ramifications for regional possibilities, but this should not be confused with granting the actual unipole an unlimited ability to shape and determine regional developments. Europe is therefore likely to continue to act mainly on its own security priorities and 'manage' the relation to the US including US demands for increased global responsibility. Also in relation to the Middle East, one should not over-estimate the power and abilities of the US. The unipolar situation enables both strong influences on peace processes like the Israel-Palestinian one and an ability to forge coalitions and intervene in extreme situations like the Gulf War, but most of the dynamics of the region will remain generated from within.

Conclusions

All three sections delivered the answer 'no' to the question of increased Western involvement and interference in the Middle East.

The first answer was a preliminary pure theory answer, the second informed by the theory guided analysis of the two complexes, and the third looked more concretely at current declarations, actions and motives. Also the third could – hesitantly – be answered with a no, but it rests to some extent on assumptions that could be questioned. The most important question is about the character and longevity of the current global (quasi)unipolarity, because it influences both developments in Europe and in the Middle East (and thereby potentially also inter-regional developments).

If unipolarity is really stable *and* widely perceived as such (and thereby motivating almost all actors to seek accommodation with the power centre), both European and Middle Eastern dynamics will be greatly influenced by US policy, and the main key to the relationship between the two regions will be US policy.

With a little more fading of unipolarity (as is to be expected), we get a clearer pattern of regional security complexes, i.e. freed of the partial overlap of a dominant unipole. It will be two extremely different complexes – one centred (Europe) and one in balance of power mode (ME); one very far to the security community end of the spectrum (Europe) and one still in conflict formation mode, even if with a chance of slight softening (ME) – but still it is most likely that their relationship will be the normal one for inter-regional relations: relative indifference. There will be some rhetoric to the opposite effect, but when it comes to actual, highly dramatized security discourse, Europe and the Middle East will not be among the dominant concerns to each other, and therefore not much mutual (or one-sided) penetration in a security mode will take place. The two regions are likely to move closer in other respects and become more closely intertwined in societal, economic and maybe even political respects, but the relative distance remains large enough to keep security concerns focused elsewhere.

List of References

Ayoob, Mohammed 1995: The Third World Security Predicament, Boulder/Colorado.

Barnett, Michael 1998: Dialogues in Arab Politics. Negotiations in Regional Order, New York.

Blackwill, Robert/Michael Stürmer 1997: Introduction, in: Blackwill, Robert/Michael Stürmer (eds.): Allies Divided. Transatlantic Policies for the Greater Middle East, Cambridge/Mass.

Buzan, Barry/Rizvi, Gowher 1986: South Asian Insecurity and the Great Powers, London.

Buzan, Barry 1989: The Future of Western European Security, in: Wæver, Ole et al. (eds.): European Polyphony. Beyond East-West Confrontation, London.

Buzan, Barry 1991: People, States and Fear. An Agenda for International Security Studies in the Post-Cold War Era, 2nd edition, Hemel Hempstead.

Buzan, Barry/ B.A. Roberson 1993: Europe and the Middle East. Drifting Towards Societal Cold War?, in: Wæver, Ole et al. (eds.): Identity, Migration and the New Security Agenda in Europe, London.

Buzan, Barry/Gerald Segal 1996: The Rise of the 'Lite' Powers. A Strategy for Postmodern States, in: World Policy Journal, 13/3.

Buzan, Barry/Ole Wæver forthcoming: Regions Set Free – The Emerging World Order?

Buzan, Barry et al. 1998: Security. A New Framework for Analysis, Boulder/Colorado.

Buzan, Barry/Thomas Dietz 1999: The European Union and Turkey, in: Survival, 41/1.

Cohen, Roger 1998: A Policy Struggle Stirs Within NATO, in: New York Times, November 28.

Chubin, Shahram/Charles Tripp 1996: Iran-Saudi-Arabia Relations and Regional Order', Adelphi Paper 304, London.

Gause, F. Gregory III 1999: Systemic Approaches to Middle East International Relations, in: International Studies Review, 1/1.

Hamilton, Alexander et al. 1911 [1787-8]: The Federalist, London.

Hansen, Birthe forthcoming: Unipolarity and the Middle East.

Huntington, Samuel 1996: The Clash of Civilizations and the Remaking of World Order, New York.

Hurst, David 1999: Where Tyranny Spells Peace, in: Guardian Weekly, March 28.

Joenniemi, Pertti (ed.) 1997: Neo-nationalism or Regionality? The Re-structuring of Political Space around the Baltic Rim, Stockholm.

Kazan, Isil 1999: Regionalization and Securitization in Turkish Foreign Policy, unpublished paper.

Mearsheimer, John 1990: Back to the Future. Instability in Europe After the Cold War, in: International Security, 15/1.

Nachmani, Amikam 1999: Turkey and the Middle East, in: Security and Policy Studies, No. 42, Tel Aviv.

North Atlantic Treaty Organisation (ed.) 1999a: The Alliance's Strategic Concept. Approved by the Heads of State and Government Participating in the Meeting of the North Atlantic Council in Washington, DC on 23rd and 24th April 1999; Press Release NAC-S(99)65, 24 Apr. 1999; <http://www.nato.int/docu/pr/1999/p99-065e.htm>.

North Atlantic Treaty Organisation (ed.) 1999b: Washington Summit Communiqué. Issued by the Heads of State and Government Participating in the Meeting of the North Atlantic Council in Washington, DC on 24th April 1999; Press Release NAC-S(99)64; <http://www.nato.int/docu/pr/1999/p99-064e.htm>.

North Atlantic Treaty Organisation (ed.) 1999c: The Washington Declaration. Signed and issued by the Heads of State and Government Participating in the Meeting of the North Atlantic Council in Washington, DC on 23rd and 24th April 1999; Press Release NAC-S(99)63; <http://www.nato.int/docu/pr/1999/p99-063e.htm>.

Posen, Barry/Andrew Ross 1996: Competing Visions for US Grand
    Strategy, in: International Security, 21/3.
Tibi, Bassam 1993: Conflict and War in the Middle East, 1967–91.
    Regional Dynamics and the Superpowers, London.
Wæver, Ole 1989: Conflicts of Vision. Visions of Conflict, in: Wæver,
    Ole/Pierre Lemaitre/Elzbieta Tromer (eds.): European Polyphony.
    Perspectives beyond East-West Confrontation, London.
Wæver, Ole 1990: The Interplay of Some Regional and Subregional
    Dynamics of Security. The Case of Europe, The Baltic Area and
    "the North" in the 1980s', in: Zeszyty, Naukowe: no. 44 – Acta
    Politica, no. 2.
Wæver, Ole 1996: European Security Identities, in: Journal of Com-
    mon Market Studies, 34/1.
Wæver, Ole 1997: Imperial Metaphors. Emerging European Analo-
    gies to Pre-Nation State Imperial Systems, in: Tunander, Ola et al.
    (eds.): Geopolitics in Post-Wall Europe. Security, Territory, and
    Identity, London.
Wæver, Ole 1998: Insecurity, Security and Asecurity in the West Eu-
    ropean Non-War Community, in: Adler, Emanuel/Michael Bar-
    nett (eds.): Security Communities, Cambridge/Mass.
Yapp, Malcolm 1991: The Near East Since the First World War, Lon-
    don.
Zunes, Stephen 1997: The Function of Rogue States in US Middle
    East Policy, in: Middle East Policy, 5 : 2 <http://www.mepc.org/
    journal/9705_zunes.html>.

Barcelona's First Pillar: An Appropriate Concept for Security Relations?

Rosemary Hollis

The Barcelona Declaration, or Euro-Mediterranean Partnership (EMP) initiative has been analysed and criticised in some detail since it was adopted at the Barcelona Conference of November 1995.[1] The initiative itself has been fleshed out through various procedural measures, dialogues and activities, the negotiation of partnership agreements between the European Union (EU) and Mediterranean partner states, and the conclusions of two further ministerial conferences, in Malta (April 1997) and Stuttgart (April 1999). Any assessment of Barcelona, in whole or in part, must take into account this process of evolution.

Existing analyses and critiques focus on three facets of EMP: the conceptual underpinnings, implementation, and interaction with other frameworks and initiatives with which it overlaps. The task

---

1 This contribution was presented to the workshop *A Future Security Structure for the Middle East and the Eastern Mediterranean*, Frankfurt, October 1999.

here is to review the appropriateness of the *concept* embodied in the first pillar or chapter for security relations. It should be clear, however, that problems encountered in implementation and overlap with other processes are often the source of criticisms of the original concept. The intention therefore, is to distinguish between means and ends and proceed on the assumption that the way a problem is defined will determine approaches to its resolution.

The first section seeks to establish the conceptual content of Chapter I of Barcelona, noting that different parties have offered contrasting interpretations. The next section will review existing critiques of this part of EMP on conceptual grounds. Thirdly, the paper explores concerns relating to implementation rather than conceptualisation. Section four will look at the range of frameworks currently in existence to deal with security needs and discuss the place of Barcelona among these. The fifth section provides a summary of prevailing assessments of security issues to be addressed in the Middle East and Eastern Mediterranean context. Against this background, the paper will conclude with an evaluation of the appropriateness of the concept of Chapter I for security relations.

The Concept

The Barcelona Declaration envisages a partnership between the 15 members of the European Union and 12 other states around the southern and eastern Mediterranean. The EU members are a bloc, the partner states are not, though Arab participants in EMP periodically coordinate their positions on issues raised in this context. The initiative identifies the Mediterranean as a geopolitical, strategic and economic space, though the EMP does not incorporate all Mediterranean countries. The identification of this space can be understood either as a vehicle for formalizing the EU's relations with its southern periphery, in parallel with the development of EU relations to the east; or, as a visualisation of a new area embracing states around the Mediterranean basin and their shared interests. The former interpretation connotes a core-periphery relationship; the latter a novel creation which cuts across existing 'regional security complexes,' as defined in the contribution by Barry Buzan and Ole Wæver in the same volume.

The three chapters of Barcelona identify three goals, which are presented as complimentary: (1) a political and security partnership to establish a common area of peace and stability; (2) an economic and financial partnership to create an area of shared prosperity (including a free trade area); and (3) a partnership in social, cultural and human affairs, to develop human resources and promote understanding between cultures and exchanges between civil societies. The language of Chapter I gives repeated emphasis to international law, human rights, democracy and respect for cultural differences, the territorial integrity of member states and non-interference in their internal affairs. It calls for the peaceful resolution of disputes and cooperation in preventing and combating terrorism and international crime.

Particularly when viewed in conjunction with the aspirations expressed in Chapters II and III, the first pillar of Barcelona embodies a concept of peace and stability commensurate with the vision of a safer, more prosperous and less conflictual world that gained currency with the end of the Cold War, the collapse of the Soviet Union and concomitant discrediting of communism, and the assumed triumph of Western notions of democracy and liberal capitalism. The language and vision also reflect two other contextual phenomena: firstly, a new European preoccupation with so-called 'soft security' threats, including economic instability, social unrest, refugee crises, international crime and drug trafficking; and secondly, the dawn of a new era of hope for resolution of the Arab-Israeli conflict, bolstered by the signing of the Oslo accords between the Israelis and Palestinians.

The specific goals identified in Chapter I deal with both 'soft' and 'hard' security issues in a way which suggests considerable optimism about the potential for cooperation between the partners to the initiative. The signatories agreed to:

- promote regional security through acting, inter alia, in favour of nuclear, chemical and biological non-proliferation through adherence to and compliance with a combination of international and regional non-proliferation regimes and arms control and disarmament regime,
- pursue a mutual and effectively viable Middle East Zone free of weapons of mass destruction,
- consider practical steps to prevent [such] proliferation, as well as excessive accumulation of conventional arms,
- refrain from developing military capacity beyond their legitimate defence requirements,
- promote conditions likely to develop good-neighbourly relations among themselves and support processes aimed at stability, security, prosperity and regional and subregional cooperation,
- consider any security and confidence building measures that could be taken between the parties with a view to the creation of 'an area of peace and stability in the Mediterranean', including the long-term possibility of establishing a Euro-Mediterranean pact to that end.[2]

Subsequent to the signing of the declaration, certain developments have led to some refinements in the vision it embodies. The Work Programme appended to the Barcelona Declaration calls simply for a continuous political dialogue to examine how the principles and objectives may be fulfilled. This dialogue has been carried forward by the committee or group of Senior Officials in the field of security,

2   Barcelona Declaration, 28 November 1995, <http://europa.eu.int/en/comm/dg1b/en/den-barc.htm>.

who are officials delegated by each of the partner governments. As of their first meeting, in March 1996, this group decided on the progressive establishment of a politically non-binding 'Action Plan,' worked out by consensus. As approved in May 1996, this plan lists six areas of dialogue: strengthening democracy, preventive diplomacy, confidence and security building measures (CSBMs), disarmament, combating terrorism, and fighting organised crime and drug trafficking.[3]

At the same May meeting the EU made detailed proposals for the dialogue in the areas of preventive diplomacy and CSBMs, which were thus in effect to be given priority consideration. In the area of strengthening democracy, it was agreed to take stock of the partners' participation in international human rights conventions. In the areas of combating terrorism and crime, it was agreed to organise preparatory meetings of experts in the framework of the third EMP area, 'cooperation in social, cultural and human affairs.' The question of disarmament was left out of consideration for the time being.[4]

Thereafter, prompted by initiatives from various countries, the security officials developed an extended wish list of proposals for action. However, when crisis in the Middle East Peace Process (MEPP) cast a shadow over EMP activities across the board, the security agenda was contracted to a more modest set of items for discussion, in the interests of preserving and protecting the core process.

The conclusions reached at the ministerial conference in Malta (Barcelona II) took note of the various activities generated by the Senior Officials in the security field (including establishment of the EuroMeSCo network of foreign policy institutes) and their draft Action Plan, which, it was also noted, is considered a 'rolling docu-

3 European Parliament, Directorate General for Research 1998: Working Document. The Mediterranean Policy after the Conference of Barcelona, Political Series POLI 103 EN (May 1998), Brussels: 7.
4 Ibid.

ment' to guide their work. The two other items singled out for mention under Chapter I were work on CSBMs and preparatory work on a charter for peace and stability, which might eventually be considered for adoption. At Stuttgart (Barcelona III) ministers gave stronger emphasis to the value of elaborating a 'Euro-Mediterranean Charter for Peace and Stability' and welcomed the guidelines submitted to them for elaborating such a document. In fact, the proposed charter has become a central feature of work under Chapter I, and as officially described, it is expected to 'serve as an instrument for the implementation of the principles of the Barcelona Declaration where issues of peace and stability are concerned.'[5] Accordingly, it was stated:

> "The Charter will provide for an enhanced political dialogue as well as the evolutionary and progressive development of partnership-building measures, good-neighbourly relations, regional cooperation and preventive diplomacy."[6]

The adoption of the term partnership building measures (PBMs), rather than CBMs or CSBMs, also marked an important development in conceptual terms, first mooted at the Malta conference. According to Italian Ambassador Antonio Badini, the transition of the nature of the work of the Euro-Med Committee from confidence building measures to partnership-building measures must be seen as an improvement.[7] In any case, the term was used at Stuttgart to encompass a variety of meetings and measures including establishing a system for disaster prevention, and exchanges of information relat-

---

5   Third Euro-Mediterranean Conference of Foreign Ministers (Stuttgart, 15–16 April
    1999), Chairman's formal conclusions, <http://www.medea.be/en/index412.htm>,
    paragraph 11.
6   Ibid.
7   Report on the Informal EuroMeSCo-Senior Officials Seminar in Bonn, 20 March
    1999, SWP, April 1999: 2–3.

ing to signature and ratification of international instruments in the fields of disarmament and arms control, terrorism, human rights and international humanitarian law. Dialogue on organized crime and drug trafficking was another expectation of Chapter I endorsed at Stuttgart.

As was apparent from Barcelona I through all subsequent refinements, the principal preoccupation of Chapter I is 'soft security' issues. This is in keeping with the logic of the whole Barcelona process. The economic programme which is the centrepiece of EMP places overriding faith in the market to generate prosperity. It is further assumed that 'political liberalisation in the Mediterranean area will follow automatically from economic liberalisation.'[8] Both together, it is understood, will produce the best antidote to the kinds of security problems identified by Europeans as emanating from the southern Mediterranean. As encapsulated by Richard Youngs:

"In designing the Barcelona process, the EU's philosophy was that economic and political objectives were symbiotic: economic reform would bring in its wake political reform, which would give a further boost to economic performance, the latter helping to stem any potential for unsustainable levels of migration and thereby enhancing security objectives."[9]

All the Europeans, northern and southern, along with their non-EU partners at Barcelona, felt able to sign up to the whole EMP concept. As various commentators have pointed out, the northern Europeans were late converts to the idea of a Mediterranean security role for the EU, but came along because they see the EU as the appropriate vehicle to push an economic agenda in the interests of security. Furthermore, they see the goals of Chapter I as complimentary to

8   Gillespie (1997: 4).
9   Youngs (1999: 17–18).

those of existing security frameworks such as NATO and OSCE. Southern Europeans felt the 'soft' security threats potentially emanating from across the Mediterranean more strongly, and in their own interests would prefer aid rather than trade as the way to generate economic remedies. Nonetheless, the southern Europeans went along with the neo-liberal approach of Barcelona, presumably in the name of unity. For the southern Mediterranean partner states, economic dependency on European markets leaves them with little choice but to be in on EMP, but they are not unaware of the hidden security agenda of the Europeans and harbour some suspicions accordingly.

Conceptual Concerns

Some criticisms of the conceptual underpinnings of Barcelona centre on the assumption that neo-liberal economics will inter alia remedy security ills. There is also concern about the in-built hypocrisy of founding a partnership with 27 members which only thinly disguises the fact that 15 of them are grouped in a powerful economic and political bloc, under the EU, which is motivated by a desire to keep the others at arms length. Espoused in the EU as a programme for its southern flank to parallel its dealings with neighbours to the east, Barcelona does not, however, offer the same incentive of EU membership to the South as it does to the East. This calls into question the coherence of the economic logic underlying EMP. Whereas Eastern Europeans can expect ultimately that the free movement of labour (people) will coexist with the free movement of goods and capital between them and the West, not so in the Mediterranean. There it is expected that the free movement of goods and capital will somehow deter the free movement of people.

In so far as Chapter I relies on the success of Chapter II, flaws in the logic of the latter undermine the conceptual underpinnings of the former. In fact, it may be that the success of Chapter II depends on measures required under Chapter I preventing or containing instability generated by the liberalisation called for under Chapter II. As was noted in a EuroMeSCo report of 1997/98, prosperity will ease ('soft') security threats, but creation of the free trade zone, at least in the short term, will not necessarily constitute a zone of peace and stability and:

> "Partners should therefore create mechanisms of political and security cooperation, within the Euro-Mediterranean area as well as with areas outside of the Partnership, thus allowing them to set up concrete measures towards this target."[10]

Another problem with Chapter I, variously seen as a conceptual or implementation issue, is the geostrategic space it defines. As identified in the same EuroMeSCo Report cited above:

> "The setting up of a Euro-Mediterranean cooperative security regime is taking place between (and overlapping with) the OSCE's longstanding experience on the northern side of the Mediterranean basin and the attempts of ACRS in the multilateral track of the Middle East peace process on the southeastern side of the same area."

Yet the EMP 'area of peace and stability' can hardly be compared to these adjoining experiences in that despite the use of the same methodology (attaining security through cooperative means) the politico-strategic contexts are basically different. While there is coincidence and a direct functional relation between the strategic context and the actors in the CSCE/OSCE and in the Middle East peace process, the same is not true in the Mediterranean where the relation is only

10 EuroMeSCo Report 1997/1998, <http://194.235.129.80/euromesco>, Reports: 11–12.

indirect. OSCE and ACRS correspond to strategically consistent regions, whereas EMP does not.[11]

The parties to the OSCE process came from an east-west divide in which the two sets of players could be considered to be in a strategic balance with each other. The state of conflict or 'Cold War' between them provided the premise for developing a set of measures to reduce tensions. Similarly, the parties to the Arab-Israeli conflict can be presumed to share an interest in reducing the possibilities of war. In the case of the Mediterranean, however, there is no comparable state of hostility between the two sides to overcome. In Europe the fear is not of attack by one or more states in the South, but rather of the potential spill-over effects of instability within or between the states in the South. Meanwhile, in the South there is no particular concern about instability inside Europe. There are, however, suspicions about the possibility of interventions or defensive actions by Western countries against the South. The creation of EUROFOR and EUROMARFOR have served to compound fears of intervention in North Africa.[12]

A third area of concern about the concept underlying Chapter I is simultaneously depicted as a source of strength. The vision espoused is so farsighted and novel as to be way ahead of its time, and therefore possibly unrealistic. According to one European diplomat, Barcelona is not just one step ahead of what has been achieved in Europe itself, and therefore of prevailing thinking on security, but several, and it is anathema to the political culture of the southern Mediterranean.[13] The problem identified here is that Barcelona assumes if not equality, then at least some sort of balance between the signatories, and more particularly it takes little if any account of the need for prior resolution of the Arab-Israeli, Cyprus and Western Sahara conflicts. Players on either side of these divides cannot enter into coop-

11 Ibid.: 16.
12 Spencer (1998: 147).
13 Unattributable interview for this contribution, August 1999.

erative security arrangements with each other as though their antag-
onisms had been resolved, because in so doing they may institution-
alise a status quo with which they are unhappy or else extend to one
another the kind of cooperative relations that currently they wish
only to develop as the fruits of peace.

Arab participants in EMP do not want to 'reward' Israel with
normal relations prior to the conclusion of a comprehensive peace
agreement, wherein Syria, Lebanon and the Palestinians will achieve
satisfaction of their outstanding claims. The Syrian government in
particular does not accept that CSBMs can aid the cause of peacemaking. Rather, they see these as enabling Israel to short-circuit the
necessary prerequisites for peace. Built into Barcelona is what one
commentator has called a 'self-denying ordinance', whereby the parties have renounced any intent to 'replace the other activities and
initiatives undertaken in the interest of peace, stability and development in the region'.[14] What this means, in effect, is that the EU has
been anxious not to cut across the US role in the MEPP. Also, the
hope has existed that crisis in the MEPP would not impede pursuit of
at least some aspects of Barcelona.

Certainly, negotiation of partnership agreements under Chapter II
has gone ahead, but only in such a way as to emphasize the isolation of
each Mediterranean partner country in its dealings with the EU. Meanwhile, full meetings of EMP participants have become embroiled in
debates about whether or not the Barcelona process can be divorced
from the MEPP. The problem is not just one of implementation. It
points to a conceptual flaw in Barcelona in so far as it ignores the existing unresolved conflicts and speaks only of establishing generic mechanisms for conflict resolution in a setting which has yet to be created.

The visionary quality of Chapter I is nonetheless depicted as one
of its strengths in some quarters. The way in which Barcelona defines
security problems is in keeping, not only with post-Cold War reali-

14   Spencer (1997: 39) quoting from the conclusions of the Malta conference.

ties, but with a post-interstate conflict setting in the Mediterranean. It is an ideal for policymakers to keep in mind, while they deal with current realities. However, in so far as they seek to implement Chapter I through the application of mechanisms which have worked in other settings, such as OSCE, they are likely to depart from the original concept.

Implementation Issues

Barcelona enjoins its participants to act in pursuit of its three complimentary goals of peace and stability, shared prosperity, and understanding between cultures and exchanges between civil societies. However, the mechanisms through which they are to proceed are different for the three tracks, which has implications for the results. Chapter I requires dialogue between all the partners and this has been undertaken by the Group of Senior Officials in the security field. The advantage of this is that individual governments are directly involved and enjoy a level of parity in the process, which would seem to be in keeping with the notion of a partnership between all 27 signatories. By contrast, realisation of Chapter II goals has been handled by the EU on the one hand and individual governments (with input from business organisations) on the other. Chapter III calls for direct civil society contacts, but funding for such activities has generally been channelled through the EU. Dialogues on such matters as drug trafficking and international crime have involved officials from all partner governments, though common positions and shared practices are more advanced on the European side. Progress on Chapters II and III is coordinated in the Barcelona Committee, wherein the European input is prepared and coordinated through a 'Med Committee' organised by the Commission.

Thus, in broad terms, implementation of Barcelona has allowed for the EU to exercise predominance. Within the EU, the Commission plays the leading role in driving the process, though the Senior Officials involved in the security dialogue are generally designated directly by their respective capitals.

The dispersal of personnel between EMP areas of economic affairs and social dialogue and the area of security partnership both in the Council and at member state level, as also in the EMP fora, gives the Commission a more important role to play as an intermediary in the overall process. Its influence is also boosted by its dual task of reporting on the one hand to the Council of Ministers, on the other to the Barcelona Committee. The Commission also drafts the reports to the Council and prepares the final declarations of the EMP Ministerial Conferences, which are first adopted in the Council before being discussed in the Barcelona Committee. There the Commission represents the Community interest while at the same time it can channel the Med Partners' ideas and criticisms to the Council through its reports. So the Commission's function reaches beyond the powers it derives from the EU Treaty (and the Barcelona Declaration). The de facto enlargement of the Barcelona Committee to the 15 EU member states could only serve to strengthen the Commission's powers of political control if on the one hand all EU member states had a national coordinator for the entire EMP process while on the other the Barcelona Committee was upgraded politically.[15]

The centrality of the Commission in the EMP process makes for coherence and efficiency in implementation, but also means that the process has been subject to some of the weaknesses in EU foreign policy-making.[16] However, mechanisms now instituted to carry forward a Common Foreign and Security Policy (CFSP) for Europe could benefit the Barcelona process, especially in so far as economic

15 European Parliament, Directorate General for Research, Working Document, The Mediterranean Policy after the Conference of Barcelona, Political Series POLI 103 EN (May 1998), authored by Martin Köhler: 37-8.
16 See Jörg Monar in the same volume.

concerns retain centrality. The EMP vision, after all, requires success in its economic agenda.

Aside from the institutional and procedural problems affecting realisation of EMP goals, there are concerns about the focus of activities under Chapter I. Perhaps because of the visionary quality of this first pillar, officials tasked with its implementation have tended to concentrate on those items on which they can register some apparent progress. This explains an early preoccupation with CSBMs, now overtaken by the potentially more appropriate notion of PBMs, and formulation of a draft charter. Some defenders of the process have claimed that Chapter I does indeed deal with 'hard' security issues, and the development of CSBMs, by whatever name, is appropriate and valuable. However, analyst Claire Spencer has argued that the elaboration of CBMs and CSBMs for the Mediterranean region "may even be detrimental to their intent in suggesting that the potential for conflict exists, or underlies the process."[17] The shift to PBMs should therefore be substantive rather than cosmetic, in developing a set of measures commensurate with the concept of partnership and the vision of the original initiative.

Overlapping Frameworks

As already noted, Barcelona is not the only framework within which the issue of Mediterranean security is being considered and pursued. The existence of multiple initiatives represents a problem in so far as this means duplication and dissipation of effort. Of even greater concern is the potential for competition and even contradiction between the various endeavours.

In addition to Barcelona, there are four prominent organisations with a remit to address certain aspects of security in the Mediterra-

17 See Claire Spencer (1998).

nean, namely: the North Atlantic Treaty Organisation (NATO), the Organisation for Security and Cooperation in Europe (OSCE), the Western European Union (WEU), and, within the MEPP, the multilateral group on arms control and regional security (ACRS). NATO, WEU and OSCE were developed in the context of East-West confrontation, but since the end of the Cold War brought a change in their thinking and focus, all three organisations have developed dialogues with non-member Mediterranean countries.

NATO's Mediterranean initiative of 1995 launched a dialogue with six countries: Egypt, Israel, Jordan, Mauritania, Morocco and Tunisia. As of the end of 1998, the WEU was engaged in dialogue with the same six, plus Algeria, Cyprus and Malta. The OSCE started a dialogue in 1994 and has granted observer status to Morocco, Tunisia, Algeria, Egypt and Israel.[18] Overlaps and distinctions are manifest on the side of the host organisations too. While the WEU, by definition, is a European body, NATO links Europe to North America and the OSCE straddles the old East-West divide. The OSCE is the most inclusive in terms of membership and dialogue. It was also the inspiration for an OSCM, or Mediterranean replica, mooted prior to the EMP. NATO and the WEU, meanwhile, incorporate in their history and identity responsibility for the defence of Europe.

By their very nature, NATO and the WEU are not best placed to develop an inclusive security framework for the Mediterranean, though the intention to subsume the WEU under the CFSP may redirect it to serving the goals of Barcelona. According to Dominic Fenech:

"Engaged in the exercise of adapting themselves to post-Cold War intra-European security, the [...] reaction of Europe's security structures, with NATO in the lead, was to address the potential implications of Mediterranean instability for Europe as a

18 Fenech (1997: 151), Winrow (1996: 52–56).

whole. Two 'arcs of crisis,' in eastern Europe and in the Mediterranean, began to be identified as centrally relevant to European security. The imagery of two arcs in symmetry is deceptive, however, for when European security organizations consider Europe's unstable peripheries, they view the East as a matter of internal security and the South as a matter of external security."[19]

In other words, when organisations tasked with the collective defence of their members enter dialogue with non-members, who are perceived as a potential source of threat, they risk reinforcing rather than ameliorating suspicions between them. Clearly, NATO and the WEU are trying to reconcile any contradictions between their fundamental responsibilities and the goal of security cooperation in the Mediterranean.

At least in terms of the economic agenda of Barcelona, EMP has a similar problem of meshing EU interests with the goal of creating a new economic space through partnership. Up to a point, the first pillar of Barcelona is more inclusive in its vision and therefore less likely to become hostage to polarization of interests. However, as was discussed above, the mechanisms by which Barcelona is being implemented have tended to reinforce the divide. A real problem exists also in finding a way to manage overlap between the security agenda of Barcelona and that of other frameworks such as NATO. Too much coordination could spell contamination for Barcelona with the in-built constraints of the other processes underway. Too little coordination may mean working at cross purposes.

Meanwhile, it is hoped that EMP proceeds in such a way as to avoid clashes with other players interested in the Mediterranean, notably the United States. Both through NATO and unilaterally, the United States has a major security presence and role in the Mediterranean. This has had implications for the Barcelona process from the moment of its inception. According to a WEU report:

19 Fenech (1997: 150).

"Although the United States attended [Barcelona] as an observer
only, it had put very strong pressure on the Europeans to gain
admittance as a participant. It was granted observer status only
and agreed to it on the understanding that the conference would
not cover conflicts which had not been resolved, particularly the
one in the Middle East. It became perfectly clear in this context
that the United States did not want to lose its monopoly in the
negotiations on the Middle East peace process. Furthermore, if
the United States had been admitted to the Conference as a participant, it is probable that Russia would have requested the same
status."[20]

If this report is accurate on the quid pro quo for keeping the United
States on the margins of Barcelona, it explains the EMP's 'self-denying ordinance' on involvement in resolution of existing conflicts. As
has already been discussed, this aspect of Barcelona has complicated
implementation of the first pillar, since, as envisaged, the security
agenda cannot be realised pending resolution of existing conflicts.
Also, since the US role in this respect is made sacrosanct, it begs the
question: What is the role for the United States thereafter? Will it be
ready to let the EMP forge ahead on all fronts if it is relegated to the
margins? US involvement in NATO's Mediterranean initiative suggests not.
    As is well documented, the United States has shown some ambi-
valence about putative plans for an enhanced European defence capability, the logical vehicle for which would be the WEU. US unease
will be an issue in so far as there is closer coordination between the
WEU and EMP. Conscious that the WEU was not invited to the Barcelona Conference or involved in any EU actions stemming from

20 Report submitted on behalf of the Political Committee, by de Lipkowski, Rappor-
    teur, to the Assembly of the Western European Union, 42nd Session, 'Security in
    the Mediterranean region,' Document 1543 (4 November 1996): 8.

this, WEU ministers have stressed the need for better coordination of their Mediterranean initiative with those of the EU and NATO.[21] The intensity which characterised competition between the WEU and NATO in the mid-1990s has dissipated,[22] but the identity of the WEU means that it reflects European policy orientations, not least on the Arab-Israeli conflict[23] and will be expected to do so. Consequently, it will give expression to European differences with the United States.

Ultimately, it makes sense that there be coordination between the Mediterranean initiatives of Europe and the United States, and of EMP, NATO and WEU. That said:

"However suitable NATO is or can become as the instrument of collective security among Europeans, it can only be marginally relevant to the Mediterranean. Its relevance is mainly negative in its other function as an alliance committed to defending its members if threatened or attacked."[24]

The new 'Strategic Concept' developed within NATO, has done nothing to assuage such concerns and disguises a disconnect between European and US thinking on the Middle East, as is discussed at length in this volume by Barry Buzan and Ole Wæver.

The experience of the OSCE in confidence and security building measures has been drawn upon already under the first pillar of Barcelona. As has already been said, this could be a problem in so far as such measures, developed in the context of East-West relations, assume or introduce misconceptions of a divide across the Mediterranean. Perhaps not surprisingly, meanwhile, Russia has called for the extension of the OSCE process to the Mediterranean, as one of

21 Ibid.: 9.
22 Fenech (1997: 158).
23 WEU Report (1996: 29).
24 Fenech (1997: 166).

the few security frameworks of which it is a member.[25] As for ACRS, conceptually this framework does dovetail with that of Barcelona, but its future is hostage to the MEPP and also, its participants are not agreed on the geographic limits of its remit, with Israel seeking to include the Persian Gulf in its agenda and Egypt set against this.

What is the Problem?

The assumption stated at the outset here is that the terms in which a problem is defined will determine its resolution. The definition of threats to peace and stability implicit in the Barcelona Declaration is echoed but not entirely replicated in other appraisals. The WEU report cited above enumerates the following regional conflicts:
- Developments in the Middle East peace process,
- crises involving Turkey, Syria, Iraq and Iran,
- crises between countries in North Africa,
- Cyprus and disputes between Greece and Turkey,
- the impact of the conflict in the Balkans on Euro-Mediterranean relations.

The same source identifies seven general problems affecting Euro-Mediterranean relations:
- The repercussions of economic, social and demographic change on Euro-Mediterranean relations,
- political Islamism,
- the fight against terrorism and organised crime,
- trends in military expenditure in the region,
- the proliferation of weapons of mass destruction and their means of conveyance,

25 Ojeda (1997: 108).

- promoting arms control and disarmament,
- the importance of public opinion.

Analysts from the RAND organisation, writing in *NATO Review* in 1996 warn of tensions in the Balkans and the possibility of growing instability in North Africa. They identify economic and demographic pressures around the Mediterranean as likely to worsen the prospects for stability, pointing to an imbalance between the total population of the current members of the EU (less than 300 million) and that of the Mediterranean littoral states in the south and east (over 350 million) in the early twenty-first century. According to this analysis:

> "This demographic imbalance, together with the stagnation of the economies of the countries along the Mediterranean littoral, has fuelled growing migration to Western Europe, above all to Southern Europe. In addition, there are some 1.5 million Turkish guest workers in Germany, roughly one third of whom are Kurds. These communities form an increasingly important economic and cultural presence. At the same time they could create growing economic, political and social problems for the countries of Southern Europe, which have become destinations as well as conduits for migration."[26]

On the southern side of the Mediterranean, population growth rates and policies adopted in the post-independence era have contributed to the rise of a small, educated middle class and a large lower class, both with aspirations which cannot be met and put their regimes under stress. In the words of Egyptian sociologist, Saad Eddin Ibrahim:

---

26 Asmus, Ronald et al. 1996: Mediterranean Security: New Challenges, New Tasks,' NATO Review No. 3: 26–7.

"A growing number of aggrieved, alienated, but articulate young-sters of the small middle class have been recruited into radical movements seeking to transform the socio-political order in the name of 'Islam'. In turn, these radical youngsters have managed to recruit many more equally alienated but less educated young-sters of the urban lumpen proletariat. It is a coalition of two emis-erated socio-economic formations."[27]

These forces are joining cause against their governments, which are charged alternately with colluding with their Western counterparts to suppress popular will and rejecting Western notions of human rights and democracy to maintain themselves in power.

Clearly there are three or four sets of security issues here: those of European governments and of European populations, and those of governments in the South and of their populations. If the instabilities in the South spill over into European countries, public opinion may turn hostile against those of immigrant descent. The more the num-bers build within the countries of the south, however, the more pres-sure will mount on the regimes to respond or fall. Leave aside the continuing interstate conflicts such as between Israel and its neigh-bours, interstate war is much less of a threat to Mediterranean secu-rity than socio-economic unrest inflamed by resentment at unresolved conflicts in the region.

These various depictions of dangers to stability in the Mediterra-nean compute with the security agenda identified in Barcelona and which EMP is supposed to solve. In other words, there is something of a consensus on what the problem is, but Barcelona represents the most visionary response.

27 Saad Eddin Ibrahim (1995: 17).

Evaluation

The central conclusion here is that Chapter I of Barcelona is visionary, but this is more of a strength than a weakness. If the problem really is more about demographics and employment than military confrontation, then the socio-political and economic goals of the whole Barcelona process make more sense than the pursuit of high technology defence systems. The principle conceptual weakness of Chapter I is that it glosses over the fact that the Arab-Israeli, Cyprus and Western Sahara conflicts are still not resolved. Full realisation of the Barcelona vision requires their prior resolution, so that south-south as well as south-north economic integration can take off.

In the meantime, making significant progress in implementation of Chapter I is bound to be difficult. Too much emphasis on achieving tangible results could encourage resort to inappropriate or counter-productive measures such as CSBMs in the military sector. As was pointed out above, the transition from CSBMs to PBMs must be substantive and that is likely to mean genuine cooperation between all the partners in areas such as environmental protection, rather than pursuit of an arms control agenda which could enshrine existing imbalances and inequalities. It is also important that distance be maintained between EMP and other mechanisms, notably NATO, with a more overt European defence agenda.

It is true that Barcelona is essentially a European response to challenges on the southern flank. However, the process has evolved and non-European partners have shown a sense of ownership of it and are looking to Europe to continue to demonstrate a serious commitment to the goals. In other words, the EU will be held to the ideals espoused at Barcelona, including building a genuine partnership, but at the same time, non-governmental groups are looking to Europe to promote pluralism, accountability and human rights despite objections from southern governments. This is especially true of intellectual and Westernised elites in Arab partner countries.

According to Saad Eddin Ibrahim:

"The Establishments on both sides of the Mediterranean are clearly keen on avoiding a Huntington 'Clash of Civilizations' and have been cooperating on narrow security issues to contain and/or pre-empt violence and terrorism. These, however, are sheer 'sedatives.' What is truly needed are drastic socio-political-economic reforms. Because the Establishment on the southern side is not democratically elected, it will not engage in such serious reform. Even if it did, credibility may still be lacking. Hence the imperative of a carrot-and-stick strategy with southern Establishments."[28]

Herein lies an obvious irony. Barcelona Chapter I is conceptually sound in its identification of the problem and its vision of a solution through partnership. However, the success of Barcelona will depend on Europe using its predominant position to push the process. In addition, Barcelona rests on the assumption that economic liberalisation means political liberalisation too and that the combination produces prosperity for all. This is more of an article of faith than a proven connection, but again ironically, it may never be put to the test, because the southern partner states will demand as much compensation from the EU as they can extract for the pain that Barcelona imposes upon their economies in the near term. In this sense they are partners in an interactive process which should not be ditched on conceptual grounds, but is beset with implementation problems.

28 Ibid.: 18.

List of References

Fenech, Dominic 1997: The Relevance of European Security Structures to the Mediterranean (and Vice Versa), in: Mediterranean Security, 2/1.

Gillespie, Richard 1997: Northern European Perceptions of the Barcelona Process, in: Revista CIDOB d'Afers Internacionals, 37/4.

Ojeda, Alfonso 1997: The Euro-Mediterranean Partnership. A Cooperation Pattern for the Persian Gulf?, in: The Iranian Journal of International Affairs, 10/1 & 2.

Ibrahim, Saad Eddin 1995: From the Battle of Tours to the Battle of Algiers, in: Civil Society, August 1995.

Spencer, Claire 1997: Building Confidence in the Mediterranean, in: Mediterranean Politics, 2/2.

Spencer, Claire 1998: Rethinking or Reorienting Europe's Mediterranean Security Focus?, in: Parks, William/G. Wyn Rees (eds.): Rethinking Security in Post-Cold War Europe, London.

Winrow, Gareth 1996: A Threat from the South? NATO and the Mediterranean, in: Mediterranean Politics 1/1.

Youngs, Richard 1999: The Barcelona Process after the UK Presidency. The Need for Prioritization, in: Mediterranean Politics, 4/1.

The Middle East Peace Process

Searching for a Sustainable Peace Settlement Between Israel and its Neighbours

Eberhard Rhein

After three years of stalemate, during which Israel has further expanded its grip on the West Bank, and which have seen major improvements of the security situation, thanks to more intensive Israeli-Palestinian cooperation, the outcome of the elections in Israel gives rise to new hope for reaching a final settlement between Israel and its neighbours in the north and east.[1]

On 5 September 1999 Israel and the Palestinian Authority have agreed to complete negotiations for the final status within 12 months. These negotiations will be extraordinarily difficult; some observers have gone so far as to qualify them as the most complex negotiations ever conducted. Indeed, their purpose is to put an end to more than 100 years, since the beginning of the Zionist movement in the late 19th century, of friction and open confrontation between Palestin-

1   This contribution was presented to the workshop *A Future Security Structure for the Middle East and the Eastern Mediterranean*, Frankfurt, October 1999.

ians and, first, Jews and after 1948 Israelis, both claiming the same
tiny stretch of mostly barren 'Holy Land' and Jerusalem as its capital. In a way, both parties are back to square one, to 1947/48 when
the international community had tried in vain to solve the dispute
peacefully by way of the UN partition plan which, the Arab side,
feeling morally and militarily strong at that time, refused to accept.
In retrospect one should say, unfortunately; the world would have
been spared investing so much futile energy in finding alternative
solutions.

More than 50 years have elapsed since; marked by two more
open military confrontations in 1967 and 1973, the peace treaty
between Israel and Egypt in 1979, continued Palestinian guerilla
activity, the 'Intifadha' of 1987, the difficult start of peace negotiations between Israelis and Palestinians in 1993 (Oslo) and the peace
treaty between Israel and Jordan in 1994. During this half century,
the balance of power has dramatically shifted in favour of Israel. It
has de facto taken control of essentially all Palestinian territory and
of the water resources contested in 1947, as well as of Jerusalem. A
new 'status quo' has therefore been imposed upon Palestinians,
Lebanese and Syrians which clearly favours Israel. That is what
makes these negotiations extremely difficult.

Israel believes it can dictate the terms of the final status and of
the peace. It is unwilling to go back to the borders of 1967, let alone
of 1947, to share Jerusalem with the Palestinians or to allow any of
the 1948/67 refugees or their descendants to return to their former
homes in Israel. The Palestinians, Lebanese and Syrians therefore
appeal to 'legality' as laid down in the various UN resolutions and to
the international community in order to support their case.

If and when successfully concluded, the negotiations with Lebanon, Syria and the Palestinians will put an end to half a century of
bitter fighting between Israel and the Arab world. Israel will by the
same token be accepted as a regional party. Whether and how fast it
will also become a respected regional partner, will depend on its will-

ingness and capacity to fully integrate in the region, to gain confidence, to cooperate on a basis of equality and, last but not least, to suppress any temptation of being an 'arrogant power'.

The international community has a vital role to play in the 'end game'. Above all, it has to see to it that the peace will be just and sustainable. This will only be the case if the Palestinians are allowed to 'breathe' more freely and to liberate themselves from the iron grip which Israel has held for so long.

This implies that:

- Israel returns essentially all of the occupied territory conquered in 1967,
- the water resources are fairly shared,
- the two societies will be allowed to interact and to cooperate peacefully and intensively.

Why is the integral return of land and an equal sharing of the scarce water resources so vital for the long-term viability of the peace?

Because the already extremely high density of population (300 people per sq. km in Israel and 500 in Palestine in 1999) will dramatically increase in the next two decades as a consequence of natural population growth and further immigration. For the year 2025 one can expect the population to rise to 400 people per sq. km in Israel and 1000 people in Palestine. Considering that most of the land in Israel/Palestine is either desert or barren mountains, their population density will reach a dimension for which there is no precedent anywhere in Europe, not even in the Netherlands with population density of less than 400 people per sq. km, but much more crop land and ample of water. And without adequate water supply the little bit of dry land of which the Palestinians will dispose will be absolutely useless. That is why they must not depend on Israeli 'control' of the water supply.

The international community must be the guarantor of a just and sustainable peace. Its main role is to see to it that a balanced compromise will be agreed upon. It would be fatal if the outcome of the peace negotiations were to produce an independent, but non-viable Palestinian mini-state which would become dependent on continued flows of massive international assistance for its socio-economic survival. That is why the international community has such a high stake in a balanced outcome and why the EU and the USA have to get deeply involved in the essentials of the negotiations.

The present paper attempts to analyse the key issues which will have to be dealt with. It offers possible 'solutions' for compromise. It does so from the rational perspective of a neutral, however committed outsider who is not inhibited by the emotional constraints of the parties. Some of the solutions suggested will be rejected as totally 'unrealistic', 'shocking' or 'naive' by one or all of the parties. Still, it is hoped that the following succinct analysis may stimulate further thinking and help to overcome one or the other mental 'blockade'.

Basic Goals of the Parties

Syria and Lebanon want to recover *all* territories occupied by Israel since 1967. Palestine wants to establish a viable independent state within the borders of 1967 and with (East) Jerusalem as the capital. Israel wants to assure the security and integrity of the country against any, even distant military risks (e.g. Iran, Iraq, coalition of Arab countries) and terrorist attacks (Palestinians) against its citizens wherever they may find themselves. The EU and the USA have essentially one convergent goal, i.e. to restore peace and normalcy in the Middle East.

Strengths and Weaknesses of the Parties

Israel can dictate the terms of peace. It enjoys complete military superiority against any Arab adversary. It is therefore in the position to dictate the terms under which it returns the lands it has occupied from its neighbours.

But the Israeli strength is not without weaknesses:
- it has international legality against it (UN Resolutions 181, 194, UN Security Council Resolutions 242, 338, 625),
- it cannot be 100 per cent certain to maintain its military superiority forever,
- it does not wish to compromise its close relations with the superpowers through excessive stubbornness,
- it has to take into account that the international business community might once again withdraw from Israel (foreign direct investment of US$ 2–3 billion p. a.) if the security situation degenerates.

Syria and Lebanon possess two assets in their hand:
- the nuisance potential through missiles/rockets on the northern part of Israel,
- the potential to form another anti-Israel coalition (with Iran and Iraq), at least in the very long term.

Palestine has by far the weakest hand. It might dream of re-starting a new 'intifadha' and thereby destabilise Israeli society and mobilise the sympathy of the international community. But this would be a dangerous weapon which is bound to hurt it at least as much as it would hurt Israel; if at all, it will therefore only be used if frustration in connection with Israel were to become truly desperate.

The EU and even the USA represent no more than a moral force. For a variety of reasons neither possesses the means to impose an agreement upon Israel. Their strength lies in their ability to have open channels of communication with all the parties and to become 'honest brokers' once the negotiations will come into force. The USA is by far the more potent external force, not only because of its privileged links with Israel but also because it has got involved in the details of the negotiations which the EU has not sufficiently done so far.

Exploring Possible Compromises

With Lebanon/Syria

The sides want a settlement, even rapidly. The sides are driven essentially by strategic and security considerations. This helps; but the
sides also have to demonstrate to their constituencies that they have
obtained their vital objectives. For Israel this means that it must be
able to feel absolutely safe against any encroachments or attacks at
its northern border. For Lebanon and Syria recovering all the territories presently occupied by Israel is the essential goal. For Lebanon
a compromise might be found around the following parameters:
- Israeli withdrawal from all of South Lebanon,
- disarming of the Hizbollah forces and control taken by the Lebanese army,
- appropriate guarantees by the Lebanese government to respect
  the inviolability of Israeli territory and vice-versa,
- possibly, a demilitarised zone along the border,
- stationing of an international peace keeping force (EU troops?)
  for a period of at least five years, until calm and confidence will
  have been established,
- normalisation of relations between the two countries.

For Syria the parameters of a compromise might look as follows:
- Israeli withdrawal, in stages, from essentially all of the Golan
  Heights.
- Israel will retain a narrow stretch of land along the northern and
  eastern shores of the Lake of Galilee in order to maintain the free
  passage around the eastern shores of the lake. It will buy this land
  on the basis of the current land price, or lease it if Syria remains
  adamant.
- Israel will retain the right to exploit the water aquifers/springs
  flowing from the Golan Heights on Israeli territory. It may have

to concede a price for those 'water rights', even if Syria, for geological reasons, will not be able to use the Golan water itself.

-   Syria agrees to keep the Golan heights permanently demilitarised (Sinai precedent) which does not exclude the right to install (passive) means of intelligence (listening devices, antennas, etc.).

-   Both sides agree to have an international (USA?) peace keeping force installed on the Golan Heights for at least five years, extendible according to the development of the situation.

-   Syria might agree to allow the settlers to stay, provided they will become subject to Syrian jurisdiction. It is more likely that both sides will agree to the evacuation of the some 20.000 Israeli settlers living presently on the Golan Heights.

-   Syria and Israel will normalise their diplomatic relations and allow for free travel of their citizens (subject to visa).

-   Israel will offer Syria to negotiate agreements on economic, scientific cooperation when relations will have normalised.

-   Both sides and Jordan will conclude an agreement on the use of the Yarmouk water.

-   Israel will raise no objections to the return of Palestinian refugees to Palestine. It will pay them compensations for the property lost/expropriated in Israel.

-   Syria will offer those who stay citizenship. The international community (World Bank, USA, EU, Japan) will offer Syria a generous loan package for the construction of housing for the Palestinian refugees wishing to stay in Syria.

-   Russia will declare its readiness to enter into negotiations for the re-scheduling of the Syrian military debt.

-   The EU will offer Syria grants and loans in the order of 1 billion Euro for the five-year period following the entry into force of a peace agreement with Israel. This will be done in the framework of the Association Agreement presently under negotiation.

With Palestine

This will be the hardest piece of work. Since 1967 Israel has changed the status quo in its favour by:
- encouraging some 200,000 Israelis to build their homes on Palestinian territory,
- installing military camps etc.,
- building some 50 km of four-lane highways and at least the same length of normal highways for its citizens living in Palestine and for transit,
- exploiting 80 per cent of the Palestinian water resources,
- severely restricting the freedom of movement of Palestinian citizens within their own territory,
- cutting the Palestinian territory into three separate parts between which Palestinians cannot travel normally.

The parameters for the future coexistence between Israelis and Palestinians might be defined in the following terms:

Statehood and Security

Israel accepts the creation of a Palestinian state, subject to a series of restrictions on its sovereignty, inter alia:
- Palestine will renounce the creation of an army or any para-military force going beyond police functions and civilian border control.
- It will equally renounce entering into defence agreements with third countries and any stationing of foreign military forces on its territory, not agreed upon with Israel.
- Israel and Palestine will negotiate an agreement which will allow Israel to continue to station military forces on Palestinian territory according to precise conditions agreed between the two par-

ties (in analogy to the agreements that have, for many years, governed the stationing of American troops in Germany).

Territorial Issues

Israel will render essentially all Palestinian territories still under its occupation. For certain territories, which either have a strategic bearing for Israel or which house Israeli settlements close to the Israeli border, there will be

- either a swap of territory with Israel compensating by other land, e.g. south of Gaza; such a compensation will have to take into account the different land value in different parts of the territory, e.g. 1 sq. km in the north may be exchanged against 2 sq. km in the Negev,
- or financial compensation by Israel (on the basis of the land price of comparable undeveloped land).

The total area subject to swap for financial compensation arrangements (including the lease of land) must not exceed a certain percentage, say ten per cent of all Palestinian lands.

Settlements

Israel will progressively evacuate all other settlements; but as of the entry into force of the final status, Palestine will be entitled to charge an adequate price (or lease) for the land occupied by the settlements. This will make living in the settlements more expensive to Israeli citizens. Israel will be entitled to financial compensation for the houses and infrastructure left behind.

Water

Two different approaches might be envisaged to solve the complex
issue of water rights and use:

- water sharing: The two sides will negotiate a new deal on how to
  share the overall water resources of which Israel and Palestine
  dispose.[2] Considering the relative populations, Palestine should
  be entitled to a share of about one third of *all* available water
  resources. In view of the unequal negotiating power of the two
  parties and the hydro-geological nature of the Palestinian water
  resources, Palestine will most unlikely obtain a satisfactory result
  out of these negotiations. Palestine will find it extraordinarily difficult to rationally use its own water resources. It may have to
  pump water up from much deeper than the 600 meters already
  practised, which will become prohibitively expensive.
- joint water management: In the medium term the use of water
  will have to be rationed by the market. A substantial part of the
  presently irrigated crops like maize and citrus will have to be
  priced out; agriculture will only benefit from sewage water for
  irrigation. For reasons of rationality, both Israeli and Palestinian
  households in the coastal plains will be supplied with desalinated
  water from the Mediterranean; the population living in the high
  lands will get their water from the Golan Heights, the Yarmouk
  and Palestinian aquifers. The supply will be managed by a jointly-
  run water company owned by Israeli, Palestinian shareholders and
  a major international water company that will be in charge of the
  water supply for the whole of Israel and Palestine. To that end, it
  will be responsible for the rational and sustainable management of
  all the waterresources in the two countries. Its pricing policy will
  be monitored by a joint Israeli-Palestinian Board.

---

2   In such a negotiation the Israeli resources must be included. Presently Palestine is
    entitled to only 15 per cent of what it considers its own Palestinian water resources.

Refugees

For political and moral reasons Palestine and Israel will have to offer the right of return to all the Palestinians who have been driven from their homes after 1947. But it is in both their vital interest to limit the number of returnees – and immigrants for that matter – to a minimum. The population in both countries combined is expected to double to about 16 millions by 2025. At that juncture, the population density will have reached levels which will most likely have a negative impact on the well-being of the people, especially in Palestine. It will, indeed, be more than twice as high as in the Netherlands, the country with the highest density in this part of the world. In order to limit the number of returnees, the host countries (Jordan, Lebanon, Syria) should be given incentives to offer their nationality to Palestinian refugees, in particular those belonging to the second and third generation. The international community should support their integration by appropriate financial packages; it should, in parallel, open generous immigration facilities for Palestinian refugees, especially for the 300.000 refugees living in Lebanon. Israel should restrict the number of new immigrants, e.g. by ceasing all promotional efforts and financial incentives. It will have to offer financial compensation to refugees who were forced to leave the country in 1948.

Jerusalem

Since 1967 Jerusalem has vastly expanded beyond the original boundaries, in particular towards the east and north into Palestinian territory. As a consequence of this expansion, done essentially through Israeli settlements, Palestinians represent today less than one third of the overall population, and the old city represents a tiny proportion of the Jerusalem metropolitan area. It will be impossible to undo this development: On the contrary, Jerusalem is bound to enlarge further, into all directions. It will sooner, rather than later, comprise all the land from Ramallah in the north and Bethlehem in the south with a population of more than 2 million people.

In this overall context, it will become easier rather than more difficult to house two capitals in the wider metropolitan area of Jerusalem; one for Israel in its present location and one for Palestine, in the south-eastern parts of the area. Brussels may serve as a successful precedent, housing three capitals in its area, for the Belgian Federation, for Flanders and for the European Union. Palestinians and Israelis will live in separate quarters but move around freely in the whole metropolitan area, including for work. This is the hardest to achieve. They will form separate municipal councils, with certain functions like transport, water, electricity, and others, to be decided upon by a joint metropolitan council or joint companies. Palestinians from the whole metropolitan area and Palestine will, of course, enjoy free access to the holy places.

Borders

Israel and Palestine will agree on borders between the two states; there will be clear separation and sovereignty over the respective lands, even if subject to certain agreed restrictions. Palestine will by the same token mark its borders with Egypt and Jordan. Palestine will assume the exclusive charge of monitoring the movement of persons and goods into and out of its country, possibly after a transition period during which this control will be exercised jointly by Palestinian and Israeli border police (cf. Gaza airport).

Movement of persons

The restrictions presently imposed upon Palestinian citizens for travel inside the Palestinian territories constitute an unsustainable limitation of their personal freedom. The final status arrangements will have to put an end to this situation. The final status agreements should also provide for free movement of persons between Israel and Palestine. This is in the vital interest of both countries, in particular for Palestine. The vision of a strict separation, as expressed by Prime Minister Barak, should be vehemently resisted by both Israelis and Palestinians. So should the idea of a fly-over between Gaza and the West Bank, the cost of which is estimated to be in the range of US$ 500 million. During a transition period, which will last as long as Israeli fears of terrorist attacks prevail, the freedom of movement may have to be restricted by security checks at authorised check points and a system of visa similar (but less humiliating) to the one presently in force at the Gaza check points. It is vital for the sustainability of peace that the separation into two states will not develop into an interruption of human contacts between the two societies. On the contrary, such contacts should by all means be encouraged. They are essential for the peaceful coexistence between the two people.

Free Movement of Workers

Israel has an economic interest in using cheap labour, especially for certain jobs which Israelis prefer not to perform, like construction, cleaning, household services. Cheap labour can either be supplied by 'immigration' from Asian countries or by cross-border facilities in favour of Palestinians. In the last ten years Israel has largely favoured the first over the second solution, essentially for security reasons. In view of the final status Israel should think of reversing the trend in favour of more Palestinian labour:

- it would avoid creating long-term problems of creeping immigration (cf. the European experience),
- it would create purchasing power in its immediate neighbourhood and boost its exports to Palestine,
- Palestine will not be able to absorb the additional three per cent annual increase of its labour force: the level of unemployment is therefore bound to grow with negative implications for the social situation and even a risk of political destabilisation.

Both sides should therefore explore ways and means to:
- allow for more Palestinian workers into Israel,
- make the conditions of entry as easy and flexible as possible,
- make sure that Palestinian workers will fully benefit from their social security contributions,
- transfer to the Palestinian Authority the full amount of the withholding taxes deducted from the salaries of Palestinian workers,
- make the security arrangements "watertight."

Movement of Goods

Under final status all goods should move freely between Israel and Palestine. They should not be subject to any customs duties nor quantitative restrictions. But the present quasi customs union should be transformed into a free trade area. For political reasons, Palestine needs to take full control of the movement of goods across its borders. Palestine will in this way become able to fully control the receipts from VAT and to grant limited infant industry protection. Moreover, both Israel and Palestine form an integral part of the emerging Euro-Med free trade area and will be subject to the same basic rules, e.g. for the origin of goods. Free trade does not make sense when it is thwarted by excessive security controls, as is the case presently. Both sides therefore will have to agree on simplified controls, comparable to those applicable in Israeli-Jordanian trade.[3] Without simplified security checks free trade with Israel is of no interest to Palestine and should be renounced. Whatever the trade regime agreed with Israel, Palestine must be free to arrange the regime of customs and trade with other third countries, in particular its two major potential economic partners, Egypt and Jordan. The borders with these two countries must be opened, without the present lengthy and excessive security checks, as a matter of top priority. For a transition period, Palestine may have to agree to the presence of Israeli security officers alongside their own staff. But it must under no circumstances agree to any disruption of charges (unloading of trucks) at its borders.

Transport and Transit

Israel and Palestine will have to negotiate a transit agreement which will allow reciprocal use of transport facilities and infrastructure. This is more in Palestinian than in Israeli interest. Without the use of Israeli ports/airports Palestinian exports to Europe will be under a competitive handicap, whatever improvements the future port and airport in Gaza might procure. The legitimate Israeli security concerns can be easily met through bonded containers, and other measures.

Cooperation in Matters of Security, Legal Matters and Currency

Israel and Palestine will be well advised to develop close links of cooperation in many areas of common interest. They should, as a matter of priority, continue and even intensify their ongoing cooperation in the field of security. In legal matters both sides have an inter-

---

3   Such as bonded containers with inspection at the factory gate instead of the border, no back to back charging, no interruption of charge, limitation of control to samples, etc.

est in establishing identical or similar legal rules concerning environment, standards, customs, transport, taxation, food safety, and
others. They should inform each other on their legislative proposals
and enter into consultations whenever one of the parties requests so.
Palestine will wish to have its own currency; Israel should not prevent it from doing so. From a purely economic point of view a Palestinian currency is not a priority and should only be introduced when
all the preconditions for stability and sound monetary and fiscal policies are being fulfilled. The currency should be informally aligned to
the Euro.

Timing

The Palestinians have a vital interest in settling their future statute as
rapidly as possible. Israel should feel in the same way in order to
avoid further frustration and possible eruption of violence in Palestine. Even if both sides agree on the urgency of a negotiated settlement, negotiations will be tough. Israel will have to take very hard
decisions which will pay dividend only in the medium term. So will
the Palestinians.

Conclusion

Peace must not be imposed on Palestine by Israel dictating its conditions. Such a peace will not be sustainable because of lack of balance
and justice. Outside players therefore have to get involved as balancing forces which should, whenever necessary, try to influence the
parties to accept or to modify certain ideas. Whatever influence is to
be exerted, it should take place through informal political contacts,
if necessary at the highest level. The EU should become a more pro-
active player, alongside and in close coordination with the USA.

It is both urgent and possible to establish peace and normal relations between Israel and its neighbours. The outcome of the Israeli elections opens a new window of opportunities. It is up to the political leadership both in and outside the region to seize it. They should jointly make the conquest of peace the top priority of their foreign policy strategies, at least for the months to come. The regional parties will have to realise that both the EU and the USA may get tired and turn their attention to other equally pressing world problems if this chance for peace will be missed again through short-sighted and nationalistic attitudes of the regional parties.

Europe and the Arab-Israeli Peace Process: The Declaration of the European Council of Berlin and Beyond

Joel Peters

"Peace in the Middle East is a vital interest of the European Union. Accordingly, the European Union is ready to play an active part in efforts to recommence the negotiations, commensurate with its interests in the region, and on the basis of its major contribution to the Peace Process so far."[1]

"[The European Union] has a *responsibility both to the region and to itself* (my italics) to put the Peace Process back on track" (Dick Spring, Foreign Minister Republic of Ireland).[2]

"We must remain involved in the Middle East Peace Process and we must be there when the time comes after the Israeli election to

---

1   Declaration by the European Union on the Peace Process, 1 October 1996.
2   Speech delivered to the 3rd Middle East and North Africa Economic Conference, Cairo, October 1996.

relaunch the efforts on all tracks. This is what the world expects from us" (Ambassador Miguel Angel Moratinos).[3]

The resolution of the Arab-Israeli conflict has always been a major concern for European leaders and has long occupied a prominent position on the foreign policy agenda of European capitals.[4] A strong consensus exists amongst both European policy makers and political commentators that Europe needs to play a more prominent and clearly-defined role in the Middle East peace process. Speeches by European leaders contain many references to Europe's willingness and desire to work with the region towards achieving peace in the Middle East; to its close political, historical, economic, religious and cultural links with the peoples and countries of the region, and to the fact that peace and stability in the Middle East are of vital strategic interest to Europe.

European leaders have sought to play a more prominent role in the peace process at both the individual and collective level, in areas such as the ongoing negotiations over final status issues between Israel and the Palestinians, and in discussions towards the resumption of talks between Israel and Syria. European involvement in the Middle East has become particularly pronounced in recent months, following the election of Ehud Barak as Prime Minister of Israel, with many European leaders visiting Jerusalem to lend their support to the peace process.[5]

European countries have always prided themselves on their 'special relationship' with the Middle East and in particular with the

3 Speech delivered by Miguel Angel Moratinos to conference on 'Recent Political and Economic Developments in the Middle East Peace Process' Centre for Applied Policy Research, Munich, 27 April 1999.
4 This contribution was presented to the workshop *A Future Security Structure for the Middle East and the Eastern Mediterranean*, Frankfurt, October 1999.
5 In October alone the Presidents of Italy and Finland, the Prime Minister of Sweden and the French and British Foreign Ministers visited Israel and the Palestinian Authority.

Arab world. Europeans have long maintained that their sophisticated understanding of the region equips them well, if not better than, the United States to develop a set of policies towards a comprehensive peace in the region. That this affinity has not always been reciprocated does not deter the Europeans. Neither are they deterred by the limitations and difficulties they have in formulating, and then implementing, a common foreign and security policy.

Europe's desire to play a greater role in the Arab-Israeli peace process stems from a long-standing dissatisfaction with its marginalisation from key negotiations within the process and with the role assigned to it by the United States and Israel, whereby it would provide the financial resources required for underwriting agreements whilst the United States would serve as sole external mediator between the protagonists.

Europe's growing irritation at being sidelined was most palpable during Binyamin Netanyahu's tenure as Prime Minister of Israel, when the peace process between Israel and the Palestinians virtually collapsed. For European leaders, Netanyahu's policies were at best unhelpful and at worst catastrophic. This sense of frustration within European capitals was best summed up by Rosemary Hollis: "Singly and collectively, the Europeans have too much at stake in the Middle East to defer to the United States' lead, if, as latterly, it seems unable by itself to rescue the Arab-Israeli peace process from a reversion towards confrontation."[6]

The desire of Europe to be more actively involved in the peace process coupled with dissatisfaction at its marginalisation has led to demands that its role correspond more closely with its importance as a political actor on the world stage and reflect the substantial financial backing it is giving the region. Accordingly, there have been calls that the EU co-sponsor the peace process and be afforded a role in the final status negotiations. At a minimum, it should at least be

6   Hollis (1997: 15–29).

more engaged in decisions that involve a financial commitment on its behalf.

The aim of this paper is two-fold:

First, it reviews the contribution of Europe to the Arab-Israeli peace process since the Madrid Conference at the end of October 1991. It argues that rather than playing a marginal role in the search for peace, the European Union has emerged from the sidelines and has succeeded in carving out a role for itself in a number of arenas.

Second, it will suggest ways in which the European Union might, in the coming months, contribute to the peace process. The paper argues that rather than seek a more prominent political role in the forthcoming negotiations and new areas of activity, Europe should deepen its activities in those areas in which it has already carved out a role for itself over the past eight years.

Future European Union policy should in particular focus on four specific areas: support for Palestinian civil society and institution building; enhancing security arrangements between Israel and the Palestinian Authority; supporting future security arrangements between Israel and Syria and Israel and Lebanon; the encouragement of regional economic development and the development of new structures for regional cooperation.

In particular, European policy should be based on the following three related principles: i) identifying issues and areas in which there is a need for action; ii) assessing whether it has the capability and capacity to act and contribute effectively in those arenas; iii) assessing if there is a European interest in undertaking such a commitment.

From Venice to Berlin

Europe's determination to carve out for itself a separate and distinct role in the quest for peace in the Middle East is not new. Attempts by the member states of the European Union to play a collective role, independent of the superpowers, in the Arab-Israeli conflict can be traced back to the early 1970s. When the foreign ministers of the six original member countries of the European Community met for the first time in the framework of the newly established 'European Political Cooperation' in Munich 1970, the situation in the Middle East was the first item on the agenda.[7]

Although there are differences in thought within the European Union as how best to play a more active role in the peace process, the policies of the member states converge around a number of shared principles, expressed in the Declarations and Statements on the peace process issued by the European Union.

It was the Venice Declaration of June 1980, issued one year after the signing of the peace treaty between Israel and Egypt, that marked the emergence of a distinct and common European stance towards the Arab-Israeli conflict and which outlined a collective position on steps to be taken for its peaceful resolution. Nearly twenty years on, the Venice Declaration still constitutes the basic principles of European policy towards the peace process.

In the preamble to the Venice Declaration, the members of the EC stated that "[...] the traditional ties and common interests which link Europe to the Middle East" obligated them to "[...] play a 'special role' in the pursuit of regional peace". The Declaration asserted that it was imperative that a just solution be found to the Palestinian problem, that this issue was "[...] not simply a refugee one", and that the Palestinian people be allowed to "[...] exercise fully its right to self-determination". Significantly, the member states called for the inclusion of the Palestine Liberation Organization (PLO) in any negotiations for a settlement. The Declaration stressed that Israel end its territorial occupation and that the EC was "[...] deeply convinced that Israeli settlements constitute a serious obstacle to the peace process" and that these settlements "[...] are illegal under

7   Joulani (1998: 5).

international law". The Declaration was equally forthright concerning the future of Jerusalem. "The Nine stress that they will not accept any unilateral initiative designed to change the status of Jerusalem".

Over the years, the Europeans have sharpened their positions on the nature of the conflict and underlined what they perceive are the prerequisites for a lasting peaceful resolution between Israel and the Palestinians. For example, on 1 October 1996 the Council of Ministers issued a statement on the rioting in the West Bank and Gaza which occurred following the opening by Israel of the Hasmonean tunnel in the Old City of Jerusalem. Laying the blame for the outburst of the violence on Israel, the European Union reaffirmed its policy on the status of Jerusalem thus:

"East Jerusalem is subject to the principles set out in UN Security Council Resolution 242, notably the inadmissibility of the acquisition of territory by force and is therefore not under Israeli sovereignty. The Union asserts that the Fourth Geneva Convention is fully applicable to East Jerusalem, as it is to other territories under occupation."[8]

The statement called upon Israel to "[. . .] refrain from any action likely to create mistrust about its intentions" and to cease "[. . .] all acts that may affect the status of the Holy Places in Jerusalem". It went on to call for a cessation of "[. . .] measures that prejudice the outcome of final status negotiations, including annexation of land, demolition of houses, new settlement construction and expansion of settlements".

Israel has constantly denounced the European Declarations on the Middle East for their one-sidedness, for pre-judging the outcome of the negotiations, and for the way in which they simply reflect the

---

8 Declaration by the European Union on the Middle East Peace Process, General Affairs Council, 1 October 1996.

position of the Arab states, making demands of Israel without expecting reciprocal compromise on the part of the Arabs. The Venice Declaration signalled a low point in Israel's relations with the European Community from which it has never fully recovered. To this day, some twenty years on, it is still seen as reflecting European bias towards the Arabs. The positions adopted by Europe in these Declarations are seen by Israel as mirroring those taken by the Arabs, thereby effectively removing Europe as a potential mediator between the two sides.

Rightly or wrongly, especially prior to the signing of the Oslo Accords, Europe was perceived by Israel as part of the problem rather than as a solution to it.[9] Whilst that view has been modified in recent years, Europe's desire to play a more prominent mediatory role in the region is still broadly dismissed by Israel.

Not surprisingly, the Arab states have derived great satisfaction from the position adopted by the European states and regard the European stance on issues such as the Palestinian right to self-determination and the illegality of Israeli settlement policy as an important element in attracting international support for the Palestinian cause. They view the Declarations as an important counterweight to the blanket support given to Israel by the United States. Accordingly, they have been eager to afford the European Union a more prominent role in efforts to resolve the Arab-Israeli conflict.

The most significant change in European Union thinking on the peace process has occurred over the past eighteen months concerning the question of Palestinian statehood. In the summer of 1998, in a statement issued by the Council of Ministers following the Cardiff summit meeting, the European Union called on "[. . .] Israel to recognize the right of the Palestinians to exercise self-determination, *without excluding the option of a State* (my italics)."

---

9   See Joseph Alpher in this volume.

One year later, at the Council of Ministers meeting held in Berlin on 24–25 March, the European Union sharpened its position with its most explicit statement yet of support for Palestinian statehood:

"The European Union reaffirms the continuing and unqualified Palestinian right to self-determination including the option of a state and looks forward to the early fulfilment of this right."
"The European Union is convinced that the creation of a democratic viable and peaceful sovereign Palestinian state on the basis of existing agreements and through negotiations would be the best guarantee of Israel's security and Israel's acceptance as an equal partner in the region. The European Union declares its readiness to consider the recognition of a Palestinian State in due course."

Not surprisingly, Israel dismissed the Berlin Declaration as a further sign of European bias and as an attempt to dictate the future outcome of negotiations with the Palestinians. Binyamin Netanyahu's response to the Declaration was unambiguous: "It is a shame that Europe, where a third of the Jewish people was killed, should take a stand which puts Israel at risk and goes against our interests."[10]

Whilst the Berlin Declaration is the clearest statement on record of European support for the creation of a Palestinian state, it also reveals that the issuing of Declarations by the European Union is not necessarily about reiterating long-held positions, but can be a valuable tool in crisis management and stabilizing the peace process. The wording of the Declaration was crafted in close coordination with the United States and was an important element in diplomatic efforts aimed at preventing a unilateral declaration of independence by the Palestinians on 4 May. Highlighting European support for Palestinian statehood turned out to be a valuable way of assuring the Pales-

10 See *Jerusalem Post*, 26 March 1999.

tinians international support for their claims to statehood and in preventing them from embarking on such a course unilaterally.

The Contribution of the European Union to the Peace Process

In the summer of 1991, following the Gulf War, international efforts aimed at re-launching the Arab-Israeli peace process were intensified, leading to optimism within Europe that an international conference would be convened and that the European Community would be invited to play a key role in the following phase of the Arab-Israeli peace process.[11] These hopes proved short-lived. The United States took it upon itself to set up an institutional framework to deal with the Arab-Israeli conflict. Whilst Madrid played host, and gave its name to the conference convened by the United States at the end of October 1991, the European Community was offered only a minor role in the proceedings. Indeed, the United States turned to Moscow, rather than Europe, when looking for a co-sponsor to the Madrid Conference, despite the fact that the Soviet Union's power was visibly declining and the country on the verge of collapse. The European Community played no part in the bilateral negotiations that immediately followed the Madrid Conference. Instead, it was invited to participate only in the multilateral talks which were set up by the Madrid Conference.

The dominance of the United States in the proceedings has been a source of great disquiet within European policy circles. But it would be false to conclude that the European Union has played only a marginal role in the Arab-Israeli peace process. Evidence gathered from the past eight years reveals that the European Union has emerged from the sidelines and carved out a role for itself in underwriting the agreements reached between Israel and the Palestinians.

11 Palmer, John: The European Community and Middle East Peace, in: Middle East International, 16 August 1991: 17–18.

The aim of this paper is not to outline in full the numerous arenas in which the European Union has been active. Rather, it will highlight three particular areas of activity which indicate the range and extent of European involvement in the peace process: the role of the European special envoy to the peace process; support for the Palestinian Authority and Palestinian institution building; the multilateral talks and the Euro-Mediterranean partnership, which demonstrate European engagement at the regional level.

The Role of the European Special Envoy to Peace Process

The clearest sign of Europe's determination to play a more active political role came at the end of October 1996, with the decision to appoint a 'Special European Envoy to the Middle East Peace Process,' a position filled since 1996 by Miguel Moratinos. Whilst the decision to appoint a special envoy to the region received much attention, it was generally greeted with scepticism. It was seen by Israel as a further sign of Europe's desire to meddle in the peace process and to win the affection of the Arabs by exerting pressure on Israel, although the appointment of Moratinos, in preference to the high profile political appointee originally envisaged by some European states, was welcomed. The Arab states questioned Moratinos' experience as well as his ability to play a significant political role and to influence events.[12] It was unclear what his specific functions would be and how his activities would complement the existing institutional frameworks for the implementation of European policy.

Moratinos' formal mandate is as broad as it is vague:
– to establish and maintain close contact with all the parties to the peace process, other countries of the region, the United States and other interested countries,

12 See Joulani (1998: 41–42).

- to observe peace negotiations between the parties, and to be ready to offer the European Union's advice and good offices at the parties request,
- to contribute where requested to the implementation of international agreements reached between the parties, and to engage with them diplomatically in the event of non-compliance with the terms of these agreements,
- to engage constructively with the signatories to agreements within the framework of the peace process in order to promote compliance with the basic norms of democracy, including respect for human rights and the rule of law,
- to monitor actions by either side which might prejudice the outcome of permanent status negotiations.

Although Moratinos has yet to broker a major agreement between Israel and any of the Arab parties (which by himself he is unlikely to do), the presence of a European special envoy has enhanced Europe's political standing and has afforded it a more prominent profile in the peace process. Despite the general scepticism experienced at the time of his appointment, Moratinos quickly gained the confidence of all parties to the conflict and showed Europe to be a valuable partner to the United States in helping mediate political agreements between Israel and the Palestinians and offered an additional diplomatic channel through which parties can operate.

The presence of a European special envoy has allowed European Middle East policy to become more visible to regional and extra-regional actors, to become more flexible and responsive to developments in the peace process and to identify specific areas where Europe can undertake practical measures to help build confidence between the parties and support agreements reached.

An example of how the presence of a European special envoy can help complement the mediation efforts of the United States can be seen in the signing of the Hebron Protocol of 17 January 1997, which provided for the partial redeployment of Israeli troops from the city and a timetable of future redeployments in the West Bank. Whilst Moratinos was not directly involved in the negotiations, he was working quietly behind the scenes helping to bridge the gap between the sides. At the time of the agreement, considerable attention was paid to the content of the letters of assurance which US Secretary of State Warren Christopher had sent both sides. These letters were seen to provide an important sense of security, thus allowing Arafat and Netanyahu to put their signatures to the agreement. Through Moratinos' efforts, the European Union also supplied Yassir Arafat with a letter assuring him that it would "[...] use all its political and moral weight to ensure that the agreement would be fully implemented."[13]

Moratinos has embarked on a number of practical, small-scale initiatives aimed at building confidence between the parties and has identified a number of areas, namely water and refugees, in which the European Union might contribute to final status negotiations. In particular, over the past two years, the European Union, through the auspices of the Special Envoy, has set up an EU-Israel Joint Dialogue in which European and Israeli experts meet at regular intervals in five separate working groups (passage of goods and peoples, labour issues, financial and fiscal issues, Gaza Port, long-term economic development) to discuss ways of overcoming obstacles to the economic development of the Palestinian territories.

The European Union developed an assistance programme which trains Palestinian security forces to support the Palestinian Authority in helping prevent terrorist activities in the territories under its control, and has set up a forum under the auspices of the special envoy in which representatives of the Palestinian security forces meet regularly with their counterparts from the European Union with the aim of developing joint cooperation on security issues.

---

13 For text of the letter see Jerusalem Post, 10 February 1997.

Moratinos has also maintained over the past three years a channel of communication between Israel and Syria at a time when negotiations have not been taking place and when no mediation efforts
were undertaken by the United States.

Financial Support for the Palestinian Authority

Since the signing of the Oslo Accords five years ago, the European
Union has emerged not merely as an interested bystander in the welfare of the Palestinian people, but as the mainstay of international
efforts in support of the Palestinian economy and the development of
Palestinian institution building. On the eve of the signing of the
Declaration of Principles, the European Community announced an
immediate aid package of thirty-five million ECU to enable the PLO
to establish minimal services and to attend to the most urgent needs
of the Palestinian population.

At the donors' conference held on 1 October 1993, the member
states of the European Union collectively pledged an additional 500
million ECU, spread over a period of five years, for the economic
recovery and the developmental needs of the Palestinian territories.
This aid package amounted to nearly a quarter of the total funds
pledged by the participants at the Washington Conference and made
the European Union the foremost donor to the Palestinians. Following the signing of the Wye Accords in November 1998, the
EU pledged a further 400 million ECU, to be distributed over the
next five years. In a report presented to the European Council
and the European Parliament, the European Commission calculated
that from 1993–1997, the European Community would have committed 700 million ECU of aid to the Palestinians and that if the
contributions of the individual member states were included,
then the total financial contribution of the European Union to

the peace process during that period would have come to over 1.68 billion ECU.[14]

European aid has focused on three complementary areas: short-term aid focussing on projects in the field of housing; micro-credit and the assistance of small-scale businesses and education; medium-term aid aimed at improving the economic and social infrastructure of the Palestinian territories; and thirdly the provision of financial support for the development of Palestinian institution building. With regard to the latter, the European Union provided 24 million ECU in logistical support for the holding of elections to the Palestinian Legislative Council held at the beginning of January 1996, and was responsible for the international monitoring operation of those elections.

In addition to the financial aid packages, the European Union signed a Euro-Mediterranean Interim Association agreement with the Palestinian Authority on Trade and Cooperation. This agreement, which came into force on 1 July 1997, offered the Palestinians a number of trade concessions and foresees the eventual establishment of a free trade zone between the European Union and Palestine by the summer of 2002. The agreement also provides for a wide range of financial measures to support the development of Palestinian industries.

The European Union has become, in the words of the European Commission, "[...] by far the largest donor to the peace process, dwarfing the efforts of all other donors."[15] In light of this level of financial support, member states of the European Union have not hidden their frustration at being denied a more active political role in the peace process and at being expected to pay for decisions over which they have no influence. Their frustration is compounded by a

14 The Role of the European Union in the Peace Process and its Future Assistance to the Middle East. European Commission Communication to the Council and the European Parliament, 16 January 1998. Com (970) 715 final.
15 Ibid.

lack of influence over political developments which have a direct bearing on the economic well-being of the Palestinian population in Gaza and the West Bank. Whilst this level of financial assistance has been critical in ensuring the short-term survival of the peace process, in so far as it covers the immediate shortfall in budget and meets the day-to-day running costs of the Palestinian Authority, it has little impact on the long-term economic development of the Palestinian territories and does little to attract private investment to the Palestinian territories.

Promoting Regional Cooperation

Denied a seat in the bilateral negotiations after the Madrid Conference, the members of the European Union were consigned to operating solely within the framework of five working groups of the multilateral talks. [16]

The multilateral talks were designed to run in parallel with the bilateral negotiations. The aim was to bring together Israel, its immediate Arab neighbours and the wider circle of Arab states in the Maghreb and the Gulf to address issues of regional and mutual concern. The idea of the multilateral talks was that by drawing the states in the region into an ever-wider web of economic, technical and welfare interdependencies, it would force them to set aside their political and/or ideological rivalries. Drawing parallels from the experience in Europe, the intention was that functional cooperation would eventually spill over into regional peace.

Europe was entrusted with the running of the Regional Economic Development Working Group (REDWG), the largest of the five working groups and the one which reflected most fully the broader goals of the multilateral track. Little interest or enthusiasm was dis-

16 Peters (1996).

played in European capitals for these talks and it was not until the breakthrough between Israel and the PLO after the signing of the Oslo Accords, that Europe paid any real attention to the running of REDWG. At the plenary meeting held in Copenhagen in November 1993, a list of ten spheres of activity was drawn up, and 'shepherds' were assigned to take responsibility for the running of projects in each of these areas. The majority of these projects focus on infrastructural development in the areas of transport, communications and energy, and on exploring areas of sectoral coordination in the realms of trade, finance, tourism, agriculture and health.

The progress at the bilateral level between Israel and the Palestinians gave a strong boost to the regional dimension of the peace process and to European engagement in the multilateral talks. The European Union began to take the lead in promoting regional ventures and in encouraging the regional parties to develop ideas about the long-term nature of their economic relations.

In the summer of 1994 four sectoral committees covering trade, tourism, infrastructure and finance were established. Membership of these committees was confined to the four core regional parties – Egypt, Israel, Jordan and the Palestinian Authority. In order to drive the process of regional economic development, the European Union helped establish in 1995 a permanent economic secretariat which is based in Amman and staffed by personnel from the region. Although embryonic in its nature and functioning, the establishment of the secretariat signalled the first steps in fashioning new common structures of cooperation, coordination and decision-making in the Middle East. In its first year of operating, it serviced over 100 meetings and workshops. However, with the breakdown of the peace process during the Netanyahu government, the activities of the multilateral talks ground to a virtual halt. REDWG has not met since May 1996 and whilst the secretariat is still operational, it has struggled to find a role for itself, and no meetings have taken place for the past three years.

The Arab-Israeli multilateral talks are not the only context in which Europe has been engaged in trying to develop new structures of cooperative relationships in the region. In November 1995, the European Union launched the Euro-Mediterranean partnership – the Barcelona process – aimed at developing a framework of peaceful and cooperative relations in the Mediterranean region. Like the multilateral talks, the Barcelona process also assumes that economic development can lead to political stability, and involves many of the same actors and addresses similar issues to those covered in the Arab-Israeli multilateral talks. In Barcelona, the member states of the European Union and its Mediterranean partners agreed to establish a common area of peace and stability, a free-trade zone by 2010, and to develop a set of institutions to foster cooperation between the civil societies of the region.

The launching of the Barcelona process received its impetus from progress made in the Arab-Israeli peace process. Designed to be separate and distinct from the peace process, the Barcelona process offered an additional diplomatic environment in which Israel and its Arab neighbours could engage in dialogue towards future cooperative arrangements. It enjoyed a distinct advantage over the multilateral talks in that it is the only regional forum in which Syrian and Lebanese officials have been prepared to sit with their Israeli counterparts. Despite the collapse of the multilateral talks at the end of 1996, Israel and the Arab states continued to meet for a while within the Barcelona framework. However, as relations between the countries became increasingly soured, the Arab states were reluctant to engage in dialogue toward cooperative ventures with Israel and the activities of the Euro-Mediterranean framework were halted.[17]

17 Peters (1998).

Looking Forward – What Role for Europe?

The previous section highlighted the range and extent of European engagement in the peace process. Over the past eight years, the European Union has succeeded in carving out a presence in nearly every dimension of the peace process – fostering the development of Palestinian institutions, supporting agreements and promoting regional economic development. Yet there remains within European policy circles a level of frustration at what it perceives as its limited political role, and its inability to actively influence the outcome of the peace process. This frustration has been matched by a desire to participate more directly in any future negotiations between the parties.

Europe's desire to play a more influential role in the Arab-Israeli peace process is not new. Nor do European leaders attempt to hide their ambitions in this respect, and they are forthcoming in offering support and services to the region. With the start of the final status talks between Israel and Palestinians, and the possibility of renewing negotiations on the Syrian track and resuming the multilateral talks, it is important that the European Union defines its role and assesses how it can best contribute in moving the peace process forward.

Rather than continuing to seek and demand a greater political role, European policy should be based on the following set of criteria:

- identifying issues and areas in which there is a need for action,
- assessing whether it has the capability and capacity to act and contribute effectively in those arenas,
- strengthening the policy instruments available,
- speaking and acting in a coordinated and unified manner.

The demand for a more prominent European role in the peace process needs to be balanced with a keener recognition of the limited capacity of the European Union to act in a coherent and effective manner as a single foreign policy actor and also with a greater awareness of the limited means at its disposal to influence events. European leaders need to construct a more nuanced set of policies than those developed previously. Future European policy in the region needs to be more responsive and adaptive to immediate developments on the ground.

If Europe is to play a more meaningful role in the peace process it will require the development of a greater level of coordination amongst the member states than has been previously demonstrated. Whilst the positions of the member states of the European Union towards the Arab-Israeli conflict converge around a number of shared principles, consensus is lacking as to how those principles should be translated into effective policy. European policy has often appeared as a series of independent initiatives by member states whose actions are driven by a desire to promote their own national and commercial interests in the region.

The presence of a Special Envoy to the Middle East Peace Process ensures that Europe's views are expressed with one voice, and that the European Union is actively and demonstrably represented in the peace process. It has also enabled European policy to respond to the immediate needs and concerns of the parties. However, Miguel Moratinos has little scope or freedom to act and initiate policies in the name of the fifteen member states of the European Union. Whilst he has developed a working relationship and personal rapport with the parties involved, his mandate and institutional constraints prevent him from developing a more effective role. As the negotiations between Israel and the Palestinians proceed, the member states of the European Union will have to decide if, and in what ways, they are prepared to strengthen the role and the tools available to the special envoy. In similar fashion, they will need to decide what role Javier Solana will play in representing European interests in the peace process. The recent flurry of visits by European leaders to the region indicates that they will be unwilling to allow their voice and national interests to come entirely under the umbrella of a common European foreign policy.

For all Europe's willingness to act as a potential mediator in the talks on the Israel-Palestinian track or between Israel and Syria, experience shows that it will not be assigned that role. The parties will continue to look to Washington rather than to the capitals of Europe for help in that realm. Europe cannot, nor should it, aspire to supplant the primary role of the United States.

Yet Europe has an invaluable role to play. Whilst the United States will be critical in driving the parties towards an agreement, it no longer possesses the capability to create by itself the necessary conditions for a comprehensive peace between Israel and the Arabs. Europe and the United States have differing and comparative advantages which they bring to the Arab-Israeli peace process. The European Union needs to reinforce and extend the degree of its strategic coordination with the United States so that its actions are seen as complementary to, rather than competing with, those of Washington. The increasing level of coordination between the US and Europe over the past few years can be seen in the drawing up of the Berlin Declaration, which served as a valuable instrument in deflecting a potential crisis in the region over Palestinian intentions to unilaterally declare independence on 4 May 1994, and in the Letters of Guarantee which the European Union has provided as part of the Hebron agreement of January 1997, and the recently signed Sharm-el-Sheikh agreement.

Europe has played an important role in supporting and sustaining the economy of the Palestinian territories in their transition from occupation to independence. In particular, it should continue to engage in a dialogue with Israel to overcome obstacles for the economic development of the Palestinian territories. It should continue to foster the conditions that will improve the prospects for the emergence of a viable Palestinian state by promoting Palestinian institution building, developing the necessary legal and regulatory environment for private investment to prosper and by creating the conditions for the development of Palestinian civil society.

The European Union should continue to underwrite any agreements, especially in respect to security arrangements reached between the parties. It should be ready to support those agreements by providing technical assistance and support for the security procedures arrived at between Israel and the Palestinians. In the short term, Europe should look at ways at providing logistical support to the safe-passage routes between the West Bank and Gaza, and be prepared to come up with ideas in negotiations surrounding Gaza port.

Whilst this contribution has primarily focussed on the Palestinian dimension of the peace process, any agreements reached on the Syrian and Lebanese tracks will result in the development of new security arrangements and guarantees on those two borders. Here Europe's wealth of experience in monitoring peace agreements and in peace keeping operations may serve as a valuable complement to the security arrangements reached between the two sides.

Finally, the European Union should work for the resumption of the multilateral track and in particular place greater emphasis on supporting the activities of the five working groups. The European Union has been a reluctant player in the multilateral talks and has preferred to focus its efforts on the Barcelona process. Yet these regional frameworks should be seen as complementary to European activity. Both frameworks have offered an invaluable diplomatic environment for Israel and the Arabs. Seemingly similar in their long-term objectives, in their agendas and participation, these two frameworks nevertheless have differing objectives. The European Union should encourage the parties to revive the activities of the Regional Economic Development Working Group and give a new impetus to the activities of the REDWG secretariat in Amman. In particular, it should develop a strategy in which the activities of REDWG can serve as an effective complement to the Barcelona process, rather than simply paying lip-service to that ideal.

List of References

Joulani, Adnan 1998: The European Union Foreign Policy and Economic Assistance to the Palestinian People (MA thesis, The University of Reading).

Hollis, Rosemary 1997: Europe and the Middle East. Power by Stealth?, in: International Affairs, 73/1.

Peters, Joel 1996: Pathways to Peace. The Multilateral Arab-Israeli Peace Talks, London.

Peters, Joel 1998: The Barcelona Process and the Arab-Israeli Multilateral Talks. Competition or Convergence in: The Political role of the European Union in the Middle East, Gütersloh/Munich.

Reconsidering the Economic Benefits of a Stable Middle East

Riad al-Khouri

Though the Middle East enjoyed strong levels of economic growth in comparison with the rest of the world up to the early 1980s, the past decade or so tells a different story. In the 1990s in particular, Middle East economic performance lagged behind all other regions of the world except Africa.[1] Furthermore, the Middle East surpassed all other regions in population growth, effectively meaning that an already weak economic performance was even worse on a per capita basis. In both major oil exporters and poorer economies, this was partly due to parochial and underdeveloped systems and processes, sometimes disguised as sources of stability. In the mid- and late 1990s in the Middle East, "stable" often meant economically stagnant.

---

1   This contribution was presented to the workshop *A Future Security Structure for the Middle East and the Eastern Mediterranean*, Frankfurt, October 1999.

In the late 1980s and the 1990s several Middle East states tried some structural economic adjustments without serious attempts at reform. These adjustments have come through limited privatisation, as in Jordan or reduction in government subsidies in the case of Iran. Nonetheless, the state's financial and coercive power in the region remains strong.

Some in the region can look back on how stable their systems have been over the past few decades. However, the steps that have to be taken today for putting these economies on the track of prosperous stability may depart markedly from those of previous eras. Liberalisation is a key factor here. This still has to be coupled with maintaining internal stability, but the day may come soon when opening up the economy will have to start taking precedence over previous stabilization policies.

The peace process is changing the economic relations of the Middle East, creating stability in some spheres, while giving rise to uncertainty in others. New forms of economic relations are being initiated between Israel and her neighbours, including regional projects, joint ventures and subcontracting arrangements. However, these and other economic benefits of a more stable Middle East have not yet made a major impact on the region. Trade between Israel and Egypt has been growing slowly, and Israeli-Jordanian commerce remains modest. The Palestine National Authority (PNA) area continues to be closely integrated with the Israeli economy, in spite of efforts being made to develop Palestinian economic autonomy. The peace process has also been responsible for some changes in the relations between the countries in the region and the rest of the world. Transnational corporations (TNCs) are setting up offices and/or facilities in Israel and other countries in the region. The European Union is actively promoting cooperation with neighbouring Mediterranean countries through various EU partnership schemes.

Regional economic relations are still hindered by many problems. These relate to business controlled by the state, government bureaucracy and complicated procedures, and non-tariff barriers and other border restrictions. Economic relations are seriously hampered by non-economic barriers as well, including political and cultural factors.

The impact of the peace process will partly be determined by programs to reform economic policies that the countries in the region, including Israel, are undertaking. It will in addition depend on the rate and extent of implementation of the peace agreements eventually reached. At the same time, other factors, such as the impact of the World Trade Organization and of the Euro-Med process, will also be crucial, as various Middle East states have entered into association agreements with the EU, and have joined the WTO or are negotiating entry into it.

The peace process will not only bring about new forms of Arab-Israeli relations, it will also result in change in the economic relations between countries of the region and the outside world. More intensive and new forms of cooperation are expected to develop, in particular with the US and the EU. In this regard, special attention should be paid to economic cooperation between the EU and the region. A peace settlement in the Middle East may also lead to greater involvement of TNCs and to increased foreign direct investment in the region, with a possible bias towards tripartite partnership (i.e. among TNCs, Israel, and other Middle East states).

The Quest for Stability 1993–1995

Since the beginning of the peace process, the potential for economic cooperation among the countries of the Middle East has often been analysed under the apparent assumption that increased integration will not only yield direct economic and social benefits, but may also ensure that peace, once attained, is stable, since the costs of disrupting it becomes prohibitive. Thus, bilateral and regional cooperation initiatives flourished in the mid-1990s, though the fruits of such efforts remain meagre. Those attempts were launched with a basically political underpinning.

Many proponents of the peace process foresee a Middle East with open borders, economic cooperation leading to economic growth, and free movement of people, goods, and services among states. Regional projects covering infrastructure, such as transport, communications, water pipelines, and electricity grids are envisaged as uniting elements. Freedom to travel, trade, and develop joint ventures are seen as a strong guarantee for a lasting peace.

All these things are probably desirable in themselves; however, in the economic context, the question arise as to whether peace brings stability and prosperity or is it prosperity that encourages peace and stability. These are two different, though not necessarily conflicting, points of view that are central to peacemaking. In any case, the attempt to promote prosperity taken in 1993–1995 did not lead to an end to conflict. Israel and others at that time incorrectly claimed that the remedy for the ills of the region was an economic solution that would bring prosperity and help those with grievances forget them. In fact, closer commercial ties may have been expected to play a role in reinforcing the peace process, but have not yet done so. The emergence of an integrated market in the region will yield economic advantages, but this is still a long way off. Today, a new political arrangement will have to come into being before any economic understanding can be effective.

At the same time, economic considerations will play a very important role in reaching a political settlement. This suggest that in doing so, a trade-off between economic and political benefits is possible, and may be even necessary in the context of achieving a just and lasting peace. However, the lesson of the mid-1990s is that the Middle East Peace Process is not and should not be driven by economics alone. Economic understanding can be effective and serve its purpose only if placed within the correct political context. By the same token, in working out a political agreement, it is essential that one knows where one is heading economically.

In any case, a boost in intra-regional trade is in the direct interest of the Middle East. Such trade will not only benefit Israel but every country in the region, especially when trade services and tourism are also taken into consideration. So far, the region's trade relations have been strongly directed at the outside, and this pattern will remain basically intact. The EU and the US dominate imports and exports. Close regional ties are only evident for the PNA for which the overwhelming majority of imports and exports are accounted for by Israel. This pattern however was forced and not based on natural advantages, although the structures created since Israeli occupation will make future preferential PNA ties to Israel more likely.

The lesson of the mid-1990s is that, in the quest for stability, economic agreements should not be used as bait or as a substitute for achieving political rights if the peace being sought is to be lasting. Peace cannot be durable if national rights are not realized. Once this happens, prosperity will also have to be more or less evenly spread among the states in the area. In all cases, peace is not likely to endure if elements of fairness and equity are absent from the final settlement and if justice is not satisfied. Given these factors, Israel must first enter into a comprehensive, just and lasting peace with her neighbors. Examples of attempts at regional economic cooperation that began during this period follow.

The Regional Economic Development Working Group (REDWG)

REDWG was formed to foster the economic cooperation attendant on the peace process. REDWG, which operates under the guidance of the EU, decided that if economic cooperation was to become effective, it was time for the four Core Parties to peace (Egypt, Israel, Jordan and the PNA) themselves to take over. Regional cooperation, it was recognized, could not be authored from outside but must have roots within the region and respond to the needs of the Parties themselves.

REDWG has tried to play a role in the peace process by promoting economic cooperation in four main sectors: finance, trade, tourism and infrastructure. In the area of Finance, REDWG focused mainly on developing a regional approach to the creation of the Middle East Development Bank. In the area of Trade, a Middle East Business Council was created to provide a regional voice for the private sector and to facilitate trade, investment and general economic activity. The primary concern of REDWG in the area of Tourism has been to assist the establishment of the Middle East-Mediterranean Travel and Tourism Association. For infrastructural transport, telecommunications and energy REDWG aimed to improve the efficiency of existing capacity, plan for future needs, and develop concrete projects for implementation.

These activities have, however, suffered because of difficulties in the peace process. Such activities, although focusing on economic cooperation, depend crucially on continuing the movement towards a just, lasting and comprehensive peace.

The Middle East and North Africa (MENA) Economic Conferences

In a major exercise in support of the Middle East peace process, annual MENA Economic Conferences were held (respectively in Casablanca, Amman, Cairo, and Doha) in 1994–1997. This process, now suspended, was more or less related to the work of REDWG. The talk in Casablanca in 1994 (and to a lesser extent in Amman in 1995) was, for example, of a major highway from Egypt to Syria via Israel, huge tourism and infrastructure schemes including a canal linking the Red Sea and Dead Sea, and other multibillion dollar projects. However, things have since changed. The grandiose visions of Casablanca in 1994 were replaced by bickering and lack of implementation in the wake of the 1996 and 1997 conferences. Nevertheless, there is now talk of reviving this process if the regional diplomatic and political climate improves.

The Israeli 'wish list' of projects presented at these conferences was a long one. As such, Israel's proposals appear to be the product of a political agenda that has thus far proved unrealistic. This is not necessarily because these projects are not technically valid or, in a situation of prosperity and stability, economically viable. The main problem is that Israel wishes to pursue "economic development" while ignoring the major political issues, which still have to be addressed. These obviously include the achieving of a just, comprehensive and lasting peace with the rest of the Arab world (in particular Syria and Lebanon) but also the satisfactory implementation of existing accords. For Israel to present projects at these conferences and other venues without regard to the overall situation in the region is unrealistic. It is also unrealistic to expect outside donors and other financiers to support such projects outside the regional political context.

Jordan Rift Valley (JRV) development

Various subregional development schemes exist in parallel to the MENA Conference and REDWG activities. The JRV, which includes Lake Tiberias, the Dead Sea, the Ghor, Wadi Araba and the northern Red Sea shore, has abundant development potential due to its unique topography, its location on a natural trade route and its rich history. Initially a bilateral Jordanian-Israeli scheme, the idea is for it to evolve and expand into a broader multilateral framework. Specific plans for the area cover new transport links and joint promotion of tourist destinations on both sides of the valley. This project is supported by the World Bank.

Extension of border services and transportation facilities along the JRV area could have a major impact on tourism and international trade, assisting in the economic integration of the region. It would give Israel easier access to other markets in the region, provide Jordan and its neighbors with the opportunity to export goods to Israel and through Israeli ports to the Mediterranean, and reaffirm Jordan's role as a transport hub in the Middle East.

The proposed Aqaba International Airport is one of the centerpieces of the JRV. If executed, this project would be a touristic gateway for the countries in this region. With funding from the US government, a US firm has completed a study on the airport and submitted proposals to the Jordanian and Israeli governments together with different scenarios. The various options would cost roughly US$ 115–225 million; the authorities in Jordan and Israel are examining them, and finance is expected to be shared.

The two sides have different scenarios regarding the way the airport should be run, and have not reached a final decision except for accepting the principle of using the facility for the region. Though things have once again begun to move forward in the wake of the ouster of the Netanyahu government, this debate is typical of the difficulties in development of regional projects, and the problems besetting attempts at regional cooperation.

In all these cases, the imposition of a false stability underpinned by unjust, non-comprehensive and fragile peace has led to distorted expectations and a waste of resources through inappropriate investments. This in turn has resulted in a negative peace dividend.

"The Triangle"

Economic integration can be an essential element in the development of small countries such as Israel, Jordan and Palestine, as it has been in the case of Belgium, the Netherlands and Luxembourg. In the Benelux triangle, the case of Belgium for example emphasizes the ability of a small country to overcome market limitations through integration and export. The country's material resource endowment was neither a necessary nor a sufficient factor for viability. Belgium provides a good illustration of how the lack of material endowment can be compensated. Integration within the Middle East region, as within Benelux, has thus been considered as a possible cure for the problem of smallness, whether in the market or the endowment of the economy. Can the Middle East profit from this example?

A Jordan-Israel-Palestine triangle of cross-border economic integration, investment and development would be a free trade zone if not a full customs union, with close coordination of monetary policy, and a variety of joint institutions to manage common resources. This scenario maintains that the extent to which the three economies vary in structure is not necessarily an obstacle to regional integration. On the contrary, the differences may provide a basis for a Jordan-Israel-Palestine triangle on the premise that advantages enjoyed in one country could be shared with another, thus raising overall output and employment.

The major lesson for the protagonists of a Jordan-Israel-Palestine triangle is a realization of the difficulties ahead in achieving a popular basis of support: this is something that cannot be obtained simply by founding supranational institutions and aiming for integrated economies. The appropriate policy for Jordan's economic integration with Israel in particular depends on several elements including the time horizon, the ideology, and the overall political culture.

The impact of time is directly related to the target rate of achieving integration. Over ten years have passed since Jordan's letter of intent to the IMF and the beginnings of structural adjustment. Yet myriad restrictions and structural problems still hamper the economy. Continuing such a time frame for growth and development and the slow dismantling of economic barriers would be inconsistent with integration with Israel and Palestine. Ideology is critical to the extent to which regional decision-makers often adopt policies that may be economically irrational, although they may be politically and socially rational.

Finally, the pattern of development must be put in the context of a general environment including both the internal forces of the economy and external conditions. The policy toward integration will suffer because the Arab economy is not underpinned by a political system that stresses the individual, and social and cultural values are not conducive to economic growth.

In my opinion, Benelux is not the appropriate model for the Israel-Jordan-Palestine region, yet the concept seems to have enjoyed considerable backing. For example, a report made after the signing of the peace treaty between Jordan and Israel by a team of Israelis, Jordanians and Palestinians, proposed a free trade agreement among the three economies, that could later "evolve into a customs union and be extended to include other countries in the region."[2] The authors went on: "they do not believe that free trade should end with the triad. On the contrary, just as the Benelux countries served as the nucleus of the European Union, so the triad should serve as the nucleus of a broader arrangement."[3] The report continues: "If free trade develops among them, the Israeli-Palestinian-Jordanian Triad is more likely to play the role of Benelux, showing the way to develop closer economic relations including overcoming the practical difficulties of setting up the necessary arrangements and the benefits of doing so".[4] The fundamental error here of course is that the Benelux countries never served as the 'nucleus of the European Union.' That role was and is still being played by the German-French axis, not Benelux. It is difficult to believe that at least some of the authors of the report cited above did not know this; more likely, in the spirit of the promotion of peace that flourished in the mid-1990s, the facts were ignored.

2   Lawrence et al. (1995: 1).
3   Ibid.
4   Ibid.: 13

Replacing the Peace Dividend 1996–1999

The above and other attempts at multilateral regional integration in the 1993–1995 period did not progress very far, even before Operation Grapes of Wrath and the coming to power of the Netanyahu government in the first half of 1996. Since then, and with the slowing down of the peace process, various attempts at bilateral integration have been made by countries of the region in trying to recoup the lost peace dividend.

Economic Integration in the Middle East

The Middle East remains relatively disintegrated in terms of the extent of economic interaction within the region and the absence of an effective framework for formulating and implementing rules and policies to boost commerce. Intra-regional trade in the late 1990s averaged about ten percent of foreign trade by Middle East countries with the world. There may thus be potential for greater intra-regional economic interaction. While countries of the Middle East will continue to deal mostly with non-regional partners, the current levels of trade within the region are below those that would be attained if economic relations intra-regionally were freer. Political factors clearly constrained integration over the past few decades, and most counties in the region continued to trade mainly with the EU, the US, and East and South Asia. Today, the short-term outlook is better. Major developments such as the Arab-Israeli peace process are part of the region's opening up economically, and a combination of firmer oil prices and easing regional tension could mean generally stronger business.

Bilateralism: the Case of Jordan

Jordan is a good supplier and customer for its neighbours. About 47 per cent of the country's exports went to Arab countries, Iran, and Turkey, and 24 per cent of imports came from there as well.[5] However, weakness in Jordan's exports to regional markets, including declining trade with neighbouring Iraq, has been among the causes of the kingdom's current economic malaise. Booming trade with Palestine and Israel is another instalment of the Peace Dividend that never got paid – though the promise of revived Arab-Israeli negotiations may now mean that exports across the Jordan River could rise soon. As multilateral integration faltered or was frozen, Jordan began to more seriously consider its bilateral options. This became more important as Jordanian exports to and imports from its two main markets – and largest neighbours – Iraq and Saudi Arabia, fell recently, as Table 1 shows.

Table 1: Jordanian Trade with Neighbouring Arab States and the World, 1997–98 (in millions of US$)

	1997		1998	
	Exports	Imports	Exports	Imports
Iraq	200	514	152	339
Saudi Arabia	198	146	145	143
Syria	36	84	22	43
World	*1,504*	*3,824*	*1,472*	*4,100*

Source: Central Bank of Jordan (1998): Annual Report, Tables 39 and 40, Amman.

5   Central Bank of Jordan 1998: Annual Report, Amman: Tables 39 and 40.

Jordan and Israel

Jordan enjoys competitive wage structures in relation to Israel. Under existing conditions, essentially political considerations and sensitivities impinge on the investment decision. Nevertheless, certain investments are considered more promising than others. For example, some Israeli businesses see the investment or joint venture potential as great as trade potential in food processing, farming and irrigation techniques, and automotive feeder industries, among others. Other Israeli business is attracted to such fields as textiles and computer software. Jordanian business sees joint venture opportunities in high technology, including medicine.

New mechanisms of industry relations and technology transfer continue to emerge, leading to a new geographical distribution of production, through bilateral arrangements such as subcontracting, joint ventures or the relocation of industries from Israel to Jordan. The newly emerging industrial patterns may result in Israel's concentrating on selected high technology products (geared mostly to Western markets) and on the transfer of technology and know-how, while Jordan may continue to promote labour-intensive and/or less technology-intensive industries, such as food processing and textile and garments. The labor-intensive textiles and garment industry has been one of the main subjects of the impact of the peace process on Jordan, in view of its significant contribution to total manufacturing output, value added, exports and employment in the country. This industry is expected to be the one most affected by the new patterns of economic relations, and is also one of the major contributors to total exports to Israel. Also, as agricultural policy is changing in Israel, away from water-intensive produce, it is possible that imports of tomato, peppers, cut flowers etc. will start to come from Jordan.

Jordan and Syria

The Jordanian-Syrian trade pact of 1999 has eliminated customs tariffs on a wide range of goods in a move that could give a strong boost to trade between the two countries. Under the agreement, the Jordanians and the Syrians expanded the list of duty-free goods imported by each side to about 200 items, the largest number in any agreement that Jordan has ever signed with another state. The extensive tariff cuts agreed were a major step towards eventual free trade. However, Jordan will retain a 35 per cent duty on imports of Syrian garments, alcoholic beverages, biscuits and chocolates to protect its own industries, and Syria will most notably continue to exclude marble, granite and vegetable ghee from the list of over 100 Jordanian products on which it waived tariffs. This agreement could lead Syro-Jordanian trade to rise sharply from its 1998 total. Along with the cut in tariffs, Syria and Jordan have taken other steps to consolidate ties, including easing formalities at border crossings and the launch of a regular train service between the two countries' capitals.

Deep Integration

Though the Middle East may not yet be so important economically to the European Union, maintenance of stability and security in the region is vital to the EU. On the other hand, Europe is a major factor in individual Middle East states' economic relations, so either way the EU has a big role to play in the region. Hence the Euro-Med Barcelona process and the Association Agreements that are being made between the EU and various countries in the north and west of the region.

However, an arrangement with Europe must be more than just a free trade area. It should also involve deep integration, and this will mean – among many other things – streamlining and simplifying the rules for international trade. A tariff-free Euro-Med free trade zone will not be worth much if real or imagined security fears slow trade in some goods and services or even prevent it in others; and unreasonably tight controls on travellers can also represent an important barrier to tourism and business.

One of the most important impediments to trade with and in the Middle East is the security element, or rather the unprofessional insecurity of customs and other border authorities. In one way or another some form of tight border security is characteristic of all countries of the region. In fact, much of this so-called security is simply the result of outdated administration.

Countries of the region have to actively engage in removing the numerous trade restrictions still existing in the Middle East, including false security measures. This can be accomplished partly through pressure from the EU, but also through the prescriptions of the World Trade Organization. Several Middle East countries – including Israel and Egypt – are WTO members; others, such as Jordan and Saudi Arabia are negotiating to join. The WTO lets a member apply legitimate security restrictions at borders, but should these start to get out of hand, problems with other members may arise.

The GCC is an example of how travel and other restrictions among some Middle East states can be eased and even in some cases abolished. This is good for business, but many security obstacles are still imposed by some GCC states. Saudi Arabia presents some interesting cases of import restrictions due to security. For example, an import license is required from the Saudi Ministry of the Interior for – among many other items – TV monitoring cameras and accessories, and closed circuit television. The import of all these items is restricted and requires a license for reasons of security. It may take up to thirty days to decide on the application depending on the case. High quality photocopiers, and burglar and fire alarms also require import licenses, to prevent import and the misuse of the items by persons who could pose a security risk. Partly as a result of the process of WTO accession, the list of such items subject to import licensing is under review.

Stabilization through Finance

The very high import surplus in many parts of the region could not be financed but for international transfer payments of various kinds. In the case of Israel these are subsidies and credit guarantees from the US, other international aid, and assistance from the Jewish diaspora. International debt forgiveness is not generally thought to be sufficient to allow a significant economic recovery in Jordan, especially since financial aid from the oil countries of the Gulf has virtually ceased. Jordan and Palestine, like Israel, also profit from American and other aid; money now being promised by the big donors is starting to push countries of the region towards the top of international league tables of per capita aid recipients.

Those directly affected by the withholding of the peace dividend seek aid. However, talk of "aid conditionality" continues to be overwhelmed by political factors. In other words, the misuse of aid funds is sometimes ignored by donors for overriding strategic reasons. Most powers want the region to remain stable, so aid flows in, but such external support may be precarious. With the threat of Communism ended, the US and Europe are less interested in addressing the long-term development of the region, even if they are involved in the Arab-Israeli peace process.

Nonviable, unproductive economies in the region remain intact largely due to the rent-seeking nature of the state, sometimes exacerbated by foreign influence. Public officials have become rent-seekers, and state-owned firms are a net drain on public finances. Government bureaucrats and their allies, including public sector managers, civil servants and ministers, and labor and business representatives with ties to the government, prefer to preserve their own interests rather than cooperate with others to benefit the country on the whole.

The Middle East is viewed in the West primarily in strategic or security terms rather than economically. While many Western institutions are far from ready to devise a global approach to the region, Europe is showing more independence from US policy in the Middle East. However, the EU still shares a common position with the US in a focus on regime stability, so aid continues to flow. At the same time, there has been increased reliance on international borrowing in Lebanon, Jordan, Egypt and Iran, among other Middle East states.[6]

Although external forces have also played a role in generating or exacerbating conflicts and instability, stagnant regional regimes bear great responsibility for the Middle East's dismal economic performance. Governments in the region are faced with a challenge: either make the necessary economic adjustments in order to compete, or continue with the status quo and be undermined. Aid helps preserve the status quo.

Future Stability: the Southern African Model

The path created by the deliberate engineering of institutions and massive infusions of aid to place countries in a tight Benelux-style union will not bring stability and prosperity to the region. On the other hand, a less formal approach that approximates the ideas of integration and association may be the way to go after a just, lasting and comprehensive peace is achieved. Such a path is being applied by southern African countries in the Southern African Development Community (SADC).

In 1992, the old Southern African Development Coordination Conference was transformed into SADC. The emphasis of the organization changed from 'development coordination' to 'development integration.' Crucially, South Africa acceded to the SADC Treaty in

6   As well as Israel: See for example Euroweek, 11 June 1999: Israel's First Euro Helped by Peace, on the launch of the country's first euro bond issue. The article links this directly with enhanced peace prospects following the election of Ehud Barak.

1994, giving SADC the opportunity to tackle issues such as sustainable regional growth. South Africa has been assigned the Financial and Investment sector of SADC as a special area of responsibility. Because the political settlement in the region was followed by South African membership of SADC, it provides a more effective instrument for member countries to move towards eventual economic integration. SADC is thus in the process of simultaneously implementing two models for regionalism: sectoral cooperation and trade integration. Although the two are distinct, success in one area tends to reinforce the other. Trade integration and sectoral cooperation contribute both directly and indirectly to sustainable economic growth and development in all countries of the region. The current mission of SADC is to find within the region the resources to overcome the legacy of apartheid, with the cooperation of the international community.

It is in South Africa's direct interest to make a substantial contribution to the economic development of sub-Saharan Africa. Not only will this make the continent as a whole more attractive to investors, but could also assist in reducing the number of other Africans seeking a better life in South Africa as illegal immigrants. South Africa has pledged itself to be a constructive participant and to contribute to the best of its ability to the improvement of conditions within the Southern African region and further afield. In this regard the initiation of planning and development activities with South Africa's neighbors is a most important issue, to be coordinated between all concerned national and provincial departments and the private sectors. South Africa's basic approach to take part collectively and as an equal partner arises not out of diplomatic modesty. The reality is that the socio-economic conditions of a majority of South Africans are, in some respects, worse than those of the citizens of a number of developing countries. Various parts of South Africa lag behind a number of other states in the region. A regional approach based on collectivity and equality is therefore in South Africa's interest.

Through close interaction the individual states of the region stand to benefit, as does the region at large. The challenges faced by South Africa are equally those of the region. (This is not the current attitude of Israel towards regional development.)

This model could only work for the Middle East region after a just, comprehensive and lasting political settlement is reached between Israel and all her neighbours. After that happens, a Southern African model can be applied, with one large economy helping smaller ones around it to the benefit of all in the region.

Conclusions

The globalization of international commerce and the technological revolution of the 1990s pose serious challenges for Middle East economies. The stability brought about by peace will allow regional states to better confront these challenges, but this will have to be real stability based on just, comprehensive and lasting peace, and not the partial measures of the mid- and late 1990s.

Reform is indispensable for the integration of Middle East countries into the global economy. Stabilization and adjustment programs demand substantial change in traditional structures. Incumbent regimes have tried a number of different reforms, without seriously jeopardizing the status quo.

Nevertheless, the impact of globalization and change is already been felt by individual countries in the region. Foreign intervention, however, has in the past fifty years promoted the political status quo in the Middle East through support for authoritarian states and arms sales to autocratic regimes. The fear of political instability fed by economic slowdown and of external threats to the state – real or otherwise – have helped justify arms purchases by the governments in the region. In the 1990–1991 US fiscal year, covering Operations Desert Shield and Desert Storm, countries of the region, including

Israel, imported more than US$ 24 billion worth of arms from the US alone.[7] High levels of spending on weapons continue, as shown in Table (2). Though this may bring short-term stability, it is destabilizing and expensive in the long term.

Table 2: Military Expenditure as a Percentage of GDP in Selected Middle East States, 1995

Iran	4 per cent
UAE	5 per cent
Saudi Arabia	11 per cent
Kuwait	12 per cent
Oman	15 per cent
Iraq	15 per cent

Source: Abootalebi, Ali "Middle East Economies: a Survey of Current Problems and Issues" in *Middle East Review of International Affairs*, September 1999, Footnote 4

The Middle East state's domination of the national economy remains largely intact and has led over the years to bloated governments with inefficient bureaucracies. The state, unwilling or unable to initiate reform, has proven largely incapable of dealing with the intricacies of the open market. Failure to reform can result in economic crises that in all probability will exacerbate instability. This will deter foreign investments, further weakening the economic status of the region in the global economy. The new international order punishes stagnation masked as stability much more than the bipolar world of the Cold War. Those interested in serious reform and regional stability must recognize that reality and adapt policies accordingly.

A Middle East enjoying just, lasting and comprehensive peace will be truly stable, not precariously so as in certain periods during the past half century. The Middle East will also be prosperous, as the

7   Congressional Record 24 January 1992, pp. E67 – E69.

peace dividend is finally paid to the majority of the region, and not just a tiny minority, including some Israeli investors.[8]

List of References

Lawrence, Robert et al. 1995: Towards Free Trade in the Middle East. The Triad and Beyond, Cambridge/Mass.

---

8 See for example Charafeddine/Smythe 1999: Tyre Developers Waiting for Peace, in: The Daily Star, 20 July 1999, Beirut, on how the success of the construction industry in southern Lebanon is linked to the prospects of security stabilization.

The Political Role of the EU in the Middle East: Israeli Aspirations

Joseph Alpher

This contribution explores the way Israelis view the role – past, current and potential – of the European Union in the Arab-Israeli peace process.[1] It makes several assumptions.

The first assumption is that we can generalise about an Israeli perspective on this issue, without addressing the diverse views of different political groups in Israel. It is not at all self-evident, for example, that at any given time the political Left and Right in Israel take the same approach to the American role in the peace process. However in the case of Europe there does appear to be a broad consensus in Israel – essentially a negative one – regarding involvement in the political peace process.[2]

---

1   This contribution was presented to the workshop *Aims and Instruments of a European Political Role in the Mediterranean Region*, Frankfurt, October 1997.
2   Having noted this, the views expressed in this paper are necessarily those of the author alone, and not of any Israeli group or movement.

194 _Joseph Alpher_

The second assumption is that – in Israel, the Arab states or Europe – there is a potential need for an EU political role. This, too, would not have been self-evident two or three years ago. Indeed, two or three years ago the necessity for an American political role was seen by most parties as minimal, in view of the success of Israelis, Palestinians and Jordanians in negotiating agreements bilaterally. Today, however, an enhanced EU political role is called for by Arab and European parties alike.

This appears to reflect a number of necessary prerequisites for third party intervention: first, the parties to the conflict are incapable on their own of narrowing the substantive and/or procedural gaps that separate them; yet second, those gaps are not so large as to preclude the hope of effective settlements; and third, alternative third parties, i.e. the United States, are not overwhelmingly successful, or are not interested, in bridging these gaps.

In the European case, the commitment to a strategy for a broad economic, social and security partnership with the Mediterranean states, made at Barcelona in 1995, is of necessity linked at least in part to the success of the Arab-Israeli peace process. This factor alone might in any case mandate greater political involvement. Certainly with that process frozen, Europe feels impelled to explore its own initiative designed to advance it. This explains much of the timing of the appointment of Ambassador Miguel Moratinos as European special envoy for the peace process. But the European Union (EU), in its earlier permutations, sought involvement in the Arab-Israeli peace process many years before Barcelona and the current stalemate. By the same token, Israeli attitudes toward this involvement were shaped decades ago. While these have evolved in many ways, particularly in recent years, the Israeli view remains essentially negative with regard to a major European political role in the peace process.

This contribution will briefly examine Israel's recent interaction with the EU, and focus on the role played thus far by Ambassador Moratinos. It will then offer an assessment as to Israel's difficulties in welcoming a more expansive EU political role. It will conclude with suggestions as to what the EU can and should do in order to be able to play a significant role in the Arab-Israeli peace process. What this paper does *not* do is discuss the Arab-Israeli peace process per se, render judgements regarding the objective accuracy of European positions, or prescribe specific short-term policy options for European involvement. Rather, it looks at the desirability and efficacy of basic European positions in Israeli eyes, against the backdrop of the expressed desire of European actors to play an enhanced political role in the peace process. Because many of the other papers in this volume state the European and/or Arab case for such a role, this one goes into some depth and specificity in outlining Israeli objections.

Israel and the EU

Israel has an extensive economic relationship with the EU. The EU is Israel's leading trading partner, accounting for 44 percent of Israel's total trade volume in 1996. Israel is the only country in the Mediterranean group that has, since the mid-1980s, completely abolished tariffs and duties for industrial products from the EU; a similar agreement with the US enables Israel to offer unique services in completing production of unfinished goods from one of these two economic giants and re-exporting to the other. Israel has also led the way in the Mediterranean in entering into scientific and cultural cooperation agreements with the EU, thereby gaining access to valuable Research & Development (R & D) funds.[3] Notably, Israel's economic relationship with the EU is lopsided in favour of the latter. From January through July 1997 Israel exported US$ 3.964 billion

---

3   Europe in Israel, Newsletter of the Delegation of the European Commission to the State of Israel, August 1997.

worth of goods to the EU, but imported US$ 8.640 billion.[4] As we shall see, this heavy Israeli debt to Europe – virtually half the EU surplus vis-à-vis the Mediterranean countries – is potentially significant when considerations of economic sanctions arise.

Meanwhile, the EU is also far and away the biggest financial supporter of the Oslo process between Israel and the PLO, and the Barcelona Process predicates a massive flow of European funds – some US$ 6 billion – to the Mediterranean region, including Israel, by the year 1999.

Perhaps most significantly, many Israelis tend to see their country as sharing in the European cultural heritage, rather than that of the Middle East. Europe is where most Israelis vacation, and (along with America) where they feel most at home outside of Israel.

Against this backdrop, the gap between the European and Israeli approach to the peace process is all the more striking. It is a long-standing gap. It commences most emphatically with the Venice Declaration of 12–13 June 1980, wherein the European Council stated its support for a series of positions: recognition of "the legitimate rights of the Palestinian people," including "the right to self-determination"; rejection of any "unilateral initiative" by Israel in Jerusalem; and the determination that "[. . .] Israeli settlements constitute a serious obstacle to the peace process [. . . and] are illegal."[5] By the time the Venice Declaration was issued, many European countries had already granted the PLO some sort of official recognition as the representative of the Palestinians.

When the Venice Declaration was published it created a considerable backlash in Israel, where virtually the entire political spectrum (save the far Left, mainly Arab parties) condemned it and rejected its contents. It is interesting to compare those contents to the most recent formulation of the EU position, at Amsterdam on 18 June

4   Central Bureau of Statistics, Jerusalem, October 1997 (direct inquiry).
5   Laufer (1997).

1997: "Europe calls on the people of Israel to recognise the right of the Palestinians to exercise self-determination, without excluding the option of a state. [...] The creation of a viable and peaceful sovereign Palestinian entity is the best guarantee of Israel's security."[6] In nearly 20 years the European position has changed little, compared to that of the United States and of both major political parties in Israel. In this regard, Europe has served in recent years as an effective catalyst of ideas for advancing the peace process. Yet the EU is no closer to playing a major mediatory role now than it was then. As Foreign Minister David Levi put it in Brussels on 22 July 1997, after meeting with Chairman Yassir Arafat under EU auspices: "It is our right to expect from Europe [...] to allow the two sides to try to resolve the matter without interference."[7]

The two most striking European initiatives toward the region in recent years are the Barcelona Process and the Moratinos mission. The former, inaugurated in November 1995, is intended to constitute a partnership in three fields: political and security, economic and financial, and social, cultural and human affairs. Because its frameworks are non-binding, and because they are backed up by a broad political-economic concept of close Euro-Med integration that Israel endorses, Israel is an active participant. At a time when the Madrid and Oslo processes are largely moribund, the 'track two' opportunities offered by Barcelona for exchange of views in security and other fields are welcomed by Israeli institutions. The Barcelona framework is today the only one that affords an opportunity for Israel and Syria/Lebanon to meet in the same forum. But the Barcelona Process per se has not sought an active role in the political peace process. It did, however, generate the momentum for the EU to appoint, on 25 November 1996, its own 'special envoy' to the process, Ambassador Miguel Moratinos.

6   Reuters North America, 18 June 1997.
7   Reuters North America, 22 July 1997.

The Moratinos Mission

Moratinos' mandate is framed in general but fairly comprehensive terms. He is empowered by the EU not only to monitor the actions of the parties and observe peace negotiations, but to offer good offices, contribute to the implementation of agreements, and discuss problems of non-compliance. He himself has no complaints about the authority given him by the European Council, and feels no need to broaden his mandate.[8] Indeed, he appears to be interpreting that authority relatively minimalistically.

One of Moratinos' accomplishments in the course of the past years has been to fill, however partially, the vacuum created by the stalemate in the process and the reduced activity of US mediator Dennis Ross in 1997. Thus at a time when no Israeli-Syrian negotiations were taking place and no US mediation effort was being attempted, Moratinos made frequent visits to Damascus and Jerusalem. These were designed, at a minimum, to defuse tensions, and at a maximum to advance the effort to find a bridging formula to enable renewal of direct negotiations. Moratinos himself acknowledges that, if and when that formula is found, it is the US that will step in to mediate. Indeed, in general it is the US that is needed for 'the hard parts', because it is the US that 'can deliver'. As for the EU, 'we know our limits'.

By the same token, Moratinos has been helpful at various times in maintaining momentum between Israel and the PLO, e.g. in providing additional assurances for the January 1997 Hebron agreement, and in arranging a Weizman-Arafat meeting. And he credits the EU with moderating Arab-sponsored resolutions at the UN.

Moratinos believes that the EU will from herein be increasingly involved in the process, though always in a secondary role. It has

---

8 Parts of the description of Ambassador Moratinos' work were provided by Ambassador Moratinos himself. Personal interview, Jerusalem, 29 July 1997.

more influence than the US with the Arabs, and it has the 'economic option', i.e. the capacity to use its economic presence in the region for political purposes. The EU is also more committed than the US to the 'global spirit of Madrid' – hence Moratinos' efforts in Damascus at a time when the US has concentrated on the Palestinians. While at least some Middle East leaders and diplomats involved in the process consider Moratinos naive and inexperienced,[9] it appears that thus far he has avoided making serious mistakes, and has contributed to the process within the modest parameters that he has defined for his mission. Because he has neither challenged American supremacy nor sought in any way to pressure Israel, his efforts have been welcomed in Jerusalem, and have enhanced European-American cooperation in the Arab-Israeli sphere. But are those efforts the outer limit of possible near-term European involvement in the process?

France, or the Lack of European Unity

Regardless of Israeli attitudes, one of the most obvious constraints upon the activities of an emissary like Moratinos is the evident lack of unity and consistency in European policy initiatives toward the Middle East. Two relatively minor illustrations of this disunity were the proposal by British Foreign Minister Malcolm Rifkind in November 1996 to set up an OSCE-type Middle East regional security forum, and Germany's abstention in the 15 July 1997 United Nations General Assembly vote to censure Israel over Har Homa (the rest of the EU 15 voted for the censure motion).

France is most consistently independent of EU policy in its Middle East initiatives. While Moratinos downplays the disruptive effect

---

9   President Mubarrak of Egypt is alleged to have said 'give him three years' (meaning, if he can survive for three years, he may bring some benefit). Private communication.

of such actions, certainly in Israeli eyes the spectre of pro-active French policies that appear to tilt strongly toward the Arabs is cause for serious doubt about the veracity of European initiatives. The most effective French initiative of the past years was Foreign Minister de Charette's shuttle diplomacy between Jerusalem, Beirut and Damascus during Israel's Operation Grapes of Wrath in April 1996, culminating in the institutionalisation of a French role in the cease-fire monitoring commission (along with the US, Syria, Lebanon and Israel) that evolved out of that operation. Here Paris succeeded in staking a claim to involvement, based on its historic links with Lebanon, despite US and Israeli reservations and against a backdrop of EU inactivity.

The most frustrating French initiative, from the Israeli standpoint, was President Chirac's October 1996 Middle East trip, in which he appeared to deliberately antagonise Israeli sensibilities by snubbing the Knesset in favour of the Palestinian Council, and by loudly complaining that Israeli security was preventing him from having direct contact with Palestinians in Jerusalem. More recently, Chirac has proposed – without offering any details – a new, jointly-sponsored American-European initiative with France in the lead: "France must seize the initiative while coordinating with the United States."[10] Nor is this independent and confrontational French approach a right wing prerogative in Paris. On 11 September, while Secretary of State Albright was meeting with President Arafat in the Palestinian Administration (PA) to urge him to take stronger measures against terrorism, and gently but firmly asking Prime Minister Binyamin Netanyahu to reciprocate, Foreign Minister Hubert Vedrine, a socialist, was terming Netanyahu's policies "[...] catastrophic [...]. This is a French analysis which is today shared by a growing number of European countries."[11]

10 Reuters World Report, 27 August 1997.
11 Reuters World Report, 11 September 1997.

This divergent and independent French position is confusing – if not downright infuriating – for those who are happy to be supportive of American efforts or of the more modestly-conceived Moratinos mission. While some would argue that it was precisely this sort of independent French activism that helped motivate the EU to appoint Moratinos, and that impels the US and the EU to pursue their efforts with greater energy, it is nevertheless seen as disruptive by both Jerusalem and Washington.

Why the EU is not an Acceptable Primary Mediator to Israel

The lack of unity and consistency in European positions that is highlighted by French policy is, however, only one of a long list of Israeli objections to a primary EU mediatory role in the Arab-Israel peace process. Others include:

The Americans don't like it. As a close strategic ally of the US, Israel is closely attuned to American wishes on this issue, regardless of the rationale. But, as the list below indicates, Israeli and American thinking are generally fairly close on most of the additional substantive reasons for objecting to European mediation.

Europe doesn't have America's clout, hence can be ignored with relative impunity. The EU is not yet integrated enough to be a superpower. It rarely behaves like a superpower. There is no large Jewish community there whose interests, influence and wealth must be taken into account. The EU has never seriously attempted to bend Israel's will the way the US has.

The Europeans take pro-Arab positions. In UN votes, for example (see above), the EU tends to vote the Arab line, while the US votes the Israeli line.

Europe is preoccupied with economic issues, and doesn't really appreciate Israel's security concerns. This view has been reinforced in recent years by the predominant European role – albeit one thrust upon it by the US and Russia – in shepherding the economically-oriented Madrid multilaterals, and also by the favourable European response to Shimon Peres' appeal to support his New Middle East vision – a strategy that in the eyes of many Israelis also ignored security concerns. The most recent instance (at the time of writing) of apparent European indifference to Israeli security concerns took place on 26 October 1997, at the close of a visit by Chairman Arafat to Germany. Foreign Minister Kinkel publicly criticised Israel's construction project at Har Homa, but avoided in any way calling upon Arafat to increase his efforts to crack down on terrorist elements with the Palestinian Authority – an omission carefully noted by Israelis. Another example of this European approach is the reticence, over the decades, of many European countries to sell weaponry to Israel. While this trend has been countered in recent years, particularly by the development of British and German strategic relationships with Israel, it nevertheless continues to rest on a sense of indifference that is best illustrated by the next point.

Ultimately, the Europeans can't be trusted. One of the most fundamental characteristics of Israel's world view is the resolute determination never again to place the fate of the Jewish people in the hands of anyone, European or American. But the US comes out far better in this equation. It was Europeans – Nazi Germany, aided by anti-Semites everywhere, including countries like France and Italy – that perpetrated the Holocaust. While Israel has overcome the legacy of the Holocaust in, for example, creating a close relationship with post-war Germany, Israelis' sense of being abandoned to their fate by Europeans has been reinforced more recently. It was France that, in 1967, dramatically turned its back on Israel at the height of the escalation to the Six-Day War. It was nearly all the EU states that refused the US overflight rights for its airlift to Israel during the 1973 war. Of course, many Arab states also perceive Europe negatively in terms of the historical legacy of its Middle East presence – from colonialism to Suez. Nor is the Israeli sense of historical betrayal by

Europeans necessarily a primary component of the Israeli view of Europe.

Europe is motivated by economic greed, at the expense of existential interests of countries like Israel. European insistence on arming Iraq prior to August 1990 is the first example. True, the US also abetted Iraq's efforts at achieving missile and non-conventional capabilities at the time. But the US learned its lesson, and is trying desperately to apply it to the second example, contemporary Iran. Yet the Europeans persist, arguing feebly that 'critical dialogue' is a better tool than sanctions, even as Iranian terrorists practice their trade on European soil and Iran moves ever closer to a nuclear capability that will threaten Europe as well as the Middle East. This perceived insistence on placing short-term economic aggrandisement above morality and strategic common sense tends to compromise the EU's positive efforts in other spheres, like the Arab-Israel conflict.

The EU seeks to channel its energies to the Muslim Middle East in part in order to mask its own abject failure to come to terms with its Muslim problems at home. According to this perception, the Barcelona Process is essentially a strategy for preventing large-scale illegal Muslim migration to southern Europe from North Africa. Some observers fear that, sooner or later, key European countries will have a significant domestic Muslim lobby, and that already their foreign policies take into account local Muslim sensibilities. Further, as a senior American diplomat put it in criticising European initiatives in the Middle East, the Europeans must first recognise that Europe will have at least two Muslim states – Albania and Bosnia – in their heartland, and bring Turkey in as a moderating influence on Europe's flank, before they can claim to act decisively in the Middle East.[12] Europe's inability to deal effectively with the Bosnian crisis, and the necessity for an American intervention therein, appear best to illus-

12 Conversation with senior American diplomat involved in Middle East issues, Washington, 19 June 1997.

trate this point. Israelis ask why they should place their trust in a Europe that was unable to solve such a serious internal conflict. Moreover, as the Israeli-Turkish strategic relationship prospers, Israel is increasingly sensitive to Turkey's perception of a biased European attitude toward its candidacy to join the EU.

Thus for European initiatives to be increasingly effective and influential with Israelis, the EU has to improve its political image in Israeli eyes. As a corollary of the weaknesses noted above, the EU should perhaps seek ways to: speak with one voice on Arab-Israeli issues; evince greater concern for Israel's security problems; take a more principled stand toward the Iranian threat; and demonstrate to the Middle East that it can begin to deal effectively and independently with its own Muslim problems.

Conclusion:
What Europe Can and Should Do in the Arab-Israeli Process

From the Israeli standpoint, the EU is not going to be the primary mediator in the Arab-Israeli conflict. If a mediator is needed, it will be the US, or no one. Yet the ongoing aggrandisement of the EU, coupled with the escalatory progression from Barcelona to Moratinos, imply that the EU will seek an ever growing role in the peace process. Moreover, Israel must recognise that the EU of 1997 is a very different, more formidable and more positive actor than Europe of 20–30 years ago. Hence Israel must seek ways to accommodate the European quest for a more significant political role.

The EU, for its part, must define its strategic options in terms of both desirability and feasibility. One option upon which Israel, the Arabs, Europe and the US can agree, is to continue along the Moratinos track: being helpful in a secondary role, and seeking to achieve complementarity of policy initiatives with the US. Clearly, however, this will not fully counter the frustration of many European policy-makers and scholars who argue that the EU, as main financial backer of the process, deserves a more significant role, particularly at a time when US efforts are less than fully effective.

A second strategy reflected in many European and Arab circles, is to drop the pretence of European neutrality that is mandated by the role of mediator, yet is at times seemingly maintained by the EU with difficulty. Europe should line up behind the demand for a Palestinian state, and apply European economic and political clout, such as it is, to a lobby effort on behalf of this formula, in much the same way that Europe contributed to the ultimate collapse of the apartheid regime in South Africa. Would this imply European economic sanctions against Israel? This is a frequent Arab demand. Given Europe's highly favourable trade balance with Israel, and the large volume of trade involved, this would be an economically counterproductive exercise for the EU.

Perhaps more important, it would almost certainly be politically counterproductive: the Netanyahu government would effectively cite this attempt to isolate Israel, and implicitly to equate it with Iraq and Iran,[13] as justification for Israeli suspicions regarding fundamental European hostility, and would thereby more effectively rally Israelis, and Jews elsewhere, around its policies.

An alternative channel where Europe has the potential to make a strong contribution to the process is in back channel diplomacy. The Oslo channel was in many ways a natural by-product of close ideological affinity and veteran friendships between Norway's socialist government and Israel's Labour Party leadership – a combination virtually inconceivable in the Israeli-American relationship. Oslo also reflects a more advanced and effective European perception of the need to involve the PLO in the process than the US was capable of at the time; in this sense it is an outstanding example of a Euro-

---

13 Indeed, Europe still *avoids* applying general sanctions to the latter.

pean contribution to the process. An Oslo-type track two channel at the time of writing appeared to be desperately missing in the relationship between Israel's Likud government and the PLO leadership. While Prime Minister Netanyahu might not have been personally or politically inclined toward such a process, others in his government might.

Yet another productive instrument is informal or alternative diplomacy. As noted, the Barcelona Process has spawned a number of successful semi-academic forums that deal with security, the environment and other issues. The Copenhagen Declaration successfully brought together informal practitioners from four countries. In recent years the Europeans appear to have formulated and initiated such enterprises at least as successfully as the US.

From the Israeli standpoint, the preferable EU strategies for dealing with the Arab-Israeli peace process are the Moratinos track, coupled with additional attempts to foster track two dialogue. For Europe to seek to impose a South African style economic boycott on Israel would be seen as unjust and prejudicial treatment, and would probably be counterproductive. In general, a more active EU role in the process requires that first Europe be seen by Israelis to adopt more balanced policies regarding Middle East issues.

List of References

Leopold Yehuda Laufer 1997: The European Union and Israel. A Political and Institutional Appraisal, Jerusalem.

Foreign Policy Making and Strategies

Institutional Constraints of the European Union's Middle Eastern and North African Policy

Jörg Monar

Political issues of the wider Mediterranean area have occupied a prominent position on the external agenda of the Western European construction since its very first steps in international political relations.[1]
This is particularly true for the Middle East: When the foreign ministers of the six original member states of the European Communities
got together for their first meeting in the framework of the newly
established 'European Political Cooperation' in Munich in 1970 the
first item of discussion was the Middle East.[2] Since then the problems in the Middle East have not only never left the European foreign
affairs agenda but have also led the Europeans, nolens volens, to
adopt a number of major initiatives in response to developments in
this area. Inevitably some of these initiatives, such as the famous

---

1   This contribution was presented to the workshop *Aims and Instruments of a Euro-
    pean Political Role in the Mediterranean Region*, Frankfurt, October 1997.
2   Nuttall (1997: 24).

Venice Declaration of 1980, have been politically controversial. Yet the European Community and later the European Union (EU) have been criticised more often for lack or inefficiency of action than for the political content of their policy in the Middle East.

The last few years have seen a multiplication of EU activities in the Middle East, ranging from more specific actions such as the support given to the preparation of Palestinian elections and the creation of the Palestine Police Force to broader initiatives such as the Union's role in the 'Regional Economic Development Working Group' (REDWG) and the emphasis placed in the 'Euro-Mediterranean Partnership' on political and economic stabilisation in both the Middle East and North Africa. Yet in practice the Union's actual role in the Middle East peace process has remained largely limited to the economic sphere, leaving high politics mainly to the US. This stands in striking contrast both with the Union's enormous resources, economic, diplomatic, military and other, and with the declarations of leading EU politicians who rarely fail to stress the political importance of the Middle East for the EU and the need for the Union to play an active role in the peace process.[3] A similar contrast has also emerged in the EU's relations with some of its North African partners.

It seems fair to say, therefore, that the Union's Middle Eastern and North African policy continues to suffer from a gap between its apparent potential to act and its declared ambitions on the one hand and its actual performance on the other. This discrepancy, which is surely frustrating for some of the Union's partners in the Middle East and North Africa but also disappointing for many EU actors, can to a considerable extent be explained by the particular institutional and procedural constraints under which EU decision-making and policy implementation in foreign affairs is taking place. These constraints result from the nature and constitutional structure of the EU system of foreign affairs.

3 See on this point Barbé/Izquierdo (1997: 130–131).

In the following we will look at the main characteristics of the EU system of foreign affairs, followed by a more detailed analysis of how this 'dual system' works in practice. On the basis of this analysis we will then – looking at some recent cases of EU policy-making – try to identify the major constraints the system imposes on the EU's Middle Eastern and North African policy and finish this contribution with some conclusions on the implications of these constraints for the future development of the Union's role in the Middle East.

The Main Characteristics of the EU System of Foreign Affairs

The European Union's system for conducting foreign affairs is singular of its kind in the history of international relations: Because of an intricate division of powers between the member states and the community institutions, the Union's foreign affairs are conducted neither entirely by its member states, which continue to be sovereign in international relations, nor by the Union with its well developed Community substructure, which has emerged as a new actor on the international stage. Whereas external "political" relations have largely remained in the realm of national sovereignty and intergovernmental cooperation, external economic relations have become subject to the supranational institutional and procedural system of the European Communities. The result has been a splitting of the rationale, the means and the decision-making procedures in the conduct of foreign affairs which makes of the Union a particularly complex actor in international relations, difficult to deal with for both those participating in the internal process and for the Union's international partners.

Evolutive Nature of the EU System

The first major characteristic of Union's foreign affairs system is its evolutive nature. The EC founding treaties of 1951 and 1957 did neither provide for the development of a common foreign policy nor did they even mention it as political aim. Yet the cooperation of the member states in the sphere of foreign affairs has been a major political evolution resulting from the Community's existence. The aim to provide for a close general political coordination of the members states' foreign policies has accompanied the development of the EC almost from the beginning: Already in 1959 the Foreign Ministers of the Six decided to meet regularly to discuss foreign policy questions. The next step, the negotiations on a 'Political Union' with close inter-governmental cooperation in foreign affairs as it was proposed in the French government's famous 'Fouchet Plans' in 1961/62, ended in a failure. But after several years of stagnation the Davignon or Luxembourg Report of 1970, following the new impetus given to the Community by the Hague Summit of 1969, successfully advocated regular meetings of the member states' Foreign Ministers and Political Directors in order to favour common action in the sphere of foreign affairs. Baptised 'European Political Cooperation' (EPC), this mechanism of intergovernmental cooperation added to its very scarce and limited initial procedures in a step-by-step approach a series of bodies and rules with the clear aim of broadening the consensus-building process in the formation of a European foreign policy and of improving its capacities of responding to external problems. Notwithstanding some very critical comments from outside disparaging EPC as a mere phrase-producing machinery, the governments valued the evolution of the new cooperation structure as a success story, especially after having had evident positive experiences with cooperation in the Conference on Security and Cooperation in Europe (CSCE) negotiations and in Middle East affairs. As a result the Single European Act of 1986 created for the time a treaty base for the 'Common Foreign and Security Policy' (CFSP) and strengthened its institutional and procedural set-up. As the external challenges and responsibilities of Western Europe increased after the end of the Cold War the member states attempted a major reform of EPC in the framework of the 1990/91 Intergovernmental Conference (IGC). They failed to agree on substantial changes to the intergovernmental basis but strengthened the security dimension and the instruments of their cooperation in the framework of the CFSP introduced by the Maastricht Treaty. The crisis in former Yugoslavia quickly revealed the weaknesses of the new CFSP and brought it once more on the reform agenda, this time on that of the 1996/97 IGC. Yet, again, the member states were only able to agree on limited procedural and institutional reforms, continuing the process of slow incrementalism which had prevailed since the start of EPC. Broadly summarising one can say that in the area of external 'political' relations the EU foreign affairs system has evolved from a rather loose to a more and more intense and sophisticated intergovernmental cooperation.

Yet in spite of the claim, first by EPC and then by the CFSP, to be the one and only foreign policy-making structure of the Western European construction the originally purely 'economic' EC system has become an international actor on its own: From the outset, the Community's treaty-making powers as laid down in the three founding treaties (European Coal and Steel Community, European Atomic Energy Community, European Economic Community) and particularly the Common commercial policy provided for in the EEC Treaty granted the Community a great potential for taking action in international relations. In the first years following its creation, to a large extent the Community only acted in response to initiatives from abroad. But then it gradually fortified its international position by a series of important trade agreements, such as the preferential trade agreements with countries in the Mediterranean region (starting with Greece in 1961) and the agreements on preferential treatment of African, Caribbean and Pacific (ACP) countries (starting with the first Yaounde Convention of 1963). The steadily continued series of trade agreements, together with the Community's coherent action within the framework of the GATT (starting with the Dillon Round in 1961), led third countries to recognise it as an important partner, able to play a decisive role as an independent entity in international relations. This was reflected, in particular, by the status acquired by the Community in important international organisations (especially in GATT and the OECD) and the fact that the Community's supranational executive institution, the Commission, saw itself admitted as a participant to the G-7 Summits and entrusted with major international tasks such as the coordination of the West's economic aid for Eastern Europe's new democracies (G-24/PHARE programme). This enormous development of the Community's external relations did not proceed without friction. Member states not only exercised tight control over the Commission in this area but also repeatedly tried to prevent the gradual extension of Community competences or even to regain some of the powers they had originally transferred to the Community. Yet these attempts largely failed due to the jurisdiction of the European Court of Justice, and in recent years the completion of the Single Market, the introduction of the European Monetary Union (EMU) project by the Maastricht Treaty and the 'pre-accession' policy towards the Central and Eastern European Countries have again strengthened the external role and position of the EC. In the case of external economic relations therefore, the evolution took the form of a gradual extension and particularly successful implementation of the supranational competences introduced by the EC founding treaties.

Yet there is still another important aspect relating to the evolutionary nature of the EU foreign affairs system: In practice, a clear separation of external 'economic' and external 'political' issues is of course impossible, and policies agreed on in the EC and CFSP structures must inevitably overlap and be correlated. This has been the case right from the beginning because the role of first EPC and then the CFSP in international relations have always been heavily dependent on the EC's economic power and instruments. Instrumentalising this economic power has been one of the key elements of the rationale for developing foreign and security policy cooperation between the member states, and since the 1980s 'consistency' and 'coherence' between the policies agreed on in the two structures have been recurrent themes in the various IGCs. As a result the links between the two structures were gradually increased by strengthening the guidance function of the European Council for both structures, the introduction of new mechanisms for the use of EC instruments by EPC/CFSP, an upgrading of the role of the Commission in EPC/CFSP and partial merger of the decision-making bodies and procedures of both structures.

The evolution of both the EC and the EPC/CFSP parts of the Union's foreign affairs system have therefore been accompanied by a parallel evolution of their interaction. This 'triple' evolution is still going on: In the 1996/97 IGC the development of both the CFSP and the EC's external competence as well as their interaction have again been the subject of protracted negotiations.

Dualistic Nature of the EU System

The above description of the evolution of the EC and EC/CFSP structures makes clear that since the early seventies the Western European construction has had two different decision-making structures in foreign affairs: on the one hand, its "external economic relations" are conducted by the Commission and the Council of Ministers in the framework of the partially supranational decision-making structure of the EC. On the other hand, foreign and security policy issues are dealt with in the essentially intergovernmental framework of CFSP which has retained the main features of old EC. As a result the European Union's foreign affairs system – this is the second major characteristic – is governed by the fundamental dualism of two structures which reside on a different legal basis, follow different decision-making rules and procedures, are different in their institutional set-up and, perhaps most importantly, gravitate around different rationales, i.e. the supranational 'Community' rationale on the one hand and the intergovernmental cooperation rationale on the other.

Mitigated Predominance of the Member States

From a formal point of view EU foreign affairs are under the responsibility of the four main institutions of the EU: the European Council, the Council (of Ministers), the European Commission and the European Parliament. The main decision-making power, however, lies with the member states which take the decisions in the European Council and the Council of Ministers.

Yet – and this is the third major characteristic – this predominance of the member states is mitigated by two factors. The first is the dual system itself: whereas in the CFSP sphere the member states can still act independently from each other, have an unlimited right of initiative and decide by consensus only, action in the EC sphere can only be taken through the Community system, on an initiative by the Commission, needs in many cases only a qualified majority of the member states and is normally implemented by the Commission. The second factor is the strength of the political and economic ties between the member states. As a result of these, most member states are normally reluctant to oppose a position backed by a strong majority of member states and prefer to compromise on a common approach, often prepared by the Commission, rather than to risk isolation and a weakening of the Union's position on the international stage.

The Union's Dual System at Work

The question of competences is central to the understanding of the entire EU foreign affairs system and needs therefore closer examination.

The EC Framework

The EC Treaties do not set out a list of the subjects falling within the Communities' competences of the kind we can find in federal constitutions. As this is the case with most international organisations, the competences of the Community are defined in a more complex manner, by confining the relevant rules and the scope of the competences, and by laying down the conditions and the methods for exercising them. This is done in order to ensure that provisions which frequently are of a general character cannot be interpreted as automatically conferring unlimited powers of action upon the Community institutions.

The EC Treaty, because of its wide economic and political scope is by far the most important of the three founding treaties, stipulates in Article 210 that the Community "[...] shall have legal personality". This provision is an affirmation of the Community's capacity to exercise powers in international relations. However, the EC Treaty does not provide explicitly for a general external Community competence over the whole range of the Treaty. It only contains a limited number of explicit provisions regarding the competence for concluding specific international agreements, the most important of these being Article 113 Treaty on the European Community (TEC) providing for the Common Commercial Policy and Article 238 TEC providing for the conclusion of 'association agreements'.

Although it is generally acknowledged that the Common Commercial policy covers both autonomous and conventional measures, the nature and the scope of Community competence under Article 113 has given rise to a number of controversies between the Commission and the member states which ended up before the European Court of Justice. As regards the nature of Community competence the Court held in Opinion 1/75[4] that the exercise of concurrent powers by the member states in this area is impossible because it would distort the institutional framework and prevent the Community from fulfilling its task of the defence of the common interest. Community competence under the Common Commercial Policy (CCP) has therefore to be regarded as exclusive, with the effect that the Community replaces the member states in their role as sovereign trade units. As regards the scope of Community competence in this field the Court has repeatedly held that the concept of 'commercial policy' has to be understood in a broad sense which takes into account changes in international trade relations requiring the extension of that concept beyond the traditional patterns of trade. In Case 45/86[5], for instance, the Court ruled that the link of the Community's generalised preference system with development policy does not cause measures taken under this system to be excluded from the CCP. In Opinion 1/94[6] the Court reaffirmed the open nature of Community competences under the CCP by holding for the first time that also trade in services can be included in Article 113 if it is limited to cross-frontier services rendered by a supplier established in one country to a consumer residing in another. However, in the same case the Court also established certain limits to the scope of Article 113 by declaring that international agreements in the field of transport are excluded from the scope of Article 113. This opinion was based on the fact that transport is the subject of a different Title of the Treaty and that the connection between intellectual property rights and trade in goods is not sufficient to bring them within the scope of the CCP.

4   Understanding on a Local Cost Standard, [1975] ECR 1364.
5   Commission vs. Council, [1987] ECR 1493.
6   Agreement establishing the World Trade Organization, [1994] ECR I-5267.

Article 238 TEC enables the Community to conclude "[...] agreements establishing an association involving reciprocal rights and obligations, common action and special procedure". The Community is competent to enter into any such agreement whose subject-matter falls within the scope of the Treaty. Yet the TEC does not give a precise definition of the notion of 'association', and this has led to a contradictory practice: For both external political reasons (considerable political implications of the concept of 'association') and internal political reasons (different majority requirements of Articles 113 and 238 and the different role of the European Parliament) agreements of an essentially commercial content have been based on Article 238, whereas in other cases agreements establishing much closer relationships between the Community and third States have been based on Article 113 only.

The TEC has left open the fundamental question whether the Community's external competence is based on the principle of enumerated competences ('compétences d'attribution') and therefore limited to the external competences expressly provided for by the Treaty, or whether its competence in external relations should be regarded as coextensive with its competence for internal purposes and therefore exist also in cases not expressly provided for by the Treaty. On this issue the ECJ has developed what is commonly called the 'doctrine of implied powers'. First established by the famous ERTA judgement and then further developed in later case law this doctrine holds that the Community's authority to enter into international commitments arises not only from an express conferment by the Treaty, but may equally flow implicitly from the duties and powers which primary and secondary Community law have established and assigned to the Community institutions on the internal level. The principle of the Community's implied external competences is therefore one of parallelism, the internal competences being paralleled by the external competences. Since the limits of internal Community competence can never be finally settled, this parallelism means that the scope of Community external competence grows in the same measure as the Community extends its internal sphere of activity and that in this sense Community external competence is indefinite and evolutionary. The doctrine of implied competences has provided, and still provides, considerable impulse for the development of EC external relations. However, because of the lack of a Treaty provision which formally establishes the parallelism of internal and external competences and because of the indefinite and evolutionary nature of the implied competences, the scope of external Community competence continues to be an inexhaustible source of conflicts between the Commission as the representative of the Community's interest and those of the member states which want to restrict Community activity in external relations. The Community, therefore, still lacks a stable and comprehensive legal basis for external activity comparable to that of which nation-states normally dispose.[7]

Not surprisingly the member states tend to be keen to preserve their residual competences against any 'pre-emption' by the exercise of Community competence and to limit, wherever possible, the practical scope of exclusive Community competence. A frequently used instrument in this respect is the practice of "mixed-agreements". From a formal point of view "mixed agreements" are simply international agreements which need a joint "mixed" conclusion by both the EC and some or all of the member states because they contain both elements which pertain to exclusive Community competence and elements still coming under the member states' jurisdiction. Yet the practical use is somewhat less innocent because the member states are quite successful in finding in many international agreements at least some elements which fall outside exclusive Community competence and justify their participation, thereby stunting the use of exclusive Community competences.

7   See on this the assessment Emiliou (1996: 43–45).

The CFSP Framework

With regard to the competences within the CFSP framework one can be rather brief: Unlike the EC, the CFSP has not been conferred upon any legal competence by the member states which remain fully sovereign in the foreign and security policy area. In contrast with its ambitious title, the CFSP is not a "common policy" according to the Community model. It establishes only a domain of institutionalised and structured cooperation between the member states.

The scope of the CFSP domain extends to all matters of foreign and security policy, yet this with two important exceptions:

In the sphere of security policy Article J.4 (4) Treaty on the European Union (TEU) provides that the CFSP shall not prejudice the specific character of the security and defence policy of certain member states and shall respect the obligations of member states under the North Atlantic Treaty.

The second exception relates to the EC framework: As a separate legal structure established outside of the framework of the EC Treaties, the scope of the CFSP is necessarily limited by the external relations competences the member states have definitely conferred upon the EC. This means in practice that the member states within CFSP cannot use any of the economic and financial instruments of the EC without a corresponding decision being taken in the EC framework. In order to facilitate interaction between the CFSP and the EC in this respect the Maastricht Treaty introduced Article 228a TEC which provides that in case of a common position or joint action of the CFSP requires action by the EC the Council shall act on a proposal by the Commission, i.e. according to normal Community rules. The member states in CFSP are therefore dependent on the Commission to have their political decisions backed up by economic measures. The political pressure on the Commission to act only as an executive agent of the member states in these cases is of course enormous, but there have been cases in which the Commission has stood its ground,

proposing measures and approaches in the economic sphere which
were not fully in line with CFSP decisions.[8]

The Dualism in External Representation

The most visible consequence of the dualism in terms of competences
is to be found in the external representation of the European Union.
By virtue of its powers under the EC Treaty (Articles 113, 228, 229)
it is the European Commission which represents the Community in
all international negotiations on matters covered by the EC Treaty.
In the CFSP area it is the member state holding the Presidency which
represents the Union in all matters of foreign and security policy.
This split in the external representation of the European Union
implies already in itself considerable complexity: It means not only
that inside of the EU a considerable effort of coordination is needed
to ensure consistency between these two sides of external representation but also that third countries have to deal with different interlocutors depending on the subject matter. In the case of CFSP, in addition, the interlocutor changes every six months because of the
rotating Presidencies. Yet in practice this complexity is made much
worse by two factors:

One is that in most international negotiations and contacts with
third countries, subject matters coming under both the EC competence and the CFSP have to be addressed. In order to respect the
internal division of competences the Union often needs to be represented in one and the same negotiation by both the Presidency and
the Commission ('bicephalous formula'). If member states' competences are concerned (for instance in negotiations on 'mixed agreements') these may even insist on having a full place at the table as
well, in which case the Presidency, the Commission and several or

8   See on this point Monar (1993: 77–78).

even all of the member states appear as negotiators on the Union side ('multicephalous formula'). It is true that the Union has developed very comprehensive coordination mechanisms which in most cases ensure adequate consistency on the Union side.[9] Yet the coordination effort is enormous and international partners are still frequently puzzled by the bewildering range of interlocutors they have to deal with on the EU side.

The second complicating factor is that both the member states (represented by the Presidency) and the Commission are anxious not to allow for any precedents that could be taken as sign of erosion of their respective external competence. As a result serious friction can arise within the system if one side is perceived to be encroaching on the other's territory. Some member states continue, for instance, to watch with distrust any step taken by the 'Heads of Delegation' of the Commission in third countries which – often treated as 'Ambassadors' by the host countries – seem to them to endanger the status and the political role of their own accredited diplomats.

The Dualism in Decision-Making Procedures

The EC and EU Treaties provide for significantly different decision-making procedures on external matters which are another distinctive element of the EU system.

The EC Framework

Community external relations are governed by the supranational "Community method" which in our context is best exemplified by a look at the treaty-making procedure under the CCP. The treaty-mak-

---

9   See Tietje (1997: 211–233).

ing procedure regulated by Articles 113 and 228 TEC is cumbersome: It is the task of the Commission to make recommendations to the Council as regards the opening of negotiations with third countries and to act as the Community's negotiator once these are opened. Yet it has to conduct these negotiations within the framework of usually very detailed negotiating directives issued by the Council and under close supervision by the Council's 'Article 113 Committee', which means that it has for most of the time to negotiate not only with the third countries but also with the member states within the Council which normally send observers to the negotiations. The Commission can initial the agreements at the end of the negotiations but cannot conclude them. The conclusion is again a prerogative of the Council who by a qualified majority on a proposal from the Commission. However, unanimity is required when the agreement covers a field for which unanimity is required for the adoption of internal rules and for association agreements.[10] Depending on the subject matter, therefore, the Commission has or has not the greater margin to manoeuvre in the Council which qualified majority voting allows for. Quite often disputes arise over the adequate legal base for an external EC measure because – depending on the legal base chosen – decision by qualified majority only may or may not be possible. The legal base determines also the role played by the European Parliament which may, however, come into the process because of its budgetary powers (see below).

This brief sketch of the EC decision-making process in external relations shows that it is aimed at striking a balance between the supranational element represented by the Commission and the interests of the member states represented by the Commission. Yet this balance comes at the price of a cumbersome interaction between the key players which in can seriously delay necessary action and often leads to complex 'package deals' on external issues between the

10 Article 228(2) TEC.

member states themselves and the member states and the Commission which may be rather puzzling and difficult to understand for third countries.[11]

The CFSP Framework

The CFSP decision-making process is much simpler from a procedural point of view. All major decisions are prepared by the Political Committee (regrouping the Political Directors of the Foreign Ministries) and taken by the Foreign Ministers meeting in the Council within the framework of very broad (and often vague) guidelines set by the European Council. For all practical purposes decisions are taken by consensus.[12] The Commission has a right of initiative but it has to share it with all the member states. In practice most initiatives come from the Presidency which is responsible both for the management of the entire CFSP structure and its external representation (see above). Various emergency procedures have been adopted in order to allow for quick reactions to international events in between the Council meetings.

The complex interaction between Commission and Council is absent in the CFSP framework and the member states do normally not have to worry over competence questions. Yet nevertheless the CFSP decision-making process produces more often than not suboptimal results and compares unfavourably with the EC process in spite of all its complexities. The main reasons for that are the consensus rule – which makes the member states to agree on the least common denominator only or even not at all – and the absence of an institutional driving force like the Commission – the rotating Presi-

11 A major example in this respect is the Union's internal struggle during the final phase of the Uruguay Round. See on this Defuyst (1995: 451–454).

12 Article J.3(2) TEU, which offers a limited possibility to decide with qualified majority on measures implementing a joint action, has never been used so far.

dencies being normally too weak for such a role. As a result the decision-making capacity of the EC structure clearly exceeds that of the CFSP with the effect that politically relevant action in external economic relations is often not sufficiently backed up or 'used' by the CFSP because the necessary consensus cannot be reached.

The Dualism in Instruments and Implementation

The systemic split in the EU foreign affairs system is no less pronounced in the area of instruments which are substantially different in the two structures: In the EC framework take the form of "regulations", "directives" or "decisions" by Council or Commission which are legally binding under EC law. In the CFSP framework only one of the instruments used, the "joint action", entails binding legal effects for the member states, yet this not under EC law but only under public international law. The legal effect of "common positions" is still subject to different interpretations, and all other texts adopted by CFSP such as the frequently issued 'statements' issued by the Presidency have only the status of political declarations.

The dualism is no less pronounced in the area of implementation. In the EC framework it is the Commission which is responsible for the implementation of external measures adopted. As a result the measures are normally administered by appropriate units of the Commission services. However, in the process of implementation the Commission remains subject to close control by the member states. This control is exercised by specific committees which – depending on the type of committee – can effectively block implementing measures proposed by the Commission.

In the CFSP framework it is the Presidency which is responsible for the implementation of common measures. The Presidency can draw on the administrative support of the CFSP Unit in the General Secretariat of the Council, but this is comparatively small (around 30 officials), and most of the implementation work is normally done at the national level in the foreign ministries. As a result EU relations with third countries are in practice administered by totally different sets of administrative structures and officials: the economic side mainly by Community officials in Brussels, the political side by national foreign ministry officials of the country holding the Presidency. Not surprisingly this often leads to problems of coordination and conflicting signals to third countries.

A special note needs to be made here about finances, certainly one of the most powerful instruments in international relations. Within the limits of appropriate budget lines external measures of the EC can be financed out of the huge Community budget. The CFSP, however, does not have a budget of its own. Its (relatively limited) administrative expenditure is charged to the Community budget. As regards the more important operational expenditure the situation is more complicated because this can be charged – by a decision of the Council – either to the member states or to the Community budget. Since the member states have had huge problems with the financing of CFSP measures out of their own budgets – there were disagreements over the scale to be applied and some of them were paid late or even not at all – they have increasingly used the Community budget for their joint actions. Yet this has caused considerable problems because appropriate budget lines were often not available and because the member states tried on several occasions to bypass the budgetary powers of the European Parliament. As a result CFSP joint actions have been affected by delays in financing and bitter arguments with the European Parliament.[13]

---

13 See on this point Monar (1997: 60–72).

The Dualism in Democratic Control

Democratic control is another peculiar aspect of the EU's dual system. In the EC framework – depending on the type of agreement – the European Parliament can be involved in three different ways in the conclusion of agreements with third countries: It may have to give its assent (association agreements and some other important types of agreements), it may only need to be informed (agreements under Article 113 TEC) or it may have to be consulted (all other agreements). In addition, it can exercise a considerable degree of control over EC external relations through its powers in the EC budgetary system (budgetary procedure and budgetary discharge). In the CFSP framework, however, the European Parliament has to content itself with a vague obligation for the Presidency to take its views "into consideration" and receiving regular information (of varying quality) from Presidency and Commission.

As a result of this aspect of the dualism there is a huge discrepancy in terms of democratic control at the European level: In EC external relations the European Parliament has some "hard" powers of control and scrutiny, within the CFSP is has none at all. Not surprisingly the Parliament has tried and still tries to make up for the absence of effective powers in the CFSP sphere by using its powers in sphere of EC external relations all the more vigorously. This has led to quite a number of cases in which economic measures of the EC (agreements, financial protocols, etc.) have been blocked or delayed by the European Parliament for foreign policy considerations which it has not been able to impress on upon the member states within the CFSP framework.

The Impact of the Institutional Constraints for the EU's Middle Eastern and North African Policy

General Impact

The above look at various aspects of the functioning of the European Union's dual system of foreign affairs has shown the extraordinary complexity of external policy making and policy implementation by the Union.[14] The institutional constraints resulting from this are always tangible. Yet they are inevitably increased if a policy touches vital interests of the Union and its member states because then the internal struggle for securing priorities and defending particular interests of all actors involved becomes all the more intense. The Union's policy towards the countries of the Middle East and North Africa definitely touches vital interests of the Union and most of its member states, from a security point of view, economically and financially. As a result this policy (if there is 'one' policy at all) puts the entire foreign affairs system under considerable strain and the impact of the institutional constraints increases.

The most important effect of the institutional constraints of the system is that it makes of the European Union a clearing house of different interests rather than a unitary actor with more or less clearly defined objectives and strategies. With the Union system lacking the single governmental structures and central authority of a nation-state actor on the international stage, its policy towards the Middle East and North Africa depends on interest constellations which vary over time and the capacity of the institutional set-up to merge these interests into decisions in the EC and/or the CFSP framework. The origins of the Barcelona initiative on the EU side are a

---

14 The author would like to thank Mrs. Laurence Auer (DG IB of the European Commission) for complementary information on this section of this paper. All assessments and interpretations are of course his own.

case in point: The early Italian and Spanish pressure to make the Mediterranean a priority area did not make much ground in 1992. Yet the idea of a new major initiative gained ground when France, trying to reaffirm its political role vis-à-vis Germany's emerging role as champion of the Eastern enlargement and increasingly worried by its immigration problems, shifted its full weight on the side of a new approach to the Mediterranean and when the four 'southern' countries (Portugal, Spain, Italy and Greece) and France started to present a reinforced policy in the Mediterranean as a strategic counterpart to the pre-accession strategy towards the countries of central and eastern Europe (CEEC) This process was helped by the increasingly ambitious Commission papers of July 1994[15] and March 1995[16], the latter of which took profit of the favourable political climate of French Presidency of 1995. It was due to this favourable developments in the member states' and the Commission's positions that not only the new initiative became possible at all but also that the old ratio of 5 : 1 in favour of the CEECs defended by the British, the Danes, the Germans and the Dutch, was in the end raised to 5 : 3,5.[17] The positive impact of the institutional set-up in this case was that it provided an established framework and set of rules for this clearing of interests towards a new policy, "channelling" so to say the diverging aspirations of the individual member states and the Commission towards a compromise. The negative impact, again related to this basic function of the institutional set-up as a clearing house of interests, was that inevitably the Union's position at the start of the Barcelona process was in every bit the result of a compromise between diverging interests under given circumstances, subject to a whole range of political and economic limitations and implying no strategic change of strategic direction of all the actors. The EU's

15 COM(94)427.
16 COM(95)72.
17 See Barbé (1996: 32).

institutional system can ease and (especially in the EC framework) even to some extent force the adoption of a common policy but, because of its essential function of a clearing house of interests, this policy is always a conglomerate of compromises made possible by a particular constellation which remains subject to all sorts of limitations imposed by diverging interests and a rather varying commitment of the different EU actors.

Another important general effect of the EU system on its Middle Eastern and North African policy is that it has what may be called an inbuilt tilt towards the economic domain. As we have tried to show above the CFSP is by far the weaker structure of the EU's dual system of foreign affairs, in terms of decision-making capacity as well as instruments. The more complex and controversial an international issue is the more difficult it becomes to achieve the necessary consensus within the CFSP for any more substantial common position or action. In the EC sphere, however, action even under these circumstances can still remain possible because of the motor function of the European Commission and the possibility of qualified majority voting. In addition, member states which are afraid of endorsing high profile "foreign policy" positions within the CFSP on a given issue might still be willing to support some economic measures within the EC framework, frequently regarded as belonging to the area of "low politics" and therefore less exposed to controversy. As a result the Union system is likely to adopt some economic measures even if it is not able to agree on a meaningful political position within the CFSP. This tilt towards the economic domain is reinforced the deep-rooted economic rationale of the European integration process. The role of the Union in the Middle East peace process during the last few years can be taken as an example for this intrinsic effect of the system: Although the Union has taken a plethora of economic and financial measures in support of the peace process, it has played only a very modest role on the political side of the process, leaving the active political role almost exclusively to the United States.

The third and final general effect of the institutional constraints of the EU system is that it creates difficulties for the Union's partners in the Middle East and North Africa in terms of its transparency and predictability. Every single element of the Union's Middle Eastern and North African policy is the outcome of a cumbersome process of compromise building between the member states themselves, the Commission and the member states and the Presidency and the Commission, to which occasionally also the European Parliament can add a powerful voice. In addition, this process takes places within institutions which are fundamentally different from both traditional national and international institutions; it is split into two because of the dualism of the system and it takes place on the basis of often rather complex decision-making rules. All this makes it difficult for third countries to adequately assess the full background of a position adopted by the Union and to adequately predict its moves in negotiations and in policy implementation. As a result the Union's partners can easily arrive at false expectations which then lead to frustration and disappointments over the Union's lack of flexibility or unexpected changes of position. The considerable disappointment shown by some of the Union's Mediterranean partners both after Barcelona and Malta is certainly in part due to difficulties in adequately assessing the Union's internal process.

Yet apart from these more general effects the EU's Middle Eastern and North African policy tends also to be affected by some more specific problems relating to its institutional set-up to which we will turn now.

The Case of the Malta Conference

With 15 member states and the European Commission often having different priorities and aims, the definition of a common priority and strategy on a particular international issue is always a cumbersome process within the Union system. Yet it becomes particularly difficult if the system has to act under time pressure because of an international event or an approaching major round of negotiations with third countries. In that case there can be not enough time left for ensuring the necessary compromise building between the member states and adequate interaction between the EC and CFSP structures.

The second Euro-Mediterranean Ministerial Conference in Malta on 15–16 April 1997 can be taken as an example for the constraints this can entail for the EU's Middle Eastern and North African policy. The European Union started early enough with the preparation for the Malta conference with the adoption of a number of reports and statements by Commission, Council and European Parliament.[18] The common tone of this preparatory work was a positive evaluation of the follow-up to the Barcelona conference combined with a number of concrete proposals for the further development of the Barcelona process. Yet this common approach was severely disconcerted following to sharp rise in Arab-Israeli tensions with the start of new Jewish settlements in East Jerusalem in March 1997. Immediately the main actors started to make rather different assessments of the changed situation and the strategy to be followed in view of Malta. The Dutch Presidency took the view, for instance, that it would be possible to convince the Arab side not to raise the issue of the settlements in Malta thereby securing a "normal" proceeding of the conference. France, however, thought this to be impossible and favoured anyway a more pro-Arab reaction on the settlement issue in the run-up to the conference. In the few weeks left the member states within the CFSP framework were not able to arrive at a comprehensive common assessment and strategy for the conference, being hampered both by the consensus rule and the lack of a strategy building institution. In the end the Dutch Presidency had to go to Malta with a

18 See, for instance, EP Doc. A4-27/97 (Sakellariou Report) and COM(97)68 (Progress Report on the Euro-Mediterranean Partnership).

weak mandate which was more concerned about damage limitation than giving a new political impetus.

The Commission had in the meantime prepared a whole package of points in areas such as economic policy rapprochement, environment and exchanges between civil societies on which it wanted to achieve progress at Malta. From the Commission's point of view making progress in these areas was not only necessary for keeping the Barcelona process going but could also form an effective counterweight to the perils the process was facing in the political sphere. Yet the Commission got little support from the member states for this approach, some being anyway not too enthusiastic about the Barcelona process, others taking the view that because of the crisis in the Middle East the Malta conference was by then much more a matter for the member states within the CFSP sphere than for the Commission and EC policies. This had a negative impact on the interaction between Presidency and Commission, and in the end the Commission's agenda was nearly totally left aside during the two days of ministerial debate, and only part of it could be rescued in the following negotiating marathon of the Ad Hoc group in Brussels in May 1997.

Put under the pressures of time and events the Union's dual system therefore failed in Malta to produce and pursue a positive strategy which would have made full use of its instruments in the EC framework.

Problems of Management: The Case of the Implementation of the Euro-Mediterranean Partnership

The broader the scope of an external policy measure of the Union the more the pressure on the institutional system increases. The sheer complexity of the system then adds to the administrative burden, with the result that serious problems of management can result. The implementation of the Euro-Mediterranean Partnership (EMP), certainly one of the most substantial external actions ever adopted by the Union, is an example for these problems.

Although the EMP is formally an intergovernmental process the member states have largely delegated responsibility for the implementation of the Barcelona process to the Commission which, according to the Barcelona Declaration, has to undertake "appropriate preparatory and follow-up work" for the meetings resulting from the Barcelona work programme. This reduces considerably the burden for the national foreign ministries and the Council secretariat, shifting it effectively to the Commission administration. The latter, however, was not prepared for this huge additional task, and needed some time for restructuring its services and for transferring officials from other sections to the units dealing with EMP issues (mainly Directorate A of DG IB). The restructuration was made more difficult by the fact that the Council did not allow for the creation of new administrative posts for the new tasks. Inevitably it came to some shortfalls in the implementation work. One of these was that some of the Mediterranean partners of the European Union failed to receive relevant documents from the Commission in sufficient time before meetings, which attracted considerable criticism.

Yet there are other problems which have emerged. Although the Commission has formal responsibility for all the meetings of the EMP implementation process, this does, of course, not change anything with respect to the internal EU division of competences. As a result, all of the meetings with the Mediterranean partners which are generally chaired by the European Union are chaired either by the Commission or by the Presidency, depending on whether the subject matter of the meeting falls primarily under EC competence or not. This sounds very straightforward. Yet in practice it means not only that the Commission, in spite of its overall responsibility for the follow-up meetings, is not consistently in the chair on the EU side – which increases the necessary internal coordination effort – but also that the EU's partners have to face different institutional actors on the EU side which often follow different practices of organisation and negotiation in meetings.

The implementation of the EMP not only involving a plethora of transversal issues (such as the fight against drugs and organised crime) but also having both a multilateral and bilateral dimension of relations with the Mediterranean partners the Union was aware of the need to simplify its internal decision-making process as much as possible in order to avoid the risk of frequent paralysis. In part it has actually been able to streamline its internal process specifically for the Barcelona process: After a working group has been able to define a common EU position on issues coming up for a sectoral meeting, this position does not go (as usual) to the COREPER but directly to the Euro-Med Committee, the COREPER only coming in in case of major difficulties. Yet the procedural requirements are still difficult enough. In the case of the MEDA programme, the economic and financial core-piece of the EMP, the guidelines for the individual MEDA programmes have to be adopted by the Council, acting by a qualified majority, on a proposal by the Commission. The decisions on financing are under the responsibility of the Commission, but each of its decisions is controlled by a 'management committee' (called 'Med Committee'), whose negative opinion, adopted by a qualified majority, enables the Council to substitute its own measures for those of the Commission. All this means a huge demand on administrative resources, not only at the level of the EU institutions (where at least eight Commission DGs, four Council DGs and several committees and subcommittees of the European Parliament are involved) but also at those of the national foreign ministries (where the 'Barcelona teams' have in some cases grown up to three times their original size).[19] One hidden management cost of the complexity of the system is that with so many institutional actors involved and so much energy absorbed by coordination

---

19 See on this point Edwards/Philippart (1997).

and compromise building in the various bodies, new ideas and approaches are always at risk of being either deprived of most of their substance in the process or even put 'ad acta' at an early stage.

Problems in the Conduct of Negotiations:
The Case of the Association Agreement with Jordan

The division of competences between the Community and the member states makes the conduct of negotiations with third countries a particularly sensitive issue of the EU's foreign affairs system. Even within the CFSP framework member states closely watch every step taken by the Presidency in contacts with third countries. Yet their control and sensitiveness reach its peak when the Commission, which they consider, after all, as not being 'one of us', is acting as the chief negotiator of the Community in matters of EC external economic relations. The procedure provided for by the EC Treaty seems straightforward enough (see above), but this does not exclude serious internal friction with a negative impact on the Union's partners, as the example of the negotiation of the Euro-Mediterranean Association Agreement with Jordan shows.

In the final stage of the negotiations on this Euro-Med Agreement the European Commission conceded to Jordan an automatic re-examination clause on the quota for tomato concentrate. The Agreement was initialled on the occasion of the Malta conference in April 1997, but two weeks later a group of member states headed by Spain severely criticised the Commission for having exceeded its negotiating mandate by granting the revision clause on tomato concentrate. Although an early signing of the Agreement was considered to be politically highly desirable, Spain and the other protesting member states insisted on a reopening of the negotiations with Jordan on this point, a highly unusual step in international relations. The incident was as embarrassing for the Commission as it was for the Union as a whole. The concrete issue at stake was that the automatic revision clause could have set a problematic precedent for ongoing negotiations on other Euro-Med agreements. Yet there was also a point of principle involved because some of the member states wanted to reassert the limits of the Commission's margin to manoeuvre in EC external relations, limits which they felt had been exceeded by the Commission on several occasions during the last few years.

As the Community's chief negotiator in the economic sphere of the EU's Middle Eastern and North African policy, the Commission's role is therefore a difficult and precarious one. It only has a rather narrow margin to manoeuvre, and even minor deviations from the position adopted by the member states in the Council can lead to a clash with the member states and *in extremis* even a disavowal of its negotiating position. As a consequence the Union's Middle Eastern and North African partners, if negotiating with the Commission, have always to take into account that in many respects their partner at the conference table is essentially negotiating on behalf of the EU member states whose common priorities and aims as well as possible concessions for the negotiations can only be secured through a complex process of internal bargaining. This can lead to delays – because the Commission needs to get back to the Council for having changes to its negotiating mandate approved – and occasionally – as the Jordanian government experienced it in the above case – even to unpleasant and embarrassing surprises for the negotiating partners.

Institutional Problems of Financing:
The Cases of EU Funding for the Palestinian Police Force and
of the Financial Cooperation with Turkey

Financial instruments are among the most important instruments the EU system can muster in international relations, and there is no doubt that they play as well an important role in the EU's Middle

Eastern and North African policy. Yet the EU's financial instruments can only be mobilised under the rules of the EC budgetary system, and the institutional constraints resulting from these rules can make it difficult for Council and Commission to implement financial decisions even after these have been formally adopted. Two cases of recent times can serve as prominent examples in this respect:

In April 1994 the Council adopted a Joint Action in support of the Middle East peace process. This action consisted, inter alia, of various measures to support the peace process at the political level, a commitment to the upgrading of Community aid to the Occupied Territories and a contribution to the creation of a Palestinian Police Force. The Community aid to the Occupied Territories, totalling ECU 500 million, could be financed in the framework of an existing Community programme and did not need any CFSP decision on financing. The creation of the Palestinian Police Force however did, and quite urgently, so that a lengthy discussion over a possible sharing of costs between national budgets was excluded. The Community budget being the only viable alternative, the Council, stressing the urgency of measure, decided that ECU 10 million be taken from the EC budget for this purpose.[20] The CFSP operational reserve in the EC budget being far too small and its transfer needing an involvement of the Parliament, the necessary funds were taken from another budget heading. At first the Commission told the Council that the 10 million could not come out of the budget line for aid to the West Bank because the latter was serving different purposes and was, in addition, fully committed. Yet under the pressure of the Council the Commission gave in and used West Bank appropriations for the police force.[21] This led to a furious row with the European Parliament, the second 'arm' of the EC budgetary authority, which –

20 OJ No L 119/1, 7 May 1994.
21 See the acrimonious remarks of MEP Titley on this subject in the EP debate of 27 September 1994; OJ Annex Debates No 4-451/36–37.

although in favour of the measure – felt that this reappropriation of the West Bank funds without involvement of the Parliament was a serious violation of EC budgetary rules and its constitutional position. Angered by similar problems in the case of the financing of the Mostar operation, the Parliament threatened to block funds in the budgetary procedure for 1995 and to refuse discharge to the Commission. It was only in October 1994 that the issue was settled by a compromise under which Council and Commission got the Parliament's approval in exchange for a formal undertaking that this sort of financial operation would be ruled out in the future. The example shows the close limits the EU's institutional system imposes on a flexible use of the EC financial instruments for political purposes.

The other case, although slightly outside of the geographical scope of this contribution, is that of the financial cooperation with Turkey. Following a resolution of 19 September 1996 which condemned Turkey for its continuing human rights problems[22] the European Parliament entered, in the framework of the budgetary procedure, the appropriations for financial cooperation with Turkey for 1997 in the reserve of the EC budget with a clause blocking these until "[...] Turkey honours its international commitments with regard to human rights".[23] In this way the European Parliament effectively instrumentalised its budgetary powers to introduce a major element of political conditionality into the EU's financial cooperation with Turkey which reflected its own foreign policy priorities but was not at all in line with the policy pursued by Council and Commission. As a result a major part of the implementation of EU policy towards Turkey after the establishment of the customs union was blocked. In a similar move the Parliament had effectively frozen the third financial and technical cooperation protocols with Morocco and Syria in 1992.

22   OJ C320/187, 28 October 1996.
23   OJ L44/1122 and 1257, 14 February 1997.

Being deprived of any real influence on policy-making within the CFSP, the European Parliament will always be tempted to use its budgetary powers in the EC framework to assert its own foreign policy priorities. At the national level the bonds and links which exist between a parliamentary majority and a government normally prevent such incidents. Yet these bonds and links do not exist between the European Parliament, the Commission and the Council. As a consequence the EU's Middle Eastern and Northern African policy is inevitably exposed to the possibility of such 'financial irruptions' by the European Parliament in the political process.

Conclusion

The internal institutional constraints of the EU system of foreign affairs clearly have an impact on the EU's Middle Eastern and North African policy and, as it seems, it is a purely negative one: Decision-making is slow, often reduced to the least common denominator of the member states' interests, sometimes even paralysed. The EU's partners have to deal with different interlocutors on different subjects, some of which are subject to the six-monthly rotation of the EU Presidency. As a result there are problems of continuity and consistency on the EU side, and both negotiations with third countries and the implementation of EU policies can be disrupted by internal problems of the Union system. One should bear in mind, however, that all this is part of the price to be paid for making common positions and policies of the Union and its member states on Middle Eastern and North African issues at all possible. Under the present system of division of powers within the Union, which combines the existence of member states sovereign in international relations with strong elements of supranationality, the Union can simply not be expected to act in relations with its Middle Eastern and North African partners like a unitary nation-state. Its partners have to accept that due to its internal institutional constraints the Union has inbuilt limitations to its capacity to act and a considerable potential for blockages in the decision-making and policy implementation process. To accept this can help reduce disappointments due to exaggerated expectations and give greater elasticity to relations between the Union and its Middle Eastern and North African partners.

This is not to say that the Union itself and its partners should be satisfied with the present state of development of the Union's foreign affairs system. The system clearly needs reform and will certainly continue to evolve. Although overall rather disappointing as regards the Union's foreign affairs system, the Treaty of Amsterdam agreed in June 1997 brings some improvements which could have a positive impact on the formulation and implementation of the Union's Middle Eastern and North African policy.[24] The establishment of the new CFSP 'Policy Planning and Early Warning Unit', for instance, could make a useful contribution to the definition of longer term strategies and a quicker assessment of major political changes in the Middle East and North Africa. The creation of the new position of a 'High Representative for the Common Foreign and Security Policy'[25] could introduce a greater degree of continuity in the Union's external representation in the CFSP sphere and provide the Union's Middle Eastern and North African partners with a more permanent interlocutor. All this will depend, however, on the member states making full use of the new possibilities offered by the Treaty which, alas, can never be taken for granted within the European Union system.

24 For an overall assessment of the new Treaty provisions see: Monar (1997: 413–436).
25 Secretary-General of the Council.

List of References

Barbé, Esther 1996: The Barcelona Conference. Launching Pad of a Process, in: Mediterranean Politics, 1/1.

Barbé, Esther/Ferran Izquierdo 1997: Present and Future Joint Actions for the Mediterranean Region, in: Holland, Martin (ed.): Common Foreign and Security Policy. The Record and Reforms, London/ Washington.

Defuyst, Youri 1995: The European Community and the Conclusion of the Uruguay Round, in: Rhodes, Carolyn/Sonia Mazey (eds.): The State of the European Union, Harlow.

Edwards, Geoffrey/Eric Philippart 1997: The Euro-Mediterranean Partnership. Fragmentation and Reconstruction, in: European Foreign Affairs Review, 2/4.

Emiliou, Nicholas 1996: The Allocation of Competence Between the EC and its Member States in the Sphere of External Relations, in: Emiliou, Nicholas/Donald O'Keeffe (eds.): The European Union and World Trade Law, Chichester.

Monar, Jörg 1997: The European Union's Foreign Affairs System After the Treaty of Amsterdam. A 'strengthened capacity for external action'? in: European Foreign Affairs Review, 2/4.

Monar, Jörg 1997: The Finances of the Union's Intergovernmental Pillars. Tortuous Experiments with the Community Budget, in: Journal of Common Market Studies, 35/1.

Monar, Jörg: Das duale System von EG und EPZ/GASP im Test – vorprogrammierte Konfliktszenarien, in: Regelsberger, Elfriede (ed.) 1993: Die Gemeinsame Außen- und Sicherheitspolitik der Europäischen Union, Bonn.

Nuttall, Simon 1997: Two Decades of EPC Performance, in: Regelsberger, Elfriede et al. (eds.): Foreign Policy of the European Union, Boulder/London.

Tietje, Christian 1997: The Concept of Coherence in the Treaty on European Union and the Common Foreign and Security Policy, in: European Foreign Affairs Review, 2/2.

The Critical Dialogue Reconsidered

Trevor Taylor

This contribution seeks to highlight the concept of the political dialogue, as a foreign policy tool which Europe uses frequently to organise its political relations to third countries.[1] The 'critical dialogue' as pursued by Europe with Iran in the 1980s and 1990s serves as a particulary relevant case study which, if analysed thoroughly, should add to the capabilities and sharpening of that instrument.

In practical terms, the political idea of a critical dialogue with Iran dates back to the then German foreign minister Hans Dietrich Genscher in 1980,[2] but the first European Council statement relating to critical dialogue was the 1992 Edinburgh Declaration which read as follows:

---

1 This contribution was presented to the workshop *Instruments of International Politics. Critical Dialogue versus Sanctions*, Frankfurt, October 1996.
2 Taheri, Amir 1996: To Influence Iran's Mullahs, Speak in One Voice, in: International Herald Tribune, 15 August 1996.

"Given Iran's importance in the region, the European Council reaffirms its belief that a dialogue should be maintained with the Iranian Government. This should be a critical dialogue which reflects concerns about Iranian behaviour and calls for improvement in a number of areas, particularly human rights, the death sentence pronounced by a Fatwa of Ayatollah Khomeini against the author Salman Rushdie, which is contrary to international law, and terrorism. Improvement in these areas will be important in determining the extent to which closer relations and confidence can be developed. [..]. The European Council accepts the right of countries to acquire the means to defend themselves, but is concerned that Iran's procurement should not pose a threat to regional stability. [...] In view of the fundamental importance of the Middle East Peace Process, the European Council also expresses the wish that Iran will take a constructive approach here."[3]

This paragraph clearly articulated a number of European concerns, some of which concerned the internal affairs of Iran. The EU was obviously interested in exploring and even having an impact on both the internal and external aspects of Iranian behaviour.

The Concept of Critical Dialogue

This contribution seeks to analyse the general concept of 'critical dialogue' which at the time of writing amidst trans-Atlantic disagreement over a coherent Euro-American strategy was often seen as the essence of EU and in particular German policy towards Iran. The EU critical dialogue has an empirical shape, mainly involving the EU Troika discussions with Iran and bilateral links between EU states and Teheran. This contribution, however, begins from a more ab-

---

3   Text supplied by DG1B of the European Commission.

stract position, exploring what might be expected of a foreign policy
of 'critical dialogue', given the ordinary meanings of the words
involved. This conceptual exploration of critical dialogue serves to
highlight, later in the text, the limited nature of the EU efforts.

The expression 'critical dialogue' suggests a discussion between
two or more entities in which each presents its own positions, along
with positive and negative arguments about the stances of the other.
Because it is designated as a dialogue, in which a statement by one
side generates a related response from the other, there should be a
flow of connected messages rather than a series of assertions.

At least implicit in the terminology, however, are two other
points. The first is that the exchange is taking place between two
entities without one side having a presumed stronger position or
superior standing. Thus an EU critical dialogue with Iran suggests
that Iran is of a similar status to the EU: they are dialogue partners.
The second is that dialogue does not imply any missionary or messi-
anic activity and thus does not appear a threat to either party: the
outcome of the dialogue should not lead to the reluctant conversion
of one to the views of the other. Using Sam Huntington's rather
unambiguous concept of civilisations,[4] a critical dialogue should not
lead to the Westernisation of Iran nor the Islamisation of the EU.
Both these implicit points in the term critical dialogue can be seen as
making the exercise more appealing in principle to Iran by providing
it with status and security.

Understanding, Empathy and Critical Dialogue

An initial and important question concerns the purposes of critical
dialogue: what is it for? In particular is it meant simply to provide better mutual understanding, or more relaxed relations stemming from

4   Huntington (1993 and 1996).

an enhanced readiness to tolerate known clashes of interest, or changed, more convivial behaviour on the part of the target state? The
terms of the Edinburgh Declaration signal that the eventual aim of a
critical dialogue was changed behaviour on the part of Teheran, but
the stress on dialogue rather than any particular threats or promises
suggested that an initial target was improved mutual understanding.

Certainly better mutual understanding can improve human relations. People and governments which do not know each other well
can fear the worst of each other. They can misunderstand or simply
not know what the other is trying to achieve, what its fears are and
so on. Continued contact prevents the dehumanisation of opponents,
and the exchange of information and views provides a framework
for empathy. Mutual, accurate understanding is more difficult if the
two have particularly different ideologies. Of necessity, people
including government officials and leaders, view the world through
some sort of ideological lens which can generate important distortions and full, careful and frank exchanges can help to clarify what
the different parties are really about. Barriers to understanding of
language and culture need to be carefully surmounted. When ideological guidance is rather inflexible, the distortions provided by the
ideological lens can be considerable. Almost 30 years ago, to erode
the fears of the Communists, the Ostpolitik of Chancellor Brandt
had the important purposes of explaining to the Soviet Union what
West Germany was aiming at and of demonstrating that the Communist message about the aggressive intent of capitalism was inaccurate.

Mutual understanding may lubricate improved relations as both
sides perhaps learn to empathise with the others' fears and ambitions. Also what conflict analysts call perceived conflicts may be
avoided or put aside if parties come to appreciate that their real
goals are not incompatible. A useful view of the national interest
denies its objective existence in realist terms and suggests instead
that its concrete form is an intellectual construct formed by thought

and debate within a state.[5] Through the provision of ideas and data from outside, critical dialogue can have an impact on how elites in a target state formulates their sense of national interest.

Critical Dialogue, Diplomacy and Foreign Policy

To assess dialogue per se, as opposed to separate foreign policy activities such as foreign aid which may be associated with it, it is necessary to return to the issue of what critical dialogue is in its essence. There are two competing views to note.

In one perspective, critical dialogue can be seen essentially as a tool of foreign policy intended to secure desired behaviour on the part of the target state. As such it would stand alongside a wide range of other possible foreign policy tools, such as economic sanctions, foreign aid, the threat and use of force, and so on, which are also meant to change the behaviour of the target state.

However, in their established International Relations text, Russett and Starr (1995) usefully distinguish diplomacy from foreign policy, using the words of a British diplomat: "Foreign policy is what you do; diplomacy is how you do it." They give this essence of diplomatic activity:

> "Diplomacy involves direct, government-to-government interactions, acting on the people in other governments who are able to do the things we want their states to do. Thus diplomacy can be considered the central technique of foreign policy implementation, the only truly direct technique. It is an instrument by which other techniques may realise their fullest potential to influence target states."[6]

---

5   Weldes (1996: 275–318).
6   Russett/Starr (1995: 138–9).

Using this second perspective, critical dialogue becomes an aspect of diplomacy rather than a tool of foreign policy. Critical dialogue, then, is part of the mediating element (diplomacy) between a range of foreign policy tools and the target state. I will next explore some of the implications of this second perspective, beginning with the content of critical dialogue and what would make it distinctive from regular, normal diplomatic activity.

The Critical Dialogue Agenda and Dialogue Partners

If mutual understanding is to be achieved, it is necessary that the agenda of the dialogue concern profound subjects including the world views and ideologies of the participants. It is not enough to address the treatment of political prisoners or restrictions on women, it is necessary to consider the whole basis and coverage of human rights. It is not enough to talk about trade, it is necessary to address the fundamentals of capitalism and of Islamic economic systems. It is not enough to discuss the Fatwa on Salman Rushdie, the meaning of sovereignty must be addressed, and so on.

If dialogue needs to be deep, it should also be as wide as the effective political establishment of the target state, i.e. it should involve many politically-relevant groups. Of international relations schools of thought, critical dialogue is clearly more compatible with pluralist rather than neo-realist ideas about foreign policy: regarding China, the US is prudently keen to include discussions with the People's Liberation Army in its discussions because it recognises the Chinese armed forces as a significant political player. Indeed, military to military exchanges are an important element in US policy towards countries, including some in Central Asia, where it feels democracy can be strengthened.[7] A policy of dialogue is unlikely to be effective

7   Perry (1996: 68–70).

unless it includes a clear view of the broad range of groups which need to be brought into discussions if possible. German enthusiasm for talking to representatives of the Iranian secret service has become well known.

In areas where governmental structures are even remotely similar, it may be straightforward to identify the groups to participate in dialogue: the military should talk to the military, parliamentarians to parliamentarians, ministers to ministers, the judiciary to the judiciary and so on. Difficulties arise when there are no obvious counterparts: there are no western equivalents to the religious authorities which are so influential in Iran.

Clearly dialogue between some groups may be more effective and open than between others. The military in many societies often find it easy to exchange views on professional concerns with other soldiers but other social-political groups may be more wary. Those planning and steering critical dialogue need patience and a readiness to enjoy varying degrees of success.

Directors of dialogue also need to take account of the potential role to be played by non-government personnel such as academics, business people, environmental lobbyists and so on. Such groups may have valuable information to disseminate and they may enjoy a different degree of credibility than government representatives. For instance, if a western state is seeking to underline the virtues of liberal democracy, it needs to include those from its own opposition in its presentations. The organisers of a dialogue should have a clear idea of who could usefully participate: if they are keen to promote the virtues of liberal democracy, they should be ready to include on their own side those whose views they may not share and whose expressed opinions they cannot control.

Although dialogue in an optimum condition should be wide, the target state has to be ready to participate and this may mean that consideration of some groups or subjects may have to be postponed until trust levels have been established and both sides have come to recognise the virtues of the dialogue. A related consideration is that the time scale associated with a dialogue should be quite long: a period of several years may be needed before any significant effects can be felt.

A different consideration relating to political structure is that, in cases where governments are completely dominated by a very small number of people, with whom it will not be possible to have sustained and open exchanges, a critical dialogue approach may not be thought feasible. This appeared to be the European stance on Libya for long, but Iran is a very different case: it is run by interlocking factions that dispute, both on ideological and pragmatic grounds, every step of policy at home and abroad.

Finally, directing dialogue towards groups which have an impact on a government may nonetheless be ineffective if the government itself is not in control of all its population. The US has presented some evidence that much terrorist activity is sponsored by wealthy individuals in the US and the Gulf rather than by governments.[8] This clearly raises a whole different series of problems where the need is for more effective government regulation of wealthy people, an issue which may well require considerable intergovernmental cooperation to track financial transactions and so on.

Implicit in the discussion so far is that 'critical dialogue' is an enhanced form of diplomacy and that variants on it can be found, not just in the Middle East, but elsewhere in world politics. The US on occasions indulges in activities similar to critical dialogue, most obviously with regard to China.

The above conceptualisation of critical dialogue suggests that the EU effort with regard to Iran has, at the time of writing, simply not been on a broad or deep enough front. The EU critical dialogue focused on twice-yearly meetings of the Troika with senior representatives of the Iranian foreign ministry with then Foreign Minister

---

8   Terrorism. Much of It Paid for Privately, in: International Herald Tribune, 15 August 1996.

Velayati on occasions being involved. There were also preparatory meetings for these gatherings and diplomatic representatives of the Troika states in Teheran also met and sometimes spoke to the Iranian foreign ministry. EU states fed developments from their bilateral contacts with Iran into European Council discussions about the critical dialogue, and the European Council also provided direction to the Troika representatives before they meet with Iran groups. This suggests that the EU diplomatic representations must have had a rather formal character, which does not fit easily with the free-flowing intellectual activity which might be associated with the term dialogue. It is little wonder that Iranians sometimes complained that the EU representatives frequently lectured their Middle East interlocutors. The content of the discussions with Iran was confidential but was understood to concentrate, not on fundamentals such as sovereignty and the philosophy of human rights which were listed above, but on the actual issues, such as the Fatwa on Salman Rushdie and support for the Arab-Israeli peace process, which dominated the contemporary diplomatic agenda. On many issues there were established Euro-Iranian differences but the opportunity was also taken to explore possible common ground on emerging matters such as Afghanistan and Central Asia.

Leaving aside the limitations of the Troika as a manifestation of EU capabilities, by focusing on the Iranian foreign ministry establishment, the critical dialogue seemed to involve insufficient people who met too infrequently to have much impact on each other's thinking. There were also some discussions among academics, albeit of a rather infrequent and small-scale nature. The rather intermittent contacts with Iran stood in contrast to the wide-ranging and structured contacts with the Warsaw Treaty states which NATO established in 1990 with the North Atlantic Cooperation Council initiative and later with Partnership for Peace. These initiatives brought defence and foreign ministry representatives, the military, parliamentarians, industrialists, scientists and even academics into regular contact with the West.

The Separation and Interaction of Critical Dialogue and Foreign Policy Tools

It is next important to underline that mainstream foreign policy tools, such as government sponsorship of trade with and investment in a target state, constitute a conceptually separate if perhaps complementary matter from critical dialogue. Foreign aid and investment and trade promotion are tools of foreign policy with a different route to influence: in particular they may build structures of interdependence or dependence whose disruption would cause the target state's economy to suffer and whose continued operation brings positive utility to both parties. Moreover diplomatic contact is fully in the hands of governments, although they can ask non-governmental personnel to contribute. In contrast, trade and investment decisions, although perhaps receiving some insurance cover from government guarantees, also involve some risk and benefit assessment from the corporate sector.

However, critical dialogue does have important implications for some specific tools of policy. Support for critical dialogue implies that there is nothing to be gained from isolating a regime diplomatically and even intellectually, indeed it suggests that something may be gained from engaging that regime in vigorous discussion. An opponent of diplomatic isolation is likely to oppose also efforts at economic isolation, despite its being a rather different sort of contact. Thus it could be predicted that EU support for critical dialogue with Iran would be accompanied by opposition to the D'Amato legislation and other American initiatives for trade and economic sanctions against Iran, but there are two different lines of thought at work. The hoped for impact of trade and investment on Iranian behaviour and attitudes involves a quite different route to the impact of critical dialogue.[9] Similarly the reported

---

9 Germany Takes Flak on Iran Policy, in: Defense News, 30 September to 6 October 1996.

German-Iranian intelligence exchanges should be viewed as separate
from, if related to, German readiness to provide intelligence training.

However, the use of mainstream foreign policy tools can make
critical dialogue efforts more effective. If the EU states, as part of the
messages which they tried to get across, argued that the EU had no
hostility towards Islam as such and that market economies bring
prosperity and welfare, those messages would have been reinforced
if the EU simultaneously was providing valued aid to Iran and generating Iranian economic development through trade and investment
based on market principles. Similarly, European assertions of good-
will towards Israel were reinforced by German apparent readiness to
provide Israel with access to Mig 29 technology so that Israel could
develop countermeasures.[10]

Critical Dialogue, Diplomacy and Foreign Policy Influence?

The use of foreign policy tools can thus reinforce critical dialogue.
But how can critical dialogue make the use of foreign policy tools
more effective?

It is helpful to look in basic terms at the roles of diplomats themselves. Diplomats have three central functions relevant to dialogue:
they collect information, they transmit messages and they negotiate.
Critical dialogue is presented here as an enhanced element in the normal diplomatic functions of communication and information collection. Both sides pass messages and so offer information about themselves. To see how critical dialogue relates to the negotiation
function and so influence it, it is necessary to see how influence can
be gained through diplomacy and relate the means of influence to
critical dialogue.

10 Germany's Emerging Role in the Middle East, in: Middle East International, 20
    September 1996: 17–18.

A useful if standard grouping says that a state can be induced to change its behaviour in a desired direction by one or more of three means: the issuing of threats and punishments; the presentation of promises and rewards; and persuasion. Threats and punishments involve commitments or actions which would hurt the target state unless its behaviour changed. Economic sanctions and arms embargoes are not uncommon forms of punishment in the contemporary world when a state behaves badly. Promises and rewards involve commitments or actions which would improve the interests and welfare of the target state if it changes its behaviour in a desired way. The US and its friends hoped that the package of energy aid designed for North Korea in 1994 would mean that Pyongyang abandoned any plans to develop nuclear weapons. Persuasion, a key element here, involves inducing a target government to change its position by providing it with information about the costs, benefits and/or probabilities associated with different courses of action. While it is true that on occasions threats can be disguised as persuasion, in principle they are discrete types of activity.

The skilled negotiator selects threats, punishments, promises and rewards with insight, but may alternatively or additionally seek to persuade by the provision of new information. How does critical dialogue relate to these categories?

Because both states should develop a good understanding of each others' positions, critical dialogue should enable both to make improved threats and punishments, promises and rewards, since each will know accurately what the other side values and fears, and will be able to frame its policies accordingly. With regard to persuasion, critical dialogue offers clear prospects of improved policy effectiveness since a state which has become accustomed to hearing another government speak frankly and accurately on one set of issues should be predisposed to listen carefully to what it has to say on other issues. Critical dialogue should have a confidence-building effect on the attitudes of the target state, leading the target state to believe rather than dismiss what its dialogue partner has to say.

This could be particularly valuable when a state wishes to play a mediating role in a dispute, as Germany did successfully in the summer of 1996 between Israel and the Hizbollah on an exchange of prisoners and combatants' remains.[11] Also, with regard to a state like Iran where groups compete for influence, the information provided may be an indirect source of persuasion, winning particular groups in the target country over to a particular point of view and then providing those groups with the information ammunition with which they in turn can win arguments in that country.

This concept of critical dialogue has implications for its relationship with traditional policy tools such as economic aid or even military sanctions. The most significant is perhaps that critical dialogue, being an activity with a different character from, for instance, economic sanctions, is not incompatible with, or an alternative for, the use of any policy tool. As Ali Massoud Assari has pointed out, the contrasting policy to dialogue is diplomatic isolation: he writes,

"Neither policy is a perfect solution, but [...] even limited and critical communication at an official level is more subtle, flexible and constructive strategy than no communication at all. Given Iran's geopolitical situation, the US policy of isolation not only remains the less constructive of the two strategies, but is an unrealistic option."[12]

In practice, individual governments as they look at the world as a whole are not predisposed to either critical dialogue or sanctions. Any one government may pursue a policy dominated by critical dialogue with one state and a policy underlining economic sanctions with another. In the present international system, the US at the time of writing was persuaded of the benefits of 'constructive' or 'compre-

11 Ibid.
12 Ansari, Ali Massoud 1996: They shall still drink Coke. In defence of Critical Dialogue, in: The World Today, August/September 1996: 209.

hensive engagement' with China and of sanctions against Libya and Iraq. A few years ago, Western states were not unanimous on the issue of whether dialogue or sanctions should be the most prominent element in policy towards apartheid-dominated South Africa.

The issue can be which takes the lead – sanctions or dialogue – because in practice both can theoretically be feasible. As the US showed with Vietnam, a period of dialogue can be needed to bring out that sanctions should indeed be eased or lifted. The US dialogue with Communist China increased in intensity from 1969, but it took until 1973 before formal US-Chinese diplomatic relations were established. Syria's transformation in the US from a pariah regime to one worthy of dialogue was achieved rather quickly because of Damascus' response to the invasion of Kuwait.

Sanctions and dialogue are however incompatible when they have fundamentally different purposes. Through the mechanisms outlined, dialogue will normally be concerned with eventually inducing a target government to moderate and modify its position. Sanctions may also be intended to secure policy amendment, but they can alternatively be directed towards an actual overthrow of a government, as has been the apparent case with Iraq. When a government introducing sanctions is dedicated to overthrowing a target regime, it will maintain only a secondary interest in how that target regime thinks and so will be little interested in dialogue. In the mid-1990s, the US apparently saw the Iranian and Libyan regimes as the major sponsors of terrorism in the world[13] and presumably thus sought their fall. Some US opinions presented relations with Iran as a zero-sum game where the possibility of cooperation for mutual benefit was absent.[14] Many Europeans, while accepting that Iran illegally

13 The Real Threat of Iranian Terrorism, in: The Independent, 20 August 1996.
14 See for instance the reported observation of Peter Rodman, from the Nixon Center for Peace and Freedom in Washington, that "anything that strengthens Iran is a menace to all of us" quoted from: Germany Takes Flak on Iran Policy, in: Defense News, 30 September to 6 October 1996.

pursued and killed its own citizens abroad, and supported terrorist strikes in the Gulf and against Israel, did not share the US zero-sum perspective and saw Iran in particular as often seeking to avoid confrontation with the West. There was a readiness in Europe to heed those who argue that the then Iranian regime in power was neither monolithic nor dogmatic in its Islamism.[15] Europeans believed there are 'moderates' in the Iranian regime whose position can be strengthened by the supply of information. On the other hand, Thomas McNamara, US Assistant Secretary of State for Political Affairs, observed that 'searching for moderates in the Iranian regime is a particularly fruitless exercise'.[16]

This point illuminates a specific source of difference between the EU and the United States on critical dialogue. One European criticism of isolation as a diplomatic approach is that isolation cannot influence a target state behaviour because there is so little contact with it, whereas there is a chance of influence if messages are being exchanged. Thus then German Foreign Minister Klaus Kinkel was quoted as saying, in opposition to the D'Amato legislation: "We think it is more correct to remain in talks with Iran [. . .] to work against the things that Iran is accused of."[17] However, seeking Iran's isolation, the US may not have sought to change Iranian behaviour but to promote the fall of its demonised government.

Against isolation as a route to the overthrow undesired regimes, a credible line of argument asserts that isolated regimes, whether that of Ghaddafi in Libya, Castro in Cuba or the State Law and Order Restoration Council (SLORC) in Burma, actually find it easier to cling on to power because their elites and general populations are denied so much contact without the outside world and their government can blame Western restrictions for their poor economic condi-

---

15 Ansari (1996: 209–211).
16 Germany Takes Flak on Iran Policy, in: Defense News, 30 September to 6 October 1996.
17 The Times, 7 August 1996.

tion.[18] Moreover there is no guarantee that an undesirable government will be replaced by anything more favourable: Islamists have been among Colonel Ghaddafi's more effective opponents in Libya.

Thus, depending on the behaviour of the target state, it may become appropriate to try to continue a dialogue in a condition of stress, even as new sanctions are being imposed, or it may be thought necessary to break off almost all contact if a regime acts in a quite intolerable manner. Then the dialogue initiator may well conclude that it no longer wishes to influence the behaviour of the target government, and instead wants to promote the establishment of a new, more favourable regime.

When and whether to underline dialogue and/or sanctions will be determined by the positions of both the target and the initiating state. The more serious are the offences committed by the target state, the more the initiating state will be drawn towards a stress on sanctions. However, the greater the cost of isolation and sanctions to the initiating state, the more reluctant it will be to endorse them. Sanctions on Iran for Germany would have been very expensive in terms of foregone economic opportunities and of the Iranian debts to Germany of US$ 8.5 billion at the time of writing. These were unlikely to be repaid while the sanctions had been in place. French anxiety to recover at least some of the money owed to it by Iraq is also apparent. Several EU states are major importers of Iranian and Libyan oil and are suppliers of oil industry equipment: sanctions threaten difficult disruptions of this trade.[19] The US was enthusiastic about dialogue with China because economic sanctions would be so expensive and difficult to arrange.

18 Roula Khalaf saying that "[. . .] by isolating a country which already seems to live in its own world and is fed a daily dose of Colonel Qaddafi's quirky theories [. . .], the sanctions have the perverse effect of bolstering the Libyan leader and reinforcing deep resentment of the US. in: Financial Times, 30 October 1996. See also Mortimer, Edward 1996: Positive Contact, in: Financial Times, 23 October 1996.
19 Europeans Pump Up Defiance to New US Sanctions, in: International Herald Tribune, 7 August 1996.

Conclusion

The Western stance in the mid-1990s, in which the EU supported critical dialogue with Iran while the US advocated isolation, probably secured the worst of both worlds. It gave Iranians and others the chance to play the EU off against the US and it meant that no coherent message from the West was delivered. As an exiled Iranian journalist wrote: "One favourite joke in Teheran [. . .] describes critical dialogue as an exercise in which the Europeans invite the mullahs to tea so that they can criticise the Americans together."[20]

It is difficult to point to solid evidence that critical dialogue has facilitated or lubricated changes in Iranian behaviour. As an Iranian critic pointed out, since 1990, more than 100 citizens of six European states have been kidnapped and held hostage in Iran or by Teheran-backed groups in Lebanon. Despite solemn pledges by the Iranian government not to sponsor acts of violence in the European Union, more than 60 Iranian dissidents have been murdered in nine EU nations. A total of 33 Iranian citizens were in jail in seven European countries on charges of terrorism. On the other hand, German diplomacy could claim some credit for securing the release of two German hostages in 1992 who had been held hostage in Lebanon, and of a German engineer in 1994 who had been held in Teheran on spying charges. While critical dialogue and conventional diplomacy were probably the ultimate means by which these changes were secured, there is obviously the possibility rather specific inducements or threats were also made to Iran. It may not have been a matter of Germany simply persuading Teheran that it would be in Iran's interest to release these people. This is the broader context to Abol-Hassan Banisadr's accusation that the Ayatollah Khomeini had signed a death warrant for the Kurdish leader, Sadiq Sharafkindi, who was assassinated with two colleagues in Berlin in

---

20 Taheri, Amir 1996: To Influence Iran's Mullahs, Speak in One Voice, in: International Herald Tribune, 15 August 1996.

1992, and to the German arrest warrant for the head of the Iranian foreign intelligence service, Ali Fallahian, who is such a prominent dialogue partner of Bernd Schmidbauer in the German Chancellor's Office.[21] A basic criticism of the EU critical dialogue with Iran is that it was pursued on such a limited scale and in such an unchallenging way as far as Iranians are concerned. Cynically it might be asked if the EU states were not actually pinning their faith on growing ties of economic interdependence as a means of constraining Iranian behaviour, with critical dialogue providing little more than a fig leaf for their materialist approach.

Cynically it might also be asked whether the few resources devoted to the dialogue did not reflect Iran's limited importance for the Europeans. On the one hand, the EU critical dialogue initiative appears part of a wider feeling, reflected in the Barcelona Conference and French/European efforts to become more involved in the Arab-Israeli peace process, that the Middle East is of vital interest to Western Europeans and that Western policy towards the Middle East should not be completely dominated by the United States. On the other hand, a German former official in DG1B of the European Commission, writing about Europe and the Mediterranean, underlined the centrality of economic development for political relations, emphasised the importance of the Arab world for Europe, noted that Israel, a model performer, will have the closest possible relationship with Europe, and judged that Europeans will not have to be excessively concerned about Turkey because of the human and natural resources which it possessed. He did not mention Iran.[22] While all this is understandable given Iran's lack of a Mediterranean coast and the official's lack of responsibility for Iran, it remains the case that Iran's relative insignificance is implicit in the arguments he offers about the importance of the EU's Arab relations.

21 Helmut Kohl's Spooky Fixer, in: Economist, 27 July 1996.
22 Rhein (1996: 79–87).

List of References

Huntington, Samuel 1993: The Coming Clash of Civilisations?, in: Foreign Affairs, 72/3.

Huntington, Samuel 1996: The West: Unique, Not Universal, in: Foreign Affairs, 75/6.

Perry, William 1996: Defense in an Age of Hope, in: Foreign Affairs 75/6.

Rhein, Eberhard 1996: Europe and the Mediterranean. A Newly Emerging Geopolitical Area?, in: European Foreign Affairs Review, 1/1.

Russett, Bruce/Harvey Starr 1995: World Politics. The Menu for Choice, New York.

Weldes, Jutta 1996: Constructing National Interests, in: European Journal of International Relations, 2/3.

US Policy of Sanctions: Prospects for Revision

Phebe Marr

In the 1990s Europe and the US have favoured different policy approaches towards Iran, Iraq, Sudan, and Libya.[1] While the US and Europe may differ over policy approaches toward the countries under discussion, they do not differ over goals and ultimate objectives. Both regarded the four countries in question as potentially destabilizing elements in their region; engaging in behaviour to a greater or lesser degree, unacceptable by international norms. This behaviour ranges in seriousness from military aggression against neighbors (Iraq) to domestic subversion of regimes of which they do not approve (Iran, Iraq, Sudan), to support of terrorism (all four). Their human rights records range from poor to abysmal. Both Europe and the US would like to see, at a minimum, a change of behaviour by these regimes, and many would also welcome a replacement

---

1   This contribution was presented to the workshop *Instruments of International Politics. Critical Dialogue versus Sanctions*, Frankfurt, October 1996.

of the regimes in the unlikely event this could be accomplished with little disturbance.

The US-European differences hinge on two issues:

First, they disagree over assessments of the nature of the regimes in each of these countries; the degree of threat they pose, and the potential for change within each regime. In general, the US policy community is more sceptical of the willingness of regimes to change behaviour. They see either little evidence of change on issues of concern (Libya, Sudan) or slow and reluctant change which has had to be compelled by forceful measures over a long period of time (Iraq). Gradual change in Iran after the election of President Khatemi has been seen as positive and has been met with some policy modifications. Hence the US has been more concerned over the short- and long-term threat posed by all four countries and rated it higher than do Europeans. The US has been more insistent on serious changes in behaviour, and unwilling to accept cosmetic or merely tactical changes. Because of its global leadership position, the US has also used sanctions to demonstrate firmness, and to send a political message to states other than the target state. Europeans have regarded these states and their regimes as weaker and more inclined to respond to traditional diplomatic and economic incentives than has the US. Europeans have appeared more sanguine about the prospects for change over the long term under current regimes and more willing to ride out the short-term difficulties while waiting for the evolution. They tend to put the emphasis on economic development and a strengthening of the middle class as the route to change.[2]

---

2   Underlying this "assessment" gap is a philosophic difference which is not confined to either side of the Atlantic. In a perceptive article on the differences between those who favour persuasion (Oxygen) and those who prefer dissuasion (asphyxiation), Franklin Lavin claims that the latter are Wilsonians who are inherently pessimists, viewing the international situation as a series of problems in need of correction. The former, exemplified by the business community, are optimists who view problems as capable of amelioration by economic growth (Lavin 1996: 152).

Second, as a result of these assessments, Europe and the US have differed over policy prescriptions. Europe has been more willing to hold out a 'carrot' (engagement, dialogue), in an attempt to shift the domestic balance in favour of 'moderates' (Iran) or to provide inducements for change. The US has generally been sceptical about the efficacy of such inducements, and more willing to adopt punitive measures and coercive diplomacy (sanctions, military actions) that compelled states to make a choice between behaviour options, and put a price on undesirable behaviour.

Underlying the different approaches, and fundamental to them, is a third factor: the different geostrategic positions of Europe and the US and the divergent roles played by them. While the US may be a reluctant superpower, it is now the only one. Much of US policy is driven by security concerns derived from this role and its function as the chief 'policeman' in the Gulf, and to a lesser extent, in the Mediterranean. The US military is the only one with the size and reach capable of performing this role, although it gets support from its allies. The US does not want to fight another war in this region and is focused on deterring conflict and preventing proliferation of weapons of mass destruction (WMD), and a buildup of conventional offensive weapons. Sanctions are seen as a robust 'containment' policy that reduces revenues for expenditures on weapons procurement.

Europe cannot match the US military posture. Rather its primary relationship with the region is commercial. Europe is more dependent on Gulf and Libyan oil than the US, and it exports more to the region to pay for the oil. In 1992, for example, almost 4 million barrels/day of Middle East oil was exported to Europe, 25 percent of all the region's production. Germany alone exported goods worth almost US$ 20 billion to the Middle East, about equal to the US. The French, Italian and British added US$ 14, US$ 13.5 and US$ 10.6 billion to that figure. Libya directs most of its oil exports to Europe.[3] This is not to

---

3   Wilson (1994: 269).

claim that the US, particularly under the Clinton administration, is uninterested in trade. The US unquestionably reaped commercial advantages from the Gulf War, a factor contributing to some tension with Europe, particularly in the highly competitive market of the Gulf, where two large markets, Iran and Iraq, are restricted by US and UN sanctions policy. But it does mean that an asymmetrical division of labor has arisen between the US and Europe. The US provides most of the military capacity for regional deterrence; the Europeans are the region's major trading partner. It is not simply that Europe must pay more attention to commercial interests; it looks on trade and economic leverage as a means of achieving its goals because that is essentially the only one open to it. The US, by contrast, has an array of options, including the military, and with its large and diverse economy, is better situated to take a harder line on sanctions.

Aims and Goals of US Policy

The US has multiple aims in applying sanctions to the states under discussion, and while they may overlap, they differ in emphasis from state to state. Hufbauer, Schott and Elliot (hereinafter HSE)[4], have suggested a typology of motives for applying sanctions. Rather than adhering to these, I prefer three broader headings, under which the HSE goals can be subsumed.

The first is a change of behaviour on key issues of importance to the US and/or compliance with internationally recognized norms of behaviour. In the case of Iraq, the changes sought are comprehensive and fundamental, and they are set forth in the UN resolutions adopted at the conclusion of the Gulf War, especially those relating

---

4   Hufbauer/Schott/Elliot (1990: chapter 3). These goals are: modest changes in target country policies; major changes in target country policies; disruption of a military campaign; impairing the military potential of a target country; and destabilizing the target country government.

to United Nations Security Council Resolutions (UNSCRs) 687 and 688. In the case of Iran, the US seeks a change of behaviour in clearly specified areas: an end to engagement in and support of terrorism, active opposition to the peace process, and pursuit of weapons of mass destruction, especially nuclear weapons. In Libya, the US has sought relinquishment of two Libyans indicted for complicity in the Pan Am bombing over Lockerbie, since complied with. Beyond this, however, sanctions have been more broadly designed to end Libya's support for international terrorism and its regional adventurism. Sanctions on Sudan have been meant to change a 'pattern of support for terrorism', although the US wants also to see an improvement in Sudan's human rights behaviour, particularly as it affects the civil war in the south, and attempts to destabilize neighbours.

A second set of motives can be subsumed under the heading of containment, that is, deterring aggression and weakening or, in the HSE phrase, 'impairing the military capacity' of target governments. In three of the four countries (Iraq, Iran, Libya), the US is concerned with the acquisition of WMD or expansion of already existing programs. Trade restrictions and constraints on investment and revenues are seen as a means of reducing the income of target states available for expenditure on arms and forcing a choice between 'guns' and 'butter'.

A third US policy aim in selected cases has been the replacement or destabilization of target governments. While the US might prefer a replacement of all four governments, this is not the explicit aim of any of the sanctions regimes. Only in the case of Iraq has the desire for a change of regime been made an explicit policy aim. Although this goal may be difficult and distant, the US is now supporting opposition groups inside and outside Iraq committed to replacing the regime. In 1998, Congress passed the Iraq Liberation Act, which appropriated funds for training, arming and otherwise supporting Iraqi opposition groups and President Clinton has signed the bill into law. However, such funds as have been spent on the opposition have been directed at non-lethal materials and civilian activities. Meanwhile, the US has specified that it "[. . .] will work to maintain [sanctions] until the Iraqi regime complies fully with all UN resolutions [. . .]".[5] Removal of the regime in Iran was never an official goal of sanctions or of US policy despite efforts by some in Congress to make it one. On the other hand there has been little interest in strengthening a regime seen as increasingly weak and in economic trouble. Since the election of Khatemi in 1997 and domestic changes in Iran, the US has moved to establish unofficial cultural exchanges with Iranians and openly called for a dialogue. In Libya, the US had made some effort to destabilize the regime, but the aim of the sanctions regime has been more limited. In Sudan, despite reports that the US began some movement in this direction by providing support to neighbouring governments who sought to undermine the Sudanese government, the State Department has denied this claim. In the offi-

---

5 Statement by Robert Pelletreau, Assistant Secretary of State for Near East and South Asia, before the House International Relations Committee, 25 September 1996. Elsewhere the administration has stated that the US would "use our veto to prevent any premature lifting of sanctions", although the US does not think that will be necessary. (Pelletreau, Robert 1995: Questions and Answers for the Record, submitted by Representative Lee Hamilton, House International Relations Committee, 6 April). Other statements indicate that the US will hinge this reservation on Iraq "demonstrating that it is no longer a threat to international peace and security. (Department of State, Economic Bureau, Press Guidance, 9 September 1996). In a 1995 statement to Congress, President Clinton laid out US conditions which would allow removal of sanctions. "I continue to be determined to see Iraq comply fully with all its obligations under the UNSC resolutions. I will oppose any relaxation of sanctions until Iraq demonstrates its over all compliance with the relevant resolutions. Iraq should adopt democratic processes, respect human rights, treat its people equitably and adhere to basic norms of international behavior." (cited in testimony by Madeleine Albright to the Subcommittee on Near East South Asian Affairs, Senate Foreign Relations Committee, 3 August 1995). In December 1999, this policy was affirmed by Thomas Pickering, Under Secretary of State for Political Affairs, at a State Department Foreign Policy Forum. He claimed that sanctions were in place because Saddam Hussein had not complied with UN resolutions.

cial view, the US aim has been to support neighbouring governments being destabilized by Sudan.[6]

There may be some logical contradictions in attempting to achieve all three aims at once. If compliance with UN resolutions or a change of behaviour is the main goal, it may be more difficult to accomplish if the target government feels the real goal is its replacement. On the other hand, if a mere change of policy is the goal, this implies a willingness to live with the 'changed' regime. Iraq is the case where the US may have to face this contradiction at some time in the future if a majority of UNSC members deem that Iraq has met Chapter 22 requirements and vote to lift the oil embargo. It is not clear that the US is yet ready to accept this logic. In practice, however, the US does not see a contradiction. Rather, it views its aims as ranging from minimal to maximum, with destabilization a tool to achieve all three.

While the Iraqi case is unique in some respects, it does illustrate a phenomenon in US sanctions policy that applies to other cases as well. Iraq's intransigence, and slowness to comply, has reinforced intransigence in Washington. While Washington's original expectations on compliance (and regime replacement) may have been reduced over time, so, too, is its willingness to change its own position. In Libya and Iran, the US has seen some change. As new, more moderate leadership has emerged in Tehran through successive elections, Iran has undertaken domestic reforms and moderated its rhetoric. It has also altered some of its international behaviour (for

6 In a Washington Post article, 10 November 1996, David Ottoway claimed that "the US government is about to send military aid to three African countries collaborating to help overthrow the militant Islamic regime in Sudan [. . .]" (Ottoway, David 1996: Wielding Aid, US Targets Sudan. Washington Post, 10 November). The State Department issued press guidance on 12 November 1996 claiming that "the article is correct in supplying some information on our non-lethal, defensive military assistance program to Ethiopia, Eritrea and Uganda. However, it draws some wrong conclusions on US policy toward Sudan". The statement flatly denied the US sought to overthrow the Sudanese regime. Rather, the aid to the three countries was "to assist them in countering Sudanese sponsored aggression." (Africa Bureau, Department of State, Press Guidance, 12 November 1996).

example, with respect to destabilizing Arab Gulf states). The US has responded with modest policy steps – moderating its rhetoric, encouraging cultural exchanges and indicating its readiness for a dialogue. The US still has serious concerns over Iranian behaviour, especially on weapons of mass destruction and its active opposition to the peace process. While US trade sanctions remain in effect, there were some steps toward easing trade in 1999 when the US permitted grain sales to Iran and in 2000 when the import ban was eased on Iranian pistachios, caviar and carpets. In Libya, the regime has finally surrendered the two suspects in the Lockerbie case for trial in the Netherlands under Scots legal principles. As a result, UN sanctions have been suspended, and there have been some moves toward normalization by some European countries. The US, however, continues its own unilateral sanctions on Libya, pending the trial's outcome and acceptable compensation for the Lockerbie victims.

Application of US Sanctions

Iraq

US policy on sanctions toward Iraq has drawn heavily on lessons learned from the pre-Gulf War experience. In the decade before Iraq's invasion of Kuwait, the US followed a cautious policy of 'carrot' and 'stick'. In 1982, after expelling Abu Nidal, Iraq was taken off the terrorist list, the only country to achieve this distinction, and was eligible for loans; in 1984, diplomatic relations, broken in 1967, were restored and the US began a policy of engagement. The US also concluded a trade agreement with Iraq, approved sales of some dual use items, and gave a green light to allies to sell arms to Iraq.[7] The US 'tilt' toward

---

7   Day, Evin 1992: Economic Sanctions Imposed by the United States Against Specific Countries 1979 through 1992, CRS Report to Congress, Washington, DC, 10 August.

Iraq in the Iran-Iraq war is well known. In the aftermath of the war, relations began to deteriorate and they became a subject of bitter partisan debate between a Democratic Congress and a Republican administration, as the spotlight was increasingly thrown on Iraq's treatment of the Kurds, its use of chemical weapons during and after the war, evidence of a developing nuclear program, and the misuse of US loan funds. But the policy was slow to change. Iraq's invasion of Kuwait took the US by surprise, and the administration subsequently paid a price in attacks from the opposition. As a result, the 'carrot' and 'stick' policy has been deemed a major policy failure, one that took a costly war to undo. Moreover, it has taken a heavy career toll on some of those involved, who have been blamed for having seen a 'change of behaviour' where there was none. Few in Washington are willing to make the same mistake again, whether in Iraq or elsewhere.

The sanctions regime on Iraq has been unique in its comprehensiveness and severity. It included an embargo on Iraq's oil exports; a freezing of its assets abroad, and export sanctions on all but food, medicine and life sustaining goods. These sanctions were imposed by the UN immediately after Iraq's invasion of Kuwait, in an effort to compel withdrawal. They failed to accomplish this purpose, but did achieve several other purposes. They helped convince waverers in the US Congress of the need for military action, and they allowed time to achieve a remarkable international coalition and to prepare for war. These sanctions were retained in the postwar period, although their effect on the population was subsequently mitigated by resolutions allowing limited oil exports for humanitarian imports. The most important provisions of the sanctions regime were embedded in UN resolutions, most importantly the cease fire resolution 687 (which falls under Chapter VII of the UN charter permitting military enforcement). This resolution included the key provision, under chapter 22, specifying that when Iraq's WMD and long-range delivery systems are dismantled, the oil embargo should be lifted. UN resolution 688 specifies that Iraq should cease repression of its people, and interference with humanitarian efforts. Under these resolutions, 'No Fly Zones' were imposed north of the 360 [parallel] and south of the 320 [parallel], the latter then extended to the 330.[8] Some easing of these sanctions for humanitarian purposes was then put into operation. Resolution 986 at first allowed for US$ 1 billion of oil to be sold over three months, renewable for a second three months, and in subsequent years it was expanded to allow more oil exports and a greater diversity of imports. These easements were accompanied by restrictions to assure that the benefits flow to the population, including an escrow account for the oil revenues; monitoring of purchases, and over 200 monitors to assure that the goods are appropriately distributed.[9]

US support for Resolution 986 and its subsequent expansion represents the way in which the US is willing to ease sanctions. Because of Saddam's intransigence and deception, distrust of him in official circles in Washington is greater than it was at the onset of the Gulf War. While the US has invested some resources in destabilization efforts, these have not been major nor been successful. The US considers that sanctions are contributing modestly to that aim. While they are surely weakening society more than the regime, problems of inflation, dwindling resources for distribution among his followers, isolation, and discredit brought about by the regime's conduct, as measured by defections and repeated, though unsuccessful plots to unseat him, all indicate some toll is being taken on the regime as well. However, the US considers that sanctions have made a major contribution to such

---

8   In addition, under 688 a safe haven was created for Kurds in the north of Iraq, monitored by a small Military Coordination Committee, consisting of US, British, French and Turkish forces, recently withdrawn. Saddam later withdrew his forces from a much larger exclusionary zone leaving the Kurds in control of this region. In the south, UNSC resolution 949, passed in October 1994, after Saddam Hussein massed his troops on the Kuwait border, has been interpreted by the US and British as establishing a "no drive zone" south of the 32o from which Republican Guard units are prohibited. See Katzman, Kenneth 1996: Iraqi Compliance with Cease Fire Agreements, CRS Issue Brief, Washington, DC, 31 October: 8.
9   Ibid. Katzman (1996: 8).

compliance with UN resolutions, although compliance, almost ten years after the war, is still not complete. Sanctions have also weakened Saddam's military and greatly reduced his potential for acquiring WMD, although the removal of inspections teams in December 1998 has probably set back this compliance. His military, although still formidable by regional standards, has gradually suffered from attrition. It has no access to high tech equipment. Lack of spare parts is eroding readiness and capacity for extended campaigns and morale is poor as evidenced by numerous defections. In the US there have been sporatic discussions of a need to review Iraqi policy, but there little evidence as yet that either the administration or Congress would favour – even countenance – a full removal of sanctions while Saddam was in power. Rather, the US is more likely to consider continued expansions of UN Resolution 986 ("Oil-for-Food") as the vehicle for easing sanctions, allowing more oil to be sold over time, but maintaining the some constraints on imports sales and their distribution. Indeed, as of December 1999, the ceiling on oil exports had been lifted and a wider array of imports allowed, beyond food and medicine. However, the Iraqi government has not been allowed to take direct control over its oil revenue, and the UN sanctions committee continues to review Iraqi purchasing contracts to make sure proscribed items are not imported.

Iran

US sanctions on Iran date from the 1979 revolution and the hostage crisis, when diplomatic relations were broken.[10] While many of

10 These included halting military spare parts shipments (8 November 1979); a ban on imports of crude oil (12 November); freezing Iranian assets in the US (14 November); a ban on all US exports (8 April 1980); an embargo on all Iranian imports (7 April 1980), and restricted US travel to Iran (7 April 1980). See Katzman, Kenneth 1994: Iran. US Containment Policy, CRS Report for Congress, 11 August, Washington, DC: 8.

these restrictions were relaxed after January 1981 when the hostage release took place, relations with Iran never recuperated and a number of restrictions were reimposed. The chief motive for sanctions was the US desire to curb or eliminate Iran's support of terrorism. Based on evidence of Iranian involvement in the October 1983 bombing of the US marine barracks in Lebanon, Iran was designated a state sponsor of terrorism, which disqualified Iran for foreign aid, sales of munitions and export/import bank credits. But in the US view, these did not curb Iranian support for terrorism, which continued in Lebanon, in Europe, in Latin America and elsewhere.[11] In particular, Iranian efforts to derail the peace process, a major US foreign policy priority, was a concern. This issue was brought into focus early in 1995 when Palestinian terrorist attacks, some from Iranian supported groups, were blamed for the failure of the Labour government to win re-election and the subsequent slowing of the peace process. A second motive was to prevent Iran from acquiring a nuclear capacity and to limit its development of other WMD and delivery systems. This issue, too, caught the attention of policy makers in 1995 when Iran conducted simultaneous negotiations with Russia and China for nuclear cooperation. The US was also concerned over Iran's buildup of missiles in the Persian Gulf and its militarisation of the island of Abu Musa shared with the United Arab Emirates. This buildup gave Iran the potential for harassing Gulf shipping.

---

11 In the US view, Iran is the primary patron of the Lebanese shi'ah militia, Hizballah, responsible for rocket attacks on northern Israel and on the Israeli supported SLA forces in south Lebanon. They have linked Iran to Hizballah's 17 March 1992 bombing of the Israeli Embassy in Buenos Aires. The Iranians have also been involved in the killing of dissidents abroad, most notably the Mykanos case in Germany. There were numerous reports that Iran is funding and training Hamas and the Palestinian Islamic Jihad (PIJ) on the West Bank and Gaza responsible for terrorist attacks in Israel. In 1996, Secretary of State Christopher stated that Iran provided up to US$ 100 million a year to Hizballah and several million a year to Palestinian groups opposed to the peace process, including Hamas and the PIJ. See ibid. Katzman (1996: 6–7.) This support, especially for Hizballah, appears to continue to the present.

To constrain Iran, the US initially focused on trade controls. In October 1987, following Iranian attacks on Gulf shipping during the Iran-Iraq war, the US embargoed imports from Iran and banned exports of military goods and dual use chemicals. These restrictions did not prevent US companies from trading in oil and other goods outside the US. By the early 1990s, the US had become a major trading partner of Iran. In 1992, exports reached a peak of US$ 748 million and by 1994, US companies bought 25 per cent of Iran's oil for sale overseas. In return, the US exported oil drilling equipment, spare parts and food.

This trend, however, was dramatically reversed in 1995 by a series of events, some initiated in Iran and some driven by domestic politics in the US. Early in 1995, both Russia and China conducted simultaneous negotiations with Iran for construction of nuclear power stations. The Russian deal included a gas centrifuge. Despite the fact that the deal fell within the Non-Proliferation Treaty (NPT) controls, the US was convinced that Iran was following the previous Iraqi path to a nuclear weapon. In March 1995, Iran further outraged US officials by publicly supporting terrorism in Israel. When Palestinian suicide bombers killed 59 Israelis, Husain Shaikolislam, a Foreign Ministry official, met with leaders of Hamas and the Palestinian Islamic Jihad, announced the collapse of the peace process and supported the action.[12] In addition, the Oklahoma bombing at about the same time, made 'terrorism' a 'hot button' issue in Washington. Both the WMD and the terrorist issue were of concern to Israel, and pro-Israeli interest groups (some of them pro-Likud) took up the issue. Partisan politics added fuel to the fire. In February 1995, House Speaker Newt Gingrich called for the removal of the regime. Pressure for taking action on Iran came to a peak in March 1995 when Tehran concluded a deal with Conoco to develop two offshore fields. The timing could not have been more unfortunate. Europeans,

12 Gerges (1996–1997: 7).

especially German Chancellor Helmut Kohl, had raised the issue of US trade with Iran while criticizing European trade and credits. Both the Republican dominated Congress and pro-Israeli groups now advocated firm action on Iran. Senator D'Amato introduced two bills in the Senate; one prohibiting US companies and their subsidiaries from doing business in Iran and the other imposing sanctions on foreign companies that were doing so. To head off further opposition, President Clinton, in May 1995, issued an executive order barring US persons and companies from financing or managing development of Iranian oil resources. This prompted Conoco to withdraw its offer, and in July, the French firm, Total, filled the gap. On May, after a review of policy, the administration announced a ban on all trade and investment with Iran. In September, D'Amato introduced the bill designed to penalize foreign companies, like Total, that were helping Iran. Negotiations with the administration finally led to a scaled-back version of the bill sanctioning foreign investment in Iran's oil and gas industry. The final version (signed into law in August 1996) penalized foreign companies that invested US$ 40 million or more in Iran's oil industry requiring the president to take at least two actions against such companies, ranging in severity from denial of export/import bank loans to a prohibition of imports from the sanctioned firm. It was this law which put the US policy into such sharp contradictions with Europeans and other trading partners.[13]

In sum, then, as with Iraq, US sanctions on Iran were designed to change behaviour (on terrorism/the peace process/WMD) and to contain its military buildup. In the US view, while there was no immediate change of behaviour, sanctions marginally hurt an already

13 This account has been drawn from Gerges (1996-1997: 7); Herzig, Edmund 1995: US Sanctions on Iran and their Effects, unpublished paper, RIIA Conference on The Politics of Sanctions, November; and Katzman (1996: 12–13). For an excellent account of the major differences in US and European approaches to this subject, see Clawson (1995).

weak economy, and contributed to a scaled-back armaments procurement program. An extremely ambitious 1989 plan to acquire a range of weapons had to be cut, at least in half. Since that time, there have been some significant domestic changes in Iran: the election in May 1997 of a moderate cleric, Ali Muhammad Khatemi, as President; continuous pressures from below for a more open society; a rapprochement with Arab Gulf countries, and official statements favouring some opening to the West. The US has responded with modest steps toward relaxing tensions. While it has not annulled unilateral sanctions legislation, including the Iran-Libya Sanctions Act, (ILSA) neither has the legislation been enforced. ILSA is due to expire in August 2001, and if Iran's domestic and foreign policy continues on its present course, the legislation may well be allowed to die a natural death. Meanwhile, a little trade has been permitted between the two countries.

Libya

The US has had a stormy history with Libya since the overthrow of the monarchy in 1969. Beginning in 1973, the US introduced a series of over 20 sanctions on Libya that banned a wide variety of activities, including transfers of weapons, foreign aid, importing Libyan oil, engaging in trade, and export/import loans. These were placed on Libya primarily because of Libya's involvement in terrorist activities. Libya was accused of providing financial or material support for a number of revolutionary groups; carrying out assassination of opponents abroad, and offering a US$ 1 million award for the assassination of Egyptian President Sadat. In December 1979, the US embassy in Tripoli was attacked and burned by government sanctioned mob violence. In 1979, Libya was put on the US terrorist list, and thereby denied aid, arms sales and loans. This was followed by a ban on US travel to Libya.

In December 1985, in near simultaneous terrorist attacks against airports in Rome and Vienna, 25 civilians, including 5 Americans were killed. The US asserted direct Libyan involvement. As a result, in January 1986, all trade with Libya was banned and its assets in the US frozen. Even more serious was the April 1986 bomb explosion in a West Berlin night club, injuring 204 people and killing three, including two US army sergeants. The US accused Libya and on 15 April, US aircraft bombed targets in Libya, killing a number of people, including Ghaddafi's infant daughter.[14]

Current US policy toward Libya centers on the same two issues as it did for Iran: terrorism and acquisition of WMD. On 21 December 1988, a Pan Am jet exploded over Lockerbie, killing all 244 passengers, 15 crew, and 11 more people on the ground. The US indicted two Libyan intelligence officers, and took the lead in securing three UN resolutions on these bombings.[15] They called for surrender of the two Libyans for trial in the US and United Kingdom, cooperation with the US, Britain and France in investigating the Pan Am and UTA bombings, severing ties to terrorism, and compensation for the victims families. UN sanctions imposed a ban on flights to and from Libya, an embargo on military equipment and support, and a limited assets freeze. However, other Western states were unwilling to join the US in an economic blockade on Libya, mainly because of their economic dependence on Libya. Libya supplied some 51 per cent of Italy's energy needs; 13 per cent of Germany's, and 5 per cent of France's.[16] Until the end of the 1990s, Libya refused compliance while suggesting alternative solutions. In 1999, Libya announced its willingness to deliver the two suspects for trial in the Netherlands

---

14 Mark, Clyde 1996: Libya. CRS Issue Brief. (CRS, Washington, DC) 1 November: 4–5; Day (1992); Joffé, George 1995: Libya. Unpublished paper for the conference *The Politics of Sanctions*, RIIA, London, November.
15 France also wanted to try these two men and four others for the explosion of a French UTA aircraft, over Niger in 1989 that killed 171.
16 Ibid. Joffé (1995: 3).

under a presumed "understanding" that no accusations would be made of any complicity in the bombing higher up the political ladder. As of writing, the trial is underway and UN sanctions have been suspended. However, unilateral US sanctions have remained and are likely to continue until acceptable compensation has been made to the Pan Am victims and Libya proves it is serious in opposing terrorism. This is likely to be difficult.

The second motive behind US policy is to curtail Libya's WMD effort. In March 1990, the US and Germany accused Libya of building a chemical weapon's center at Rabta, (subsequently destroyed by fire) and in February 1993, the US said Libya was building another one at Tarhunah. Libya seemed to be also attempting to secure a nuclear weapon. In a statement in April 1996, then Secretary of Defense, William Perry, implied, in a public statement, that the US would consider military action to remove the Tarhunah facility.[17] Among the US sanctions on Libya are those that ban transference of conventional weapons and an embargo on chemical and biological exports. The US has been desirous of expanding and tightening sanctions against Libya and getting more cooperation from Europeans on this. The US has a small, but very vocal domestic lobby interested in this case in the form of victims' families. These have organized and succeeded in keeping the issue alive. At the time the D'Amato legislation was being passed, this group successfully lobbied the Senate to include Libya in the bill sanctioning foreign companies. This legislation remains.

Sudan

In Sudan, US sanctions have been a relatively new phenomenon, although relations have been on a downward trend for some time, and have worsened as the decade of the 90s ended. Sudan was once

17 Ibid. Mark (1996: 4).

the largest sub-Saharan recipient of US aid, but then received only US humanitarian assistance. Other aid was terminated for several reasons: Sudan's arrearages on its debt; its links to terrorist activities; its on-going civil war; its human rights violations, and deepening disagreement over political philosophy.[18] The chief cause for the imposition of the sanctions has been Sudan's support for terrorism. After an 180-day review, the State Department announced in August 1993, that it was placing Sudan on the list of countries sponsoring terrorism. The US claimed Sudan had been allowing its country to be used as a sanctuary for terrorists, including Abu Nidal, Hamas, Hizballah, and the Egyptian Islamic Group. A member of Sudan's mission to the UN was named as an intermediary in the conspiracy trial of Shaikh Omar Abd al-Rahman in New York for plotting to blow up the UN headquarters and other facilities in New York, and was expelled. The US was most concerned about Sudan's support for attempts to destabilize Egypt and to spread radical Islam across borders. In June 1995 an attempt to assassinate President Husni Mubarak in Ethiopia resulted in the perpetrators fleeing to Sudan. Sudan denied any involvement in that episode but it supported and harboured the violent Islamic Group responsible for the act.

Although US officials claim that US policy was to "[. . .] isolate, pressure and contain Sudan and to compel it to modify its behavior [. . .]"[19] press reports claimed that the US was sending military aid to three African countries attempting to overthrow the Sudanese regime. All three supported Sudanese groups operating in the south in the continuing civil war. The US government has denied this aim, claiming that the military equipment was to assist the three countries in countering Sudanese sponsored aggression. The government of Sudan has provided direct support to Eritrean and Ugandan opposi-

---

18 Epstein, Susan 1995: Sudan: Civil War, Famine, and Islamic Fundamentalism, CRS
    Issue Brief, Washington, DC: 1.
19 Ottoway (1996).

tion movements: the Eritrean Islamic Jihad and the Ugandan West Nile Bank Front and the Lord's Resistance Army. Sudan also provides haven for some Ethiopian and Egyptian opposition groups.[20]

As a result of being placed on the terrorist list, Sudan cannot receive development or military assistance or loans. This is a moot point since the US ceased supplying aid since 1991, and since November 1992 there has been a ban on US commercial exports to Sudan. As a result of a worsening human rights record and brutality in prosecuting its civil war with the south, additional sanctions were imposed on Sudan in November 1997 by executive order. These blocked Sudanese assets in the US, banned bank loans and trade with Sudan and prohibited US investment in Sudan's oil industry. US trade with Sudan amounted to about US$ 4 million.

Sanctions and the Role of the Domestic US Environment

In addition to these foreign policy issues, domestic factors drive US sanctions policy, perhaps increasingly so. Some of the difference between the European approach and the American can be attributed to differences in political style, philosophy of government and even institutional arrangements, as well as the emergence of new political actors in Washington. But more is to be attributed to public opinion, particularly as it is crystallized by organized interest groups.

Satisfaction of Domestic Interests Groups

Domestic interest groups have played some role in encouraging sanctions legislation in all four cases. Compared to Europe their influence was probably greater in the US system: with power diffused between

20 African Bureau, Department of State, Press Guidance, 12 November 1996.

the executive and legislative branches (and increasingly shifting to the latter); with increased influence of the media on policy and greater availability of access to it; and with a shift of power from government to non-governmental actors and human rights groups. Among the most important of these have been groups supporting Middle Eastern governments or opposition groups. The most effective, of course, has been the Israeli lobby, which has, increasingly, focused on the threat from Islamic fundamentalism, a thread that runs through much of the fear of terrorism. Their influence has been strongest on Iranian legislation, especially the D'Amato bill (ILSA), but they also supported sanctions on Iraq, Libya and Sudan. Their support for sanctions on Iran hinged largely on Iran's support for Palestinian terrorist groups operating inside Israel, and for Hizballah in Lebanon. Since these groups were active in attempting to derail the US sponsored peace process, these interests strongly coincided with those of the US. Second, Israel fears nuclear rivals in the region. With Iraq under strict international controls, Iran now poses the most serious long-term WMD threat to Israel. Hence, the Israeli lobby has pushed to contain Iran.

Other domestic interest groups have played a role in supporting sanctions policy. Chief among these have been Iraqi exile oppositionists dedicated to the replacement of Saddam's regime. They have stressed the need for democracy and pluralism in Iraq, a theme that strikes a responsive chord in Congress and in some sections of the administration. The Kurdish parties, until they began fighting, were also effective in reaching Congress, the media and official circles with a similar message. NGOs and human rights groups have also played a significant role in keeping Iraq's appalling human rights record before the public. These groups have convinced some, but by no means all, in the foreign policy establishment that destabilization and regime replacement is not only desirable, but feasible. While they have not been able to achieve their goal in Baghdad, they have acted as a bar against any change of policy that might appear 'soft on Saddam'.

On the Iranian front, the People's Mujahidin have played a similar role. They have mounted a daily public relations campaign, focusing on Iran's human rights record, its terrorism, its WMD acquisitions, and other themes likely to resonate in policy circles. Its aim has been to encourage a tougher policy toward Iran. This group has supporters in Congress but none in the State Department which has not recognized them because of past terrorist activities.

While not all of the aims and goals of these groups have been accepted by US policy-makers, they have helped shape the US perception of the domestic environment in the countries in question and thus the US assessment of the regimes and the threat they pose. They have had a subtle, but profound, influence on policy.

Sanctions legislation has also been affected by a new domestic interest group, that of the victims of terrorism. The most potent group has been organized by the Pan Am families who have been effective in lobbying for sanctions on Libya. They reportedly saw to it that Libya was added to D'Amato's legislation on Iran. They were able to be more effective because the terrorist issue had achieved an increasingly higher profile in the US in the wake of the World Trade Center bombing in New York, and the Federal Building bombing in Oklahoma City. These incidents, until then very rare in the US, created rising public concern and stronger support for doing something about it.

Some Middle East allies have also been effective supporters of sanctions. Not surprisingly, the front-line states of Kuwait and Saudi Arabia have been strong supporters of continued restrictions on Iraq. There have also been advocates of a stronger policy toward Iran, particularly allies who fear subversion and are interested in deflecting attention from domestic opposition. These included Saudi Arabia, Bahrain and Egypt. Recently, the first two have undertaken a cautious rapprochement with Iran, as Iran has moderated its policy, and thus deflected former destabilization efforts from Iran. But regional allies have also been ambivalent about the measures to be taken against neighbours with whom they have had to live. A classic example is Egypt, whose support for legislation against Sudan is lukewarm. Few support destabilization policies precisely because the effects could spill over into their backyards, and they fear a backlash from the countries involved, should such attempts fail.

New Political Actors and a New Political Style

More intangible domestic factors have also had a bearing – indirectly – on the increased resort to sanctions and punitive measures. One is the emergence in Washington of a new generation of politicians with different backgrounds and a different outlook than its predecessors. For most of the period, the White House has had a President in his late 40s and staffers ranging in age from 20 to 40. In Congress, 70 per cent of the new entrants in recently elected Congresses have been in their 30s and 40s. Many of the movers and shakers in the new group come from the midwest and south; in short, from the American heartland. Few hail from the East or West coast, the intellectual base of the traditional foreign policy establishment. Lastly, few have had any experience in foreign affairs before coming to Washington. While the Clinton administration has in its midst some strong activists, willing to intervene abroad for humanitarian and other goals,[21] for the most part they have had to take second place to those busy reforming the domestic political and economic structure, priorities that perfectly coincided with the mood of the public. As a result, neither Congress nor the administration has devoted much time or attention to labouring in the diplomatic vineyards. Indeed, the State Department has had to spend an inordinate amount of its time, not on foreign affairs, but cultivating Congress, lest its budget, its projects, even parts of its organization, disappear. Congressional

---

21 Some of the most important of these were part of the top security team.

budget cuts have slashed foreign aid, overseas missions and the US contribution to the UN, undercutting US diplomatic instruments.

The politics of engagement and dialogue espoused by Europeans require just such diplomatic tools and talents. The hard work of creating change through persuasion, contact and diplomacy appear to have little appeal to the new political elite, which sometimes shows a proclivity for wielding power without the effort of exerting influence. Any number of political commentators have noted these traits and their impact on diplomacy. A former National Security Council director wrote: "American foreign policy has not only become passive and diminished, but also has become more narrow-minded, shortsighted and increasingly, go-it-alone [. . .]. In common with isolationism, however, the new unilateralism reflects an unwillingness to do the hard work of exercising leadership, and an urge not merely to share, but to shed its burdens [. . .]. The new unilateralism underlies a foreign policy approach which holds that we will deal with the world when we must, but only in our own way, in our time, and on our own terms."[22] Such a mindset is more likely to favour coercive diplomacy rather than long-term engagement, sanctions rather than dialogue.

Washington, with its nearly constant political campaigns, is also increasingly vulnerable to the short-term perspective. The Europeans claim that the best route to a change in behaviour is economic development and the emergence of a middle class with an economic stake in the West, is too long-term a perspective. Sanctions appear to be a quicker 'fix' for the new political elite and the Washington electoral cycle. If they do not generate immediate change, at least they 'contain' the situation. They may be easy to invoke. They can sometimes be advanced by executive order without much consultation with Congress, or by invoking already existing legislation. They are ideal

22 Scowcroft, Brent/Arnold Kanter 1995: The Perils of Going It Alone, Washington Post, 3 February.

for appeasing local constituencies; expressing outrage and frustration, and showing 'leadership'. It is noteworthy that, in a press briefing prepared by Secretary of State Christopher to explain the President's 1995 executive order on Iran, his final words were: "The reason the President took this decision was because it enables him to project American leadership. This is all about American leadership [. . .]. I hope other countries will respond to that leadership [. . .]."[23] While sanctions can be and sometimes are an effective diplomatic tool, their imposition needs to be more carefully considered and their effectiveness better measured.

List of References

Clawson, Patrick 1995: What to Do About Iran. Middle East Quarterly, December, Washington, DC

Fawaz, Gerges 1996–1997: Washington's Misguided Iran Policy, in: Survival, 38/4.

Hufbauer, Clyde/Jeffrey Schott/Kimberly Elliot 1990: Economic Sanctions Reconsidered, Washington, DC

Lavin, Franklin 1996: Asphyxiation or Oxygen. The Sanctions Dilemma, Foreign Policy: 104.

Wilson, Rodney 1994: The Economic Relations of the Middle East. Toward Europe or Within the Region? In: Middle East Journal, 48/2

23 Christopher, Warren 1995: Press Briefing on the President's Executive Order, Department of State, 1 May.

Europe, the US and Iran

Anoushiravan Ehteshami

"In the circumstances we faced, seeking to negotiate, in combination with economic sanctions, was the right course. To think otherwise ... is mistakenly to equate talking with yielding. ... Any predetermined strategy, slavishly followed, could draw us to nightmarish results ... The decision to probe and negotiate was sorely tested in Iran, where our efforts to inject reason were met only by insolence and insults. Nevertheless, in the end it was not force of our arms but the force of our arguments – along with our economic and diplomatic leverage – that ultimately prevailed. It was the policy of steady, methodical probing for a negotiated result that brought the [hostage] crisis to an end. And I believe we should take the crisis as a clear vindication of talking as a means to resolve international disputes."

Warren Christopher, in American Hostages in Iran: The Conduct of a Crisis (New York, 1985), p. 20.

Revolutionary Iran, similar to other revolutionary states of this century, was born with a chip on its shoulder.[1] First of all, it was convinced of the justness of its cause; its revolution was to change the world. Secondly, it had scores to settle, particularly with those who had made it their business to humiliate the 'proud Islamic Iranian nation'. Thirdly, it was so proud of its achievement that it sought to export to the rest of the Muslim world its message of liberation. Lastly, for all its apparent strength and the sabre-rattling of its founders, it had taught its adherents that they had to be ready to defend it against the inevitable conspiracies of the 'satanic' forces that would be unleashed against the revolution. This revolutionary psychology was to contribute to the republic's self-perception, to its infant personality, and to its view of a world which had chosen to embrace the Shah and his regime without regard for the people's aspirations.

For this complex sets of reasons, therefore, from its birth the Islamic Republic of Iran was at loggerheads with the international community, in particular with the US-led Western axis. Having started life under difficult circumstances, with diplomatic isolation and embargoes following its birth, the post-revolution Islamist regime quickly developed the ability to resist outside pressures, be these economic, political, diplomatic, or military. Over time, therefore, Tehran, acquired the skills to acclimatise to external pressures, to respond to them and, wherever prudent, to exploit them fully to its own advantage at home. The new elite became quite skilful in finding ways to minimise the impact of external pressures on its home front and in its relations with other states.[2]

The sense of siege that followed the revolution was compounded by the Iraqi invasion of Iranian territory in September 1980 and the

---

1   This contribution was presented to the workshop *Instruments of International Politics. Critical Dialogue versus Sanctions*, Frankfurt, October 1996.
2   The ability to find appropriate responses to external pressures has been a useful genetic skill which seems to have been passed down to Ayatollah Khomeini's lieutenants who are in power today!

American military's attempt to rescue the US hostages. A combination of these events gave real substance to the instinctive fear Iranians exhibit of outside intervention that might lead to domination and manipulation of their country. But on another level, these developments enabled the new regime to establish and express its independence from, indeed disdain for, the great powers – this being a revolutionary aspiration supported by the anti-Shah rainbow coalition. In the course of these struggles the regime managed very quickly to turn its lack of regard for international norms and customs into a virtue. This was to mark, as much for its domestic audiences as for its international detractors, the new Islamist regime's crowning moment, its arrival on the international stage as the only non-Marxist anti-imperialist player. Was this behaviour consistent with the new regime's overall profile?

The US Hostage Crisis

The taking hostage of American citizens on 4 November 1979 marked the start of tensions in revolutionary Iran's relations with the United States and the former's uncomfortable position in the global order. The subsequent suspension of trade in oil between Iran and the US on 12 November 1979 and US' demand for economic sanctions, recommended by the United Nations' Security Council to be introduced against Iran in January 1980, indicated the beginning of Islamist Iran's unhappy relationship with the Western-dominated international system.[3] Although Iran's isolation was more or less

3   The US suspended delivery of military equipment to Iran on 9 November, stopped buying Iranian oil on 12 November and took steps to freeze all assets of the Iranian state under its jurisdiction on 14 November. The latter act deprived Iran of access to some US$ 12 billion in bank deposits and gold assets. For details see Assersohn (1982), Rubin (1980). See also report of US House of Representatives 1981: *The Iran Hostage Crisis. A Chronology of Daily Developments*, Washington, DC.

complete, back in the days of the Cold War it could still hope that
the two superpowers' rivalries would leave it a great deal of room
for manoeuvre. Its assessment was a correct one; the US' call for the
imposition of UN sanctions on Iran on 13 January 1980, for example, could have become an internationally binding measure had it
not been for Moscow's veto of the resolution – which had enjoyed
majority support with a vote of ten-to-two in favour.

Frustrated with lack of progress in the American hostages problem, Washington severed diplomatic relations with Iran in April
1980 and followed up this decision by imposition of an economic
embargo against the country. Following the US' decision, the foreign
ministers of the European Community countries endorsed US' unilateral act and declared their own (more limited) economic embargo
against Iran in May 1980.[4] The Europeans' most significant gesture
was to halt all military contacts with Iran. The International Court
of Justice's judgement, finding Iran guilty of violating international
norms gave further impetus to implementation and maintenance of
sanctions until such time as the American hostages were, uncondi-
tionally, released.

So, in a matter of months not only had the revolutionary Islamic
Republic managed to become an international pariah state, but had
managed to alienate almost all of its main trade partners as well (see
Table 1). The damage caused by a group of anti-American Islamist
'students' taking US citizens hostage was so extensive that it took
Tehran several years in the 1980s to re-establish its international
trade links.

---

4   An action that received support from Iran's other major trading partners as far
    afield as Asia, particularly Japan and Australia.

Table 1: Iran's Direction of Trade Flows, 1977–1981 (%)

	1977	1978	1979	1980	1981
Exports					
Industrial Countries	82.0	80.3	75.9	61.3	54.7
Developing Countries	17.3	18.9	23.5	36.9	44.8
Imports					
Industrial Countries	84.4	87.2	76.2	67.0	68.3
Developing Countries	11.5	8.7	16.2	23.8	23.1

Source: United Nations: Handbook of International Trade and Development Statistics, New York, various years.

Alleged Iranian Government Pursuit of the Regime's Opponents Overseas

Tehran has acquired a reputation since the early 1980s for relentless pursuit of its political opponents overseas. At first, it was the Pahlavi regime's officials and the Shah's allies who were its target. But since 1982 it is said to have extended its surveillance and intelligence operations to cover the activities of its non-monarchist opponents as well, allegedly seeking to silence these organisations' exiled leaders and activists. As many such individuals live in Europe and, to a lesser degree, in several of Iran's neighbouring countries, the Iranian state's long security and intelligence arm has been most active in these parts of the world, in many instances directly affecting its relations with other countries. Iran's extraterritorial claim on its active political opponents has more than once disrupted its diplomatic relations with several western European countries, most notably with Austria, Britain, France, Germany, Italy, Switzerland and some Scandinavian countries. In almost all of these cases the European power concerned sought assistance from the law enforcement agencies of its European partners but, in the end, chose to deal with the problem unilaterally. The most publicised of such cases are those affecting Iran's relations with Austria (over the murder of the Iranian Kurdish Democratic Party's leaders in Vienna in 1989), France (over the murder of former Prime Minister Shahpour Bakhtiar in Paris in 1991) and Germany (over the murder of the KDP's post-Qasemlou leaders in Berlin in 1992).[5]

Western Hostages in Lebanon

In January 1984 the US State Department placed Iran on its list of states purported to be sponsors of international terrorism. A direct result of this decision was imposition of statuary sanctions against Iran, which included prohibition of arms sales, and economic and technical assistance. Once again, Iran was being punished for its regional policies. The backdrop to the US decision was the Western involvement in Lebanon in 1983 and suicide bombing of Western country barracks in Beirut by suspected Iranian-sponsored Islamists.[6]

But, in May 1985, the US started relaxing its rules and began encouraging military contacts between Iran and its Western allies (Israel, to be precise) as a way of freeing its citizens held hostage in Lebanon and of strengthening what was regarded as the moderate faction in the Iranian political establishment. By January 1985 the

---

5 Amid rising tensions in German-Iranian relations, a German public prosecutor, Bruno Jost, on 15 November 1996 demanded life sentences for one Iranian and four Lebanese charged in the 1992 shooting. To the dismay of the German government, the prosecutor in the case has implicated Iran's top leaders, Khamenei, Rafsanjani and the head of Iran's intelligence organization, Ali Fallahian, for their role in the assassinations. For official Iranian and German responses to the case see UPI's daily reports.

6 Joffé (1991).

US had initiated direct contacts with the Iranians and direct shipments of weapons followed – this episode in Iran-US relations came
to be known as the Irangate scandal. Its exposure marked the end of
covert US-Iranian contacts.

But before this sorry chapter on Iran-Western relations in Lebanon could be closed, the crisis of the Lebanese hostages had to be
resolved. With several Westerners held hostage, again by Iranian-
supported groups, the prospects of warmer Iranian-Western relations
was a distant hope.[7] Noteworthy in this period was the French
response to the holding of its citizens hostage in Lebanon, whose
number seems to have increased between 1985 and 1987 in direct
response to Paris' treatment of known Islamist terrorists in its cus-
tody. As George Joffé notes, change of government in France in
March 1986 presaged policy changes towards Iran and Syria which
resulted in freeing of all its citizens by May 1988.[8]

Again, Iran, for its part in the Lebanon hostage crisis, was isolated and marginalised. When it did suit it, however, Tehran did
intervene on behalf of 'friendly' Western powers to secure the release
of their citizens. But Iran's dependence on Syria for access to its
Lebanese allies was consistently underestimated by the West and, by
the same token, its ability to dictate to the hostage-takers was over-
estimated. Inevitably, for its lack of compliance with international
norms, the Islamic Republic was subjected to some (unsystematic)
political and diplomatic Western pressure. In the end, however, by
the late 1980s the hostage issue had run its course and before it
could turn from a profitable venture into a major liability, Tehran set
about 'resolving' the issue with the West. By 1989, with the end of
the Iran-Iraq war (in 1988) and the arrival of a new order in Iran
(death of Ayatollah Khomeini and emergence of Hojjatoleslam Raf-

7   A total of 96 foreigners were held hostage in Lebanon between 1983 and 1988, of
    which 25 were Americans, 16 French, and 12 Britons. See Burgin (1988).
8   Joffé (1991).

sanjani and Iran's first executive president) and in Lebanon (the Taif accords), the Lebanon hostages issue no longer featured as a problem between Iran and the West. A new storm, however, had already started gathering – this one was to become known as the Rushdie affair.

EU-Iran Tensions over Salman Rushdie's The Satanic Verses Novel

The Rushdie affair, as this crisis has been known, flared up as a result of the violent responses by large sections of the British Muslim community and their counterparts in India and Pakistan to the publication of Salman Rushdie's new book. Iran, though slow in responding, 'bandwagoned' and proceeded to adopt the harshest line on this book, its author and publisher in the Muslim world. Several months after the publication of 'The Satanic Verses' and radicalisation of Muslim opinion in Britain and on the Indian subcontinent, Ayatollah Khomeini issued his famous edict condemning the author to death for apostasy.

The West's response to this new challenge from Iran was not only slow in coming, but when it did it was rather weak and confused. While some countries came out condemning Iran from the outset others, including Britain, struggled hard to appear evenhanded and sensitive to Muslim sensibilities at home and abroad. France came out most strongly against the edict, with President Mitterand labelling Iran's threat against the author and his publishers an 'absolute evil',[9] and West Germany became the first EC country to recall its head of mission from Tehran. Italy too took a hard line on the issue. Thus, by mid-February 1989, within a short period of the passing of Ayatollah Khomeini's edict, the twelve EC countries had reached agreement that a concerted response was in order and so, in a joint exercise, their Foreign Ministers recalled their ambassadors from

9   Pipes (1990: 158).

Tehran. Unusually, the Soviet Union expressed broad support for the Western position and, while condemning the edict, encouraged dialogue between Iran and the EC. Also, interestingly, most Muslim states chose to distance themselves from Iran's position, even though a majority within the Islamic Conference Organisation continued to criticise Rushdie for writing such a book and the West for harbouring him.

Unlike previous ruptures in Iranian-Western relations, however, the Rushdie affair proved to be a relatively brief one: the diplomatic tensions between Iran and the Community as a whole lasted for one month. On 20 March 1989 the EC Foreign Ministers decided unilaterally to return to Tehran and normal operations were resumed. But, while the problem of Ayatollah Khomeini's anti-Rushdie edict at the time of writing was put on the back burner, it was far from resolved, and continued to be used as a political football in Iran as well as by those countries looking to punish Iran for its foreign policy excesses. As such, therefore, the Rushdie affair did continue to cloud Anglo-Iranian relations in particular and warmer EU-Iranian relations in general, casting suspicions on Iranian micro-policies in the West and on the behaviour of its representatives and sympathisers in Europe.

US-imposed 'Dual Containment' Sanctions

Relations between Iran and the US have been going from bad to worse in the 1990s, a situation not helped with the return to the White House of a Democratic administration whose leaders had never forgiven the Islamic Republic for its part in humiliating President Carter in 1980 and for helping to keep the party out of power for all of the 1980s. Thus, from May 1993, under the leadership of President Clinton and Secretary of State Warren Christopher, the US put in motion an intricate strategy to isolate Iran for its 'roguish' behaviour.[10] This new US policy towards Iran formed part of its overall strategy towards the Persian Gulf region: to 'contain' Iran (and Iraq) and to prevent these states from harming America's interests and its allies in the Middle East, and to provide direct military and security assistance to its GCC allies. Freezing Iran out of the Arab-Israeli peace process was another stated objective of the containment strategy. The overall objective of the containment policy was to force Iran to reform: to revise its rejectionist stance on many regional issues, change its behaviour internationally, and become a 'good citizen'. In short, to become a 'normal state'. For the most part, the policy of containment in its early years resembled more a statement of intent rather than adoption of actual measures against the Islamic Republic. Despite the White House's protestations about close economic ties between Iran and the US' Western allies, the US' own trade links with Iran had approached the US$ 1.0 billion mark by the mid-1990s.[11] This was an embarrassing reality which may have caused an acceleration in Washington's tougher line on Iran, and allowed the Congress to force the Clinton Administration's hand on Iran.

In May 1995 Clinton signed an Executive Order (No. 12959) banning all US trade and investment links with Iran. Under pressure from the White House, Conoco withdrew from an exploration deal with Iran in March 1995. Despite EU protestations (for instance its official protests of 6 May and 19 July) and direct attempts by the Union's representative in Washington to plead with senior member of the US Congress, on 5 August 1996 the Iran and Libya Sanctions Act of 1996 became law.[12] This was an escalation in the US'

---

10 See Kemp (1994), Gerges (1996–97).
11 According to Iranian Ministry of Commerce figures, Iran's imports from the US had been in excess of US$ 800 million in 1993/94, barely US$ 200 million short of Britain's exports to that country.
12 This bill threatens penalties against non-US companies investing in excess of US$ 40 million a year in the hydrocarbon sectors of Iran (and Libya).

attempts to isolate the Islamic Republic and marked a departure from its policy of unilateral action against the country, which had included the allocation of US$ 18 million a year by the US Congress to finance efforts to undermine the Iranian regime[13] – a measure that was not only against the letter of UN conventions but also in contravention of the 1980 bilateral agreement between Tehran and Washington that the US would in future not interfere in Iran's internal affairs.[14] The EU lodged a formal protest against the US on 8 August 1996 and its trade commissioner, Sir Leon Brittan, promised to fight the US action on behalf of the Union through such international bodies as the World Trade Organisation. In October, the EU threatened to enact legislation in order to protect European companies from the reach of US law.[15]

Since President Clinton's re-election in November 1996, slight changes in the US approach towards Iran could be detected. While Tehran continued to be 'enemy number one' in Washington, the prospects of holding direct talks with the Iranian leadership were mentioned by some US Administration officials, to the dismay of some powerful Washington insiders.[16] Where this might lead remains unclear at the time of writing, but is indicative of a re-appraisal of the US position on Iran. Such a re-appraisal may be part of a bureaucratic exercise designed to assess the effectiveness of American diplomacy in this regard, or could in fact be a direct response to the mounting domestic American pressure as well as international diplomatic and

13 The sum of US$ 18 million a year is in addition to the CIA's US$ 2.0 million a year allocation for covert operations against Iran. Although this measure did not have the support of the White House and the CIA, its adoption by the Congress in early 1996 has meant that the US administration is now committed to financing covert operations against the legitimate government of another sovereign state.
14 See earlier section of this contribution.
15 Buerkle, Tom 1996: EU Steps Up Campaign Against US Sanctions, in: International Herald Tribune, 2 October 1996.
16 Opposition to any revision of the US policy towards Iran is articulated in a newspaper editorial entitled: Why Ease Up on Iran? See Washington Post, 11 November 1996.

commercial protest against the D'Amato Bill of 1996. On the diplomatic front, it is interesting to note that not only the US' trade partners in Asia and its political allies in the developing world came out against the US legislation, but so too had its closest European allies. This should not be too surprising, considering the fact that four EU countries (Britain, France, Germany and Italy, plus Japan) formed Iran's main trading partners[17] and consumed most of its oil output.[18]

On the business front, most Western companies greeted the D'Amato Bill with horror. As one advertisement in an edition of the influential Financial Times illustrated, multinational businesses applied pressure on the US administration to review its policy of secondary boycotts.[19] A Mobil advertisement stated that 'the use of secondary boycotts to achieve foreign policy objectives should be avoided', a line of argument that first appeared in the New York Times and was taken up by other influential newspapers.[20] Until the D'Amato Bill of 1996, the EU companies seemed content to sit back and take advantage of the US' unilateral trade and investment embargo on Iran,[21] which partly explained the US Senate's decision to raise the stakes and adopt the D'Amato Bill. Although the 1995 and 1996 American legislative moves against Iran have had a degree of adverse effect on the Iranian economy, particularly with regard to the stability of its currency against Western currencies and in less tangible psychological terms, their direct economic impact remained far from apparent. Clearly, so long as the US' Western allies (in Eu-

17 See International Monetary Fund (1995): Direction of Trade Statistics, Washington, DC.
18 See Oil and Gas Journal, 8 May 1995.
19 Mobil, Secondary Boycotts: Squeeze Plays that Hurt Everyone, in: Financial Times, 5 November 1996.
20 See editorials in: The New York Times, 1 July 1996 and the Financial Times, 12 July 1996.
21 The French oil company Total, for instance, moved in to replace Conoco when the US administration banned the American firm from entering the Iranian hydrocarbons sector in 1995. The contract is worth US$ 600 million.

rope and in Asia), Russia and China continued to trade with and invested in Iran, at the same time as fighting the US action, the D'Amato Bill remained a blunt instrument.[22]

Impact of International Responses on Iran

In broad terms, looking at international responses from Tehran's perspective, their impact can be said to have been limited, in that they have failed to force Iran to change its ways. But, one can argue that international pressure caused some amendments to its policies and brought about a review of some of its more unrealisable ambitions. What can be sensed with clarity, however, is that international responses to Iran's norm violations have tended to leave a lasting mark on the Iranian state, as an examination of the US hostages crisis illustrates.

This crisis, I would argue, left a deep scar on the Iranian political elite's psyche, and in a fashion has been interpreted by the regime as a sign of its strength, independence and righteousness. The hostage crisis forms an important element of the regime's revolutionary political folklore. Iran continues to this day to celebrate the regime's defiance of the 'Great Satan' by a ritual of orchestrated demonstrations and other activities outside the 'den of spies' (the former US embassy compound). In particular, the settlement terms (specifically the American commitment not to interfere in Iran's internal affairs) seemed to vindicate the Islamist forces' rejectionist policies.

22 The continuing support given by European and Japanese businesses to Iran's strategic industries in recent years indicates how ineffective US pressure has been. One example of such support is the November 1996 agreement reached between Iran's National Steel Company (NISC) and a consortium of European and Japanese banks to provide US\$ 561 million in credit for a number of steel industry-related projects in Iran. Italy's state-controlled Mediocredito Centrale has guaranteed financing for the new projects. See Dow Jones Business News, 10 November 1996.

In more practical ways too the crisis has left a deep mark on Iran. Firstly, it showed Iranian leaders how vulnerable the country was to Western power and how insignificant its voice could be in the key international fora. Since then, Iranian leaders have been trying very hard to reduce their regional isolation by cultivating ties with both state and sub-state forces in the Middle East and beyond, largely through such alliances, as with Syria for example, and support for Islamist groups like Hizbollah, and others. Secondly, it was apparent to all that the crisis had cost the country dear in terms of its hard currency reserves, perhaps to the tune of US$ 10 billion, thus depriving it of a vital economic asset. Thirdly, the sanctions had cut Iranian access to vital US (and some) Western imports, and virtually all its military-related needs, a problem that has been alleviated today by closer contacts with Russia, China and North Korea, but persists to this day in terms of Iranian military relations with the Western world. The economic and military impact of the hostage crisis, thus, are still reverberating in the Iranian economy and in its politico-military relations with the outside world. In domestic political terms too, the hostage crisis was a harbinger for change. It brought to an abrupt end the ascendancy of the 'liberal' elements in the revolutionary coalition and soon eroded their legitimacy as a credible political force. Without legitimacy and credibility their demise was inevitable.

With respect to Iran's international relations, the hostage crisis must be viewed in the context of its changing foreign policy priorities after the revolution. Briefly, these were based on its 'neither East nor West' (non-aligned) principle – with a heavy emphasis on equal distance from the superpowers – closer ties with the Third World, support for (particularly Islamic) liberation movements, diversification of trade partners, and export of its brand of Islamic revolution through cooperation, subversion and cooptation. With these principles guiding its foreign policy priorities, a run-in with the US-led West was almost inevitable. But did these principles really guide the republic's foreign relations? On reflection, the answer has to be a qualified no, for from the outset Iranian leaders injected a great deal of pragmatism in their policies. This point can be demonstrated with the aid of a few examples: opposition to the 'American-Islam' of Saudi Arabia was tempered by close ties with America's Muslim allies, Pakistan and Turkey; its hostility towards Ba'thist Iraq was balanced by its alliance with equally Ba'thist Syria; it confronted the US, and yet strove to maintain close relations with the US' European allies; it attacked both superpowers for their 'arrogance' and yet ensured at all times that the route to Moscow would not become blocked; it preached Islamic brotherhood and yet developed strategic ties with communist China and North Korea.

Reactions of Third Parties

Reaction of third parties should be examined in the context of the crisis concerned and the prevailing global balance of power. The bipolar world of the 1980s did give Iran a degree of mobility and ability to use the international balance to its own advantage. Pressure from the West thus was reduced through the availability of safety valves in the East. This situation no longer exists, however. In the 1990s, with a unipolar military system on the one hand and a multipolar economic system on the other, while countries like Iran may find it more difficult to escape from the US, they can still use the elasticity of the system to manipulate it and also use it to their own advantage.

When assessing third party reactions to Iran's policies overseas, therefore, we must take stock of the changes in the international system. This though is insufficient in itself. In Iran's case we are dealing with several crises with different outcomes. So, for a fuller understanding of third party reactions we must allow for each to be examined in turn. Only through such a method will one be able to appreciate third party reactions to Iran's violation of international norms.

As we saw, during the US hostages problem, the world was united in condemning Iran's behaviour and, for the duration of the crisis, the West was able to form a (pro-US) united front against Tehran. But during the Lebanon hostages problem and rise of Middle East-linked terrorist activities in Europe the West was acting as a divided camp, with France and Britain representing the two poles of European opinion: while the British government refused to 'negotiate with hostage-takers', the French and German governments were prepared to cut any reasonable deal with the hostage-takers that would ensure the safe return of their citizens. A degree of unity in response to the anti-Rushdie edict was in evidence. Western countries rallied around Britain and unreservedly condemned Ayatollah Khomeini's incitement to violence against the British novelist. But today the Rushdie affair seems to be a problem in Anglo-Iranian and not in EU-Iranian or broader Western-Iranian relations.

In the 1990s the Western unity which had prevailed earlier has disappeared, with it pursuing two competing, and at times contradictory policies towards Iran. The significant issue here is that the West has been allowing new divisions to appear in its rank at a time when the international system itself has been undergoing some fundamental changes. Clearly, the dynamics of the post-Cold War international system have not helped Washington's position, and the American superpower has been finding it hard to adapt itself to the countervailing pressures that are an inevitable product of today's multipolar international economic system. More specifically, US' advocacy of 'containment' of Iran has been matched by the EU's 'critical dialogue' initiative, and with other major powers refusing to toe the American line, Iran has been left with plenty of options. Lack of a united Western response, as evidenced by European reactions to the D'Amato Bill, has allowed countries like Russia, China and other Asian powers, as well as the West's Middle East regional allies, to develop their own policies towards Iran and follow a path that is distinct from the two main Western positions. It is noteworthy that for the non-western world the policy of unreserved cooperation with Iran has applied. This policy has shown signs of alteration only when prompted by the US, or when pressurised by the West.

Policy Options

A considered view of the above, it seems to me, can lead to two divergent perspectives on the effectiveness of the two approaches used by the West: one that recommends forcing Iranian policy changes through isolation and punishment, and another, that views a carrot and stick policy which would bring about gradual, but concrete, change. Despite their differences, however, the two approaches had one major factor in common: both strategies calculated that the route to influence the Iranian leadership passed through the Iranian economy. Is this assumption a fair one?

On balance, one has to answer with a qualified yes. Lets look at one factor of vulnerability: Iran's external debt problem which arose out of its spending spree of the early 1990s quadrupled since 1989. Iran's foreign debt in the mid-1990s was hovering above the US$ 25 billion figure, standing at around 36 per cent of its GDP, costing the country an average of US$ 4.0 billion a year in debt servicing.[23]

Table 2: Iran's Foreign Debt, (Selected Years, US$ Billion)

	1980	1988	1990	1991	1992	1993	1994
Long-term	4.5	2.1	1.8	2.1	1.8	5.8	16.0
Short-term	0.0	3.8	7.2	9.3	14.3	17.6	6.7
Total	4.5	5.8	9.0	11.3	16.0	23.4	22.8
Export credits	–	3.1	7.8	8.8	8.7	9.1	10.1

Source: World Bank 1996: World Bank Debt Tables, Washington, DC.

23 Economist Intelligence Unit 1996: Iran Country Report. 2nd Quarter 1996, London.

Although, according to the World Bank, Iran was relatively successful in tackling its foreign debt problem (successfully reducing it to
just under US$ 20 billion in 1996), and, thanks to firmer oil prices in
1996, its foreign exchange reserves were showing signs of recovery
(reaching US$ 8.5 billion), its foreign debt obligations still left the
state rather vulnerable to external financial pressures. This heavy
financial burden was compounded by the Iranian economy's heavy
dependence on hydrocarbon exports and by its need of capital goods
and industrial (and consumer goods) spare parts imports.

If it is believed that applying pressure is a prudent policy, then
one could do much worse than combining affirmative action, in the
form of critical dialogue, with threatening to balance support for
Tehran's financial and hard currency difficulties in Western financial
institutions against evidence of 'normal' behaviour.[24] Anecdotal evidence from the 1980s suggests that such approaches, if followed
patiently and consistently, could produce positive results.

For Iran, economic prosperity through reconstruction of its shat-
tered economy was and is an imperative that cuts across all schools
of thought within the elite. There is even broad agreement amongst
the establishment that reconstruction can occur only in an open-mar-
ket economic environment. The dilemma is should this process be
helped or should it be hindered. Support for this process, some
argue, may be interpreted by Tehran as condoning Iran's norm violations. Moreover, the success of its reforms, the same line maintains,
will embolden the regime to misbehave internationally. For this
group of analysts and policy-makers, Iran's economic successes, especially under its pragmatist leadership, will spell disaster for regional
stability and normal relations.[25] As might be expected, this school of
thought regards isolation of Iran as central to its strategy.

24 Note, for instance, that one of Tehran's main grievances against the US is Washing-
    ton's refusal to release several billion dollars in Iranian assets in the US frozen
    since 1980.
25 Clawson (1993).

In a multi-centre system, like today's post-Cold War setting, however, attempts to isolate a regime can have the effect of encouraging the growth of radical factions within it, as well as effectively driving the subject state towards other international players or blocs. Far from imposing an effective isolation regime, therefore, one could be forcing realignment of forces at the international level. Moreover, in a world where increasingly economics determines foreign policy, such unilateral measures as that of the US towards Iran can only cause unnecessary divisions between political and economic partners and bring about discord in such powerful Western-dominated groupings as the OECD and in EU-US relations. I note with more than a hint of irony that divisions in the Western bloc occurred in the 1990s not over bilateral or multilateral disputes, but over treatment of less important third parties[26] – over relations with Iran, Cuba and Libya for example. This perspective seemed to be lost on those advocating the strengthening of sanctions against Iran. This much we can glean from the words of one senior Washington insider, who stated in late 1996 that with regard to Iran, "Europe can either be part of the problem or part of the solution".[27]

The above prevailing view notwithstanding, past experience shows that issue-based negotiations with Tehran – like over the US hostages, the renewal of the NPT, introduction of a global ban on chemical weapons, international population control efforts, environmental issues, etc. – could bear fruit and provide a bounty of opportunities for broader dialogue and exchange of views with Iranian leaders. The experience of recent years has shown that dialogue is also needed between the Western powers themselves over their policies towards countries like Iran, which are not subject to UN sanctions and yet violate international norms.

26 See also Huntington (1996).
27 Statement of Gregg Rickman, Senator D'Amato's legislative director, at a conference in London held in early November 1996. See Gulf States Newsletter, 18 November 1996.

In conclusion, let me raise some broader issues with a bearing on this case study. Internationally, Iran's position is undergoing some changes. Iran is, in my view and at the time of writing increasingly finding itself moving towards the Euro-Asia orbit – even though it continues to function within the US-dominated international and regional systems – and promotes closer economic ties with the rest of the Third World. In practice, in the post-Cold War emerging international system, this means deeper Iranian economic (and wherever permissible political too) interactions with the European Union states, Russia, China, India and Japan, and further distance from the United States. While the trend of accommodation may be good news as far as Iran's overall role in the international system is concerned, it does mean, however, that in regional terms the more structural the US-Gulf Cooperation Council axis becomes, the further east in the Middle East region the Arab-Israeli peace process spreads. And the closer Washington draws itself towards the Asian CIS republics, perhaps the less likely Iran and its pro-American Gulf Arab and Central Asian neighbours will travel within the same regional and international framework, making easy interaction between Iran and its two neighbouring regions more difficult and integration less certain in the future.

The West, therefore, needs to ask itself, in such fluid conditions as is witnessed in West Asia today, is it prudent to have such a geopolitically important country as Iran forcibly frozen out of the power balance, or should it, as the then British Foreign Minister Malcolm Rifkind suggested,[28] be aiming to create an OSCE-type regional system (lets call this the OSCME) which ties countries like Iran more directly into the fabric of regional structures, and build on their domestic needs for international cooperation to make them more conformist?

---

28 Gardner, David: Rifkind Calls for New Forum on Mideast, in: Financial Times, 5 November 1996.

List of References

Assersohn, Roy 1982: The Biggest Deal. Bankers, Politics and the Hostages of Iran, London.

Burgin, Muskit 1987: Foreign Hostages in Lebanon, in: Merari, Ariel/Anat Kurz (eds.): International Terrorism in 1987, Boulder/Colorado.

Clawson, Patrick 1993: Iran's Challenge to the West. How, When, and Why, Washington, DC.

Gerges, Fawas 1996/97: Washington's Misguided Iran Policy, in: Survival, 38/4.

Huntington, Samuel 1996: The West. Unique, not Universal, in: Foreign Affairs, 75/6.

Joffé, George 1991: Iran, the Southern Mediterranean and Europe, in: Ehteshami, Anoushiravan/Manshour Varasteh (eds.): Iran and the International Community, London.

Kemp, Geoffrey 1994: Forever Enemies? American Policy and the Islamic Republic of Iran. Washington, DC.

Pipes, Daniel 1990: The Rushdie Affair. The Novel, the Ayatollah, and the West, New York.

Rubin, Barry 1980: Paved With Good Intentions. The American Experience and Iran, New York.

Transformation and Legitimacy

Legitimacy and Economic Reform in the Arab World

Emma Murphy

"The inculcation of a sense of legitimacy is probably the single most effective device for regulating the flow of diffuse support in favour of both the authorities and the regime. A member may be willing to obey the authorities and conform to the requirements of the regime for many different reasons. But the most stable support will derive from the conviction on the part of the member that it is right and proper for him to accept and obey the authorities and to abide by the requirements of the regime. It reflects the fact that in some vague or explicit way he sees these objects as conforming to his own moral principles, his sense of what is right and proper in the political sphere."[1]

The search to establish legitimacy is a universal characteristic of nation-state regimes. For some, the task is relatively easy; for others

---

1   Easton (1965: 278)

it is a constant and uphill struggle.[2] But for all states legitimacy is considered to be a critical ingredient for preserving political stability and a regime's long-term survival. In times of crisis the need to establish the legitimacy of both the ruling elite and the political system itself becomes all the more important.

Legitimacy can be defined in a general way as the widely and publicly acknowledged right to rule. Lipset is more specific, defining legitimacy as "[. . .] the capacity of the system to engender and maintain the belief that the existing institutions are the most appropriate ones for the society".[3] Any such capacity relies upon a congruence of values among different groups in society, a common perception of what is needed from the state's leadership and the methods by which it should be achieved. The other end of the legitimacy bargain is that the regime should be responsive to that 'basket' of values and means. In his study of the Arab world, Hudson goes further, drawing on Rustow's prerequisites for political modernity,[4] and asserting that legitimacy requires the three pillars of authority, identity and equality. A regime must have an acknowledged right and capacity to exert authority, it must express a "[. . .] distinct sense of corporate selfhood [whereby] the people within a territory must feel a sense of political community which does not conflict with other subnational or supranational communal identifications" and it must operate in a manner that corresponds to aspirations for freedom and equality.[5]

Hudson, writing in the 1970s, identified legitimacy as being the central problem of Arab government and the principal cause behind the volatile and unstable character of Arab politics. The Arab world

2 This contribution was presented to the workshop *Economic Transformation and the Role of the State in the Middle East and North Africa*, Rabat, October 1996. A later version of this contribution appeared in the Journal of North African Studies, 3/3, Autumn 1998.
3 Lipset (1960: 77).
4 Rustow (1967).
5 Hudson (1977: 4).

has hardly been less crisis-ridden since that time, although new debates and controversies have wracked the region as a whole and played a part in exacerbating existing dilemmas. While Hudson identified a commitment to socialism as a requisite for regime legitimacy in the past, that particular ideological ingredient would appear to have passed its sell-by date. The failures of regimes elsewhere in the world to achieve a successful socialist transformation, success being defined in terms of economic well-being and representative political structures, has rebounded on Middle Eastern states which never really got beyond state-centred capitalist policies.

This contribution is principally concerned with the Arab world, since it is a simpler task to identify common and collective legitimacy problems and strategies among those states alone than to broaden the analysis to the non-Arab Middle East. Yet it is worth considering that Turkey, Iran and Israel have all ultimately adopted a variation on the 'Washington consensus' as the economic strategy of the 1990s and beyond. While they share some of the Arab world's dilemmas, they also face specific additional problems that relate to their own historical and national evolution. They will be referred to in this text, where it is appropriate to do so, but a more in-depth analysis of legitimacy in each particular case must be left for another time.

Legitimacy in the Arab World

In the Arab world there are a number of recognisable commonly (but not necessarily universally) held corporate values which have provided legitimacy for regimes in the modern era. These might be briefly categorised as follows, although it should be borne in mind that they frequently overlap or even impinge upon one another:

Traditional and/or inherited rights to rule. This category includes monarchical regimes, which in the case of the Middle East draw upon tribal lineage and alliances. Regimes claiming this brand of legitimacy today include the Gulf sheikhdoms, Jordan and Morocco. It should be borne in mind, however, that monarchies and Beydoms evolving in Egypt, Iraq, Libya and Tunisia were delegitimised by a combination of factors including colonial collaboration, fiscal profligacy and resistance to social transformation. Traditional or inherited legitimacy is rarely enough without a regime response to other values within the 'basket', one of the most critical of which is the desire for the leader to distribute patronage, albeit in the form of defence of a client, economic wealth or access to opportunities.

Patronage itself is not confined to monarchies or 'traditional' political systems in the Middle East. Weberian concepts of patrimonial leadership are often considered to be peculiarly appropriate to the region. In instances where the state has developed as a modernised and extended form of localised patriarchal traditions, the ruler or leadership elite demand loyalty to the institutions of the state almost as they would demand it for themselves in a more traditional political form. In return, they take upon themselves the task of taking care of the needs of their 'subjects'. The bureaucracies of the Middle East, from the highest ministerial levels to the lowest administrative functions, have evolved in a manner which expresses the personalisation of function, loyalty and responsibility such that patronage is not considered as a form of corruption or nepotism as much as a rational system whereby loyalty is exchanged for reward. This characteristic is as prevalent in populist bureaucratic states as in traditional monarchies and derives from political and social traditions which seep into and through the bodywork of government.

Anti-colonialism and anti-imperialism. The historical experiences of many Arab states included a struggle to expel colonial powers and to untangle their webs of influence. The legitimacy of Nasser was undoubtedly initially greatly derived from his early success in persuading the British to withdraw from Egypt, both through treaty and ultimately through successful resistance to the Suez invasion. Bourguiba's Tunisia and Ben Bella's Algeria claimed the same credentials and, in today's world, there is still much to be gained by a regime in articulating popular antipathy to Western interference in Middle Eastern affairs. The popular Arab 'street' response to the US-led coalition's war against Iraq was a clear demonstration of the legitimacy dilemmas involved for regimes committed to their Western alliances.

Arab nationalism. While to some extent this aspect of legitimacy derives from the same anti-colonialism and anti-imperialism pursued by individual states, it also has its own dynamics. Arab nationalism assumes a uniqueness to the collectivity of Arab states, a trans-state identity within the Arab world and an era of past glory which can be recaptured.[6] Legitimacy here is established through foreign policy, most notably through hostile positioning vis-à-vis Israel, although Saddam Hussein also used the Arab cause to rally support for his war against Iran in the 1980s. Inevitably, while the appeal of Arab nationalism has been felt from the Atlantic to the Arabian Peninsula, and from Sudan to Lebanon, its usefulness as a legitimacy tool varies from state to state. Front-line states such as Assad's Syria and Nasser's Egypt were able to deflect criticism for poor domestic performance by focusing attention on their Arab nationalist credentials. In contrast, Bourguiba's Tunisia was able to strike a more moderate, pro-Western pose not least by virtue of geographic distance between Tunis and Tel Aviv.

The reverse side of both the anti-colonialist/anti-imperialist and Arab nationalist demands made upon Arab regimes, is the requirement that regimes should represent a corporate national identity which expresses the relationship between populations and territory. Not surprisingly, this is often difficult given the ethnic cocktail of states such as Iraq, Sudan, Lebanon and Algeria (as well as the non-

6   Fred Halliday has identified this link between legitimacy and a return to the past in the teachings of Ayatollah Khomeini of Iran, indicating that the era of Islamic unity and greatness, however much romanticised, can be used to create legitimacy in a rejection of all things modern, even beyond the Arab world. See Halliday (1988: 33).

Arab Iran, Turkey and Israel). Even so, Nasser was at pains to promote an Egyptian identity which distinguished Egyptians from other Arabs, while the reluctance of Syria and Iraq to suppress national identities to Ba'thist internationalism, illustrates the desire of regimes to consolidate territorial equations. Preserving territorial integrity, while it disappoints disaffected minorities, remains a key to overall regime legitimacy.

Populism and economic reform. In the immediate post-colonial era new regimes sought and won legitimacy on the basis of social reform and wealth redistribution. The regimes of Egypt, Tunisia, Algeria and later Syria, Iraq and South Yemen were all legitimised by their commitments to these two goals. In the Arabian peninsula also regimes were pressed to respond to demands that the oil wealth be shared, that welfarism should triumph and that education and health services be universally available. The domination of Israeli coalition governments by the Israel Labour Party for thirty years and the success of the Iranian revolution indicated that these two popular concerns remained intact elsewhere in the region. Given the meagre tax-base which existed within most Arab countries, and the erosion of even that by so-called socialist policies, the ability to distribute wealth has derived in large part, although to a varying degree across the region, from the rentier nature of the Arab state. While a lengthy discussion of the features and dynamics of such states is beyond the province of this contribution, it is critical to note that public expectations of a rentier state focus on provision rather than representation, and (given the patrimonial characteristics of the Arab state) that the largesse of the public official or the prince has come to be a measure of his (or her) credibility, even when the public purse becomes confused with the private. Indeed the public sector earns merit not simply for its efficient functioning but for its role in absorbing the aspirations of the upwardly mobile. Informal access to public officialdom, and the distribution of benefits and 'rent' through such access, is perfectly acceptable. Indeed, as was mentioned earlier, it becomes 'the system' as much as the formal functioning of the bureaucracy.[7]

Islam and religion. Islam is an odd man out in this list of legitimising values, largely because it has the additional merit that a regime can barely be legitimate without Islamic credentials of some sort or other. To reject Islam entirely, would be a virtual death sentence to the modern Arab state. The Islamic claims of a regime may reach from the extreme of Iranian theocratic rule, through the Wahhabi credentials of the al-Sauds, the holy lineage of Hassan of Morocco, the institutional role of Sharia law, to the less weighty incorporation of Islamic symbols in an essentially secular state (Ben Ali's Tunisia, Mubarak's Egypt and Hussein's Jordan). Ataturk and Bourguiba may have vigorously defied the synthesis of politics and religion but neither could defy the Muslim character of their populations and many of the aspirations that consequently were laid at their doors. Even in Israel, where religious symbolism was initially used to buttress the nationalist unity of a secular state, we are witness today to the demands which a simultaneous religious identity can make upon a regime. Given the traditional role of the clerics in defending the social and economic welfare of the masses, often coming into confrontation with the secular authorities in doing so, James Bill and Carl Leiden unsurprisingly remarked that: "In every Middle Eastern country, political and social change must accommodate itself to the religious consciousness of the country's inhabitants and to the vested interests of its clerical class".[8] The issue is complicated, however, by the fact that the monotheistic religions have rarely been able to display internal unity. Islam is subject to division among sects and interpretations, with legitimacy being claimed by diverse social forces. Thus the legitimacy assumed by regimes adhering to one branch of Islam may yet be declared to be un-Islamic by competitors for religious 'truth'.

7   Beblawi (1987: 49–62).
8   Bill/Leiden (1984: 48).

Democracy and popular consent. Democracy, (although not necessarily the liberal parliamentary variety) and the will of the people are increasingly seen as a tool for establishing legitimacy within the region. Consultative assemblies, national assemblies and national elections, for example, have become a common feature of Middle East politics. There remain serious limitations to the real efficacy of such institutions in the Arab world, albeit in the form of restricted suffrage, candidacy qualifications, electoral or selection processes, legal obligations of ruling elites to submit to the will of assemblies or restrictions on the press and free expression. The three non-Arab states are as guilty as their Arab neighbours in this respect. Military intervention in Turkish civilian politics, Israeli discrimination against its Arab minority and Iranian theological qualification of candidates all prove the weakness of democratic structures in the Middle East.

The popular desire for democracy is nonetheless apparent. Education, modernisation, urbanisation and internationalisation have all played a part in the development and consolidation of civil society with a corresponding impact upon socio-political demands and their articulation. Issues of civil, political and human rights have become the domain of the masses rather simply the intellectuals and, while they may as yet be unwilling to countenance genuine power-sharing, regimes can ill afford to disregard entirely the apparel and mechanics of (democratic) accountability.

Arab regimes have attempted to derive legitimacy from acceding to varying combinations of these values. Equally, they have undermined their own claims to legitimacy by ignoring or rejecting other socially-based values. In Saudi Arabia, for example, legitimacy is derived from a cocktail of inherited and tribal tradition, Islamic credentials, and wealth distributive functions. Yet regime legitimacy is compromised by the un-Islamic behaviour of elites, cooptation to Western interests, and most recently by economic difficulties resulting from declining oil revenues, the negative implications of which are unevenly felt. In Syria, Assad has sought legitimacy through social reform, wealth distribution and Arab nationalism. Ironically, his legitimacy rating has suffered from a political preference for the Alawite minority, unwillingness to accommodate developing civil society and poor economic management which results in less wealth to distribute. In Algeria's case, initial FLN legitimacy which derived from anti-colonial activity, Arab nationalism, and populist policies has given way under the pressures of economic crises, a failure to accommodate the will of the people (cancellation of elections), and a regime rejection of politicised Islam.

A word must be said here about the role of ideology in establishing legitimacy. Rustow asserts that ideologies are the "foundations of politics"[9] and certainly the Middle East has provided a battlefield for the playing out of a number of indigenous and exogenous ideologies. Arab Nationalism, Socialism, Communism, Ba'thism, Nasserism, Wahhabism, Khomeinism – are but a few of the 'isms' which have appeared to articulate and alternatively shape Middle Eastern politics. In essence, however, they can be reduced to variations of the political demands which have been outlined above. Their messages may be uniquely clothed in the language of a charismatic individual, a religious sect, geographic specificity, sub-or-transnational identity, but the capacity of any given ideology to provide legitimacy to a ruler or elite will, in the end, come down to the same basic basket of values.

Political Systems, Patronage and Social Contracts

A number of related points need to be emphasised before the discussion can move on to assess the impact of economic liberalisation on regime legitimacy. Firstly, regime legitimacy in the Arab world has tended to ultimately derive from the satisfactory fulfilment of specific state-delegated functions, two of which are particularly relevant

9 Rustow (1971).

to this discussion. The state in both traditional and populist countries has taken on the role of provider, responsible for ensuring economic growth and for distributing the benefits. Such distribution has
taken place either through channels of patronage based on personal
loyalties and traditions, or through populist state structures such as
welfare networks, subsidies, guaranteed employment schemes, and
others. In effect, social contracts have developed between state
regimes and populations whereby provision is exchanged for loyalty.
Political demands are channelled through loyalty-based vertical
structures – be they tribes, dominant parties, or functional bodies
coopted to the state itself. Thus the social contract is corporatist
rather then democratic. Indeed, "no taxation, no representation"
becomes the subliminal message of Arab regimes. In the 1950s,
1960s and early 1970s, the state's ability to provide from the top-
down shielded it from value-demands from the bottom-up.

The second point to make here is that Arab regimes were
entrusted with another value demand which seems in retrospect to
have been disproportionate to any benefits which might possibly
have derived from it for specific populations (other than the Palestinians). Regime commitments to Arab nationalism in the 1950s and
1960s provided a primary source of legitimacy for numerous regimes.
Much as with Islam, to reject Arab nationalism entirely was unthink-
able, although some regimes, such as that of Nasser, undoubtedly
were prepared to put ideals into action rather more than others.

By the 1980s it was clear that regimes were beginning to very
obviously fail their populations on both these accounts. On the one
hand, ill-fated ISI policies, excessive borrowing and subsequent crip-
pling debt, inflated bureaucracies, high military expenditures, rapidly
expanding populations and stagnating oil revenues combined to stifle
economic growth and ultimately plunge a number of countries into
economic crises. As regimes found it ever more difficult to fulfil their
side of the bargain with society, their legitimacy was increasingly
under threat. The problem was compounded by the fact that regimes

had become obviously self-serving, corporatist structures being undermined by elite corruption, authoritarian tendencies and political immobilism. Single parties, originally intended to mobilise populations behind regimes committed to populist agendas, became more interested in their own preservation and monopoly on power than in implementing any agenda set by the grass roots. They ceased even to care about mobilising the population, seeking only to ensure their continued hegemony through utilisation of the state's monopoly on the coercive mechanisms of the state. Apparent concessions to political pluralism, such as the legalisation of (approved) alternative political parties (as in Egypt, Jordan and Tunisia) did not include the introduction of genuine competition into the political system and served only to coopt and incorporate emerging bourgeois elements. In the Gulf sheikhdoms, a similar process was apparent when, for example, the Kuwaiti amir felt inclined to suspend the National Assembly in 1976 and 1986 and when the Bahraini legislature was dissolved indefinitely in 1975. The Iranian government under the Pahlavi Shah also yielded to the autocratic whims of its ruler. While privileged elites enjoyed an oil-sponsored economic boom and social liberalisation on a dramatic scale, the regime lost touch with the increasingly alienated and marginalised popular masses. Israel too became stymied in bureaucratic red tape, inflationary over-expenditure, systemic dysfunction and its own disregard for its Arab minority.

The 1980s were also a bad decade for Arab nationalism. The peace treaty reached between Egypt and Israel had created deep divisions within the Arab world, and it proved impossible to re-establish any effective front to counter the Israeli invasion of Lebanon in 1982, or indeed to reach a consensus on responses to the Iran-Iraq war. When the Palestinian Intifada broke out in December 1987 it seemed clear that the Arab world had failed the Palestinians and they now had no chance of freedom other then through their own actions. With the Arab world bitterly divided, the rallying cry of Arab nationalism rang hollow for many of the populations of the region. It seemed incomprehensible that Syria should align itself with Iran against Ba'thist Iraq in the first Gulf War, unbearable that Iraq should invade and pillage neighbouring Kuwait and intolerable that Arab regimes should line up their forces with those of the US-led coalition to subsequently punish Iraq even as Arab lands remained occupied by Israel.

Impact of Economic Liberalisation on Regime Legitimacy

By the mid-1980s it was clear that there were serious legitimacy problems throughout the Arab world. As the financial crisis in particular dug in, austerity measures brought frustrated and unempowered protesters out onto the streets. So-called bread riots, in response to the removal of subsidies on basic goods, spread through Egypt (1977, 1984), Morocco (1978, 1980, 1981 and 1984), Tunisia (1984), Sudan (1985), Algeria (1988) and Jordan (1989, 1996). As strategies of macroeconomic stabilization and structural adjustment were adopted to remedy the economic crisis, it became clear that such policies were an imposition by regimes of policies which did not have popular and grass-roots support, upon populations who felt that the costs incurred fell unequally and unfairly upon their shoulders. If such economic reforms are truly the solution to restimulating economic growth in the region, one must ask why they seem so at odds with popular sentiment and values that they deepen, rather then reduce, the legitimacy crisis for regimes.

The most obvious problem with structural reform is that its principal aim is to reduce the intervention of the state in economic activity. As Hazem Beblawi and Giacomo Luciani pointed out ten years ago: "The public must be convinced that it has to pay for the state, not rely on it."[10] In other words, the state is withdrawing from its

10 Beblawi/Luciani (1987: 2).

side of the bargain struck with society that it should play the role of provider. Guaranteed employment is abolished, price subsidies are withdrawn, welfare provision is reduced, public sector salaries are frozen, firms fail under the impact of competition (resulting in growing unemployment), public sector investment in utilities and services is reduced and the individual is thrown back into the market place to earn his survival. At the same time, however, tax systems are reformed to broaden and deepen the tax base. Prices rise in the absence of price controls and with devaluation increasing the cost of imports. Citizens are expected to make new contributions to health and education. Labour protection legislation is watered-down or removed. In short, life becomes harder and more expensive just as the state divests itself of the responsibility for easing the burden. Oil wealth has proved to be no barrier to economic crisis and the rentier states of the Gulf have experienced many of the same dilemmas, although usually with a moderated impact, as their poorer neighbours.

To make matters worse, this new burden is spread unevenly among populations attuned to the language of social justice and evenly redistributed wealth. Commercial middle men and entrepreneurs appear to reap the benefits of trade liberalisation and the new sponsorship of the private sector even as those lower down the income ladder feel squeezed by the reforms. Income gaps widen and poverty for some becomes more visible just as others become rampantly consumerist. In essence, a restructuring of interests takes place. One way of understanding this is to consider that, as the capitalist mode of production becomes more firmly entrenched, there is greater distinction between owners of means of production and the means of production themselves, notably labour. The position of one citizen vis-à-vis another is no longer determined by his relationship with the state, or its party arm, but by his relationship to capital. In practical terms this means a citizen locates himself within the society by virtue of his income and economic status. Income distribution is no longer determined by social justice but by place in the hierarchy of capital. Thus social stratification becomes increasingly horizontal rather than functional, creating a dislocation between the vertical structures of the political system and the horizontal 'class' interests of the population.[11]

Corporatist structures already under pressure from authoritarian regimes and self-interested or corrupt parties and elites, become redundant. Political systems are no longer compatible with economic system as primary interests cannot be articulated or mediated by existing structures. Thus, it is not simply a particular ruler whose legitimacy comes into question, but entire political systems which have evolved on the basis of values, assumptions and functions which are now under threat.

Another, associated, feature of economic reform is that, in reducing the scope of state intervention in the economy, the regime reduces its own ability to gain legitimacy through distributing patronage. This is as true in monarchies like Saudi Arabia as it is for populist corporatist regimes such as Egypt and Tunisia. For example, prominent positions in state-owned enterprises (SOEs) have traditionally served as political rewards. When SOEs and civil service departments are given administrative independence as part of reform packages, and when merit becomes the criteria for advancement rather than political reward, the state obviously has fewer 'jobs for the boys' to hand out. The removal of subsidies to producers, such as farmers, to enable them to sustain standards of living, is a further example of a policy which can subsequently reduce the dependence of interest groups on the largesse of the state, and result in frustration and disappointment with the regime.

In the oil-rich monarchies, the lack of distinction between public and private purse adds an interesting dimension to this. When the

---

11 For a full discussion of the impact of economic liberalisation on the Middle Eastern state, see: Ehteshami/Murphy (1996: 753–772).

state must rein in its spending, the largesse of the ruling family itself becomes relatively more important. On the one hand this can reinforce the legitimacy of a ruling family relative to the state, but when the families are seen to have accumulated vast personal fortunes, there is inevitably a corresponding perception that the ruling elite have enriched themselves at the expense of the rest of the population.

The question of ownership of assets can prove to be particularly thorny when privatisation is introduced onto the agenda. The prospect of the state selling 'the family silver' is bad enough. It becomes almost criminal in the eyes of many when they perceive the prices set for sales to be too low. While a 'bargain' sale will attract purchasers in what are still most frequently essentially unattractive business environments, it appears to the populations who count themselves to be the true, collective owners of such enterprises as the government selling property on their behalf, without their permission and at less than the true value of the asset. Meanwhile the principal beneficiaries are either already wealthy domestic investors or, even worse, foreign capitalists. This problem of perception has not been confined to the developing world[12] and the potential to counter it in the Arab world through stock market floatations open to small local investors has been severely restricted by the small size of local stock markets and the slow pace of financial reforms which can enable them to expand and operate efficiently.

Nationalist credentials of regimes are also damaged by economic liberalisation. The perception that structural adjustment programmes are imposed by international financial institutions funded, managed and dominated by the developed 'West' or 'North' feeds grievances over the injustices of the international system and the weaknesses of its division of labour. When many believe that international trade is already structurally biased in favour of the developed

12 Letwin (1988: 52–55).

world, the opening of less developed economies is seen as exposure to more powerful and self-interested forces which in reality seek only to exploit the weaker party. Rather than liberal trade regimes fuelling a trickle-down effect of mutual enrichment, critics argue that the long-term result will be a new form of economic imperialism. Middle Eastern states will be reduced to playing the role of sources of cheap labour and markets for the consumer products of the developed world. A net transfer of wealth out of the region, reinforced by the continuing problem of debt repayment, will serve only to impoverish the Middle East to the advantage of those very powers which now advocate liberalisation. Regimes may thus be perceived as having 'sold out', acting as a comprador class whose own interests lie in advancing the interests of the metropole rather than those of their own peoples.

Critics also point out that, even as the developed world is bullying the less developed states to lower economic borders, it is itself reforming into regional blocs that exclude the Middle East. NAFTA, ASEAN and the EU are perhaps the strongest of many such blocs, including among their ranks the states which currently account for most Middle East business. The case of the EU is somewhat different, since it has specific policies towards its regional neighbours designed to ultimately create intra-regional free trade. Middle East/North African (MENA) states have consequently been lining up to knock on the EU door for, if not entry, at least preferential trade status through association agreements. In the absence of an existing MENA economic community, at least in terms of any substantive form of cooperation, integration or common policy, MENA states are often seen as entering negotiations for association from a position of weakness. The implications of association are profound: in Tunisia, for example, it has been estimated that as many as one third of all Tunisian businesses will fail as a direct result of free trade with Europe. Finding a language to explain the 'no pain, no gain' economic philosophy behind this kind of action that will convince populations of its virtue is inevitably profoundly difficult. Moreover, when countries such as Morocco, Tunisia and Egypt find themselves competing with one another to satisfy the demands of a European market, often on terms which are disadvantageous in the first place, then there are bound to be assertions that the Arab regimes are fragmenting the Arab world, rather then uniting it.

One way of both countering such accusations and strengthening the hand of the Arab collective is to advance towards regional economic integration. Substantial efforts have been made in this direction, especially since the failure of previous efforts at Arab unity have shown that political integration is an unlikely scenario. Yet even subregional economic organisations such as the Gulf Co-operation Council and the Arab Maghreb Union have achieved only very limited success and have increasingly become primarily security-related institutions. At the wider level, regional economic integration raises the thorny question of Israel. The post-Oslo peace process initially appeared to offer opportunities for negotiated entry of Israel into any developing MENA economic institutional and organisational framework. To some extent, private enterprise forged ahead with making contacts between Israeli and Arab companies, while the Jordanian and Egyptian governments led the way in establishing governmental economic cooperative links. Much of this has fallen by the way during the government of Benjamin Netanyahu, whose intransigent and destructive policies destroyed any developing consensus for regional economic cooperation. The economic conference in Doha 1997, and the absence of any official representation by the majority of Arab states, indicated that regimes are sensitive to the lack of popular support for any economic activity which appears to be dictated by the US and Israel when the latters' policies are so obviously detrimental to the Arab world. Yet there were still unofficial, business representatives from almost all the Arab states, with regimes not seeking to restrain their business allies from advancing the process. The irony of regional integration is thus that it can have both legitimising and de-legitimising effects, potentially strengthening the Arab economic position but equally being seen to weaken its political independence of action.

A third and equally negative impact of economic liberalisation is the perception by many within the Arab world that it represents a cultural assault by the West on traditional and religious values and norms. Pro-liberalisation regimes are seen as having been coopted into an alien value-system which is inappropriate for the social needs and spiritual welfare of Arabs and Muslims. It would be wrong to attribute the entirety of Islamist revivalism to a response to specific economic policies, but there is strong reason to believe that Islamist political movements have been able to articulate widely felt social anomie that results from the material effects of structural adjustment plans. Not only has the state reneged on its half of the bargain (political support for egalitarian economic development), but what secular opposition exists has failed to offer substantive alternatives. Leftists and communist parties lost credibility in the wake of the collapse of the Soviet Union. Liberal and bourgeois parties are often either off-shoots of dominant and what were single parties which evolved around disgruntled individuals, or they represent essentially the same privileged elitist interests as the regime itself in the era of liberal economic reform. The only political movement left which sustains the familiar principles of social justice and collective responsibility is that of Islam, which has the additional benefit of articulating such demands from within the context of culturally authentic language and identity.

Unlike other religious opposition to structural adjustment programmes and general economic liberalisation such as, the support in Latin America of the poor and socially marginalised by the Catholic church, or the campaigning of Christian Aid against SAPs in Africa, Islamic opposition carries with it the additional weight of its own aspirations for political power. Islam itself sees no separation between the public and private functions of religion and the political aspirations of Islamist movements are entirely legitimate within a doctrinal context. Any effort by the regime to counter or suppress Islamist opposition inevitably risks being interpreted as an attack on Islam itself, and regimes are thus caught in the double bind of being at fault for their economic policies and then again at fault for resisting efforts to challenge those policies. The Islamists, in contrast, have the advantage of both an essentialist legitimacy and a legitimacy derived from their opposition to the specific economic policies of the regime.

Strategies for Legitimising Economic Liberalisation

Beblawi and Luciani asserted that the painful decisions associated with economic liberalisation had in some developing countries been given the approval of populations, despite the numerous ill-effects which they would themselves experience. Most often, this had been the case when the decisions were taken in emergency situations by credible leaders.[13] Given then, that policies of economic reform pose serious legitimacy problems for regimes already struggling to project some aura of credibility, what strategies can be adopted to counter the negative implications of adjustment and project an aura of regime legitimacy?

One strategy which has prompted analysts to make grand associations between economic reform and democratisation, has been to restructure the state-society bargain. A process of carefully stage-managed political reform, including introduction of political party pluralism and competitive elections, is used to substitute for the state's economic obligations, introducing a new element of legitimacy into what is otherwise an ideologically bankrupt political system and creating the semi-illusion of 'taxation with representation'. This apparent pro-

13 Beblawi/Luciani (1987: 2).

cess of democratisation serves to broaden the base of responsibility for difficult decisions, and wins legal opposition parties over to the regime's side with the possibility of access to power. This apparent new 'democratic bargain' may ultimately be a tactical manoeuvre rather than a genuine effort to open up the political arena to allow serious challenges to the regime or its policy. In the Tunisian, Egyptian and Algerian cases, the success of the strategy so far has depended upon the regime's ability to 'fix' elections, either through complicated candidacy procedures, through selective legalisation of alternative parties, or through limited competition within the new system.[14] Religious and class-based parties are specifically excluded from the game since they are most likely to be able to mobilise real opposition. Jordan has also adopted the 'democratic bargain' approach, although in a modified form,[15] and in this case the opening of the political arena to Islamist candidates resulted in a limited period of Islamist domination of the government. The Islamists proved, however, no more able to wish away the endemic economic problems than their secular colleagues and to some extent the challenge to the regime was dissolved through a later electoral procedure.

Even the Saudi monarchy has increased the importance of the advisory council to give the impression that, while liberal democracy on the Western model is not appropriate for the kingdom, decision making should now be more evenly shared with technically competent citizens. In the Kuwaiti case, and following not least from the demands made upon the monarchy after the liberation of the country, an active parliament was re-established in which anti-government (including Islamist) factions have been able to dominate. Even so, only 15 per cent of the population are legally entitled to vote.

14 For a discussion of the limitations of the attempt at a 'democratic bargain' in Egypt, see: Brumberg (1992: 73–104). For a study of the Tunisian case see Murphy (1998).
15 For an explanation of the early linkage between economic liberalisation and political reform in Jordan, see Brand (1992: 167–188).

An associated manoeuvre for establishing regime legitimacy is to formalise new political bargains through national pacts which bind actual and potential opposition to a common agenda (principally that of the regime) in return for regime concessions to include them in a consultation process. This strategy, which was behind Assad's National Front and Ben Ali's National Pact, has the added advantage of creating the impression of unity in the face of adversity. The population is led to believe that there remains a national consensus over the values and principles of government and that, in the interests of preserving political stability at a time of economic crisis, all political parties are willing to suppress their individual agendas to that of the common good. Again, for the opposition, it provides a route to legalisation, consultation and a share of the political pie which they would otherwise most likely be denied. In the Tunisian case, there can be no doubt that the 1988 National Pact did indeed provoke widespread public support for the regime and was considered at the time to be a genuine attempt to recreate and bring the government in line with a national consensus. Subsequent failures of the regime to do more than consult with the opposition and indeed a recent tendency to actively harass even the legal opposition, have served to undermine the National Pact and reduce its efficacy in mobilising support for the regime.

Both these strategies have an additional benefit for regimes which have developed around a single post-independence party. Parties such as the Front de Libération Nationale (FLN) in Algeria, the Arab Socialist Union (ASU) in Egypt, the Rassemblement Constitutionnel Démocratique (RCD) in Tunisia and the Ba'th in Syria, have proved to be resistant to economic reform which threatens their own powers of patronage and control. Party bureaucracies which developed bourgeois characteristics and which expanded their reach into state bureaucracies and the public sector, have had their wings severely clipped by national pacts and competitive party systems, however limited these may prove to be. The president and his pro-reform elite, a group referred to by some as the 'change management team'[16] can rise above the party, assume a degree of relative autonomy from it, and advance their own agendas at the expense of reactionary party cadres.[17] Their apparently politically liberal actions are inevitably going to arouse public support, strengthening their hand and their legitimacy at a crucial point in time. Chadli ben Jedid's introduction of democratic elections were intended to achieve precisely this effect. His mistake was on the one hand to underestimate the electoral strength of Islamist opposition, and on the other to miscalculate that the army would not interfere in civil politics to defend the FLN's position. His accelerated political reforms failed where Ben Ali's more gradual version, in neighbouring Tunisia, has been more successful. In the latter case, the president was able in his first years in office, to draw immense public support through his National Pact, his conciliatory moves towards the opposition (including the Islamists) and his determination to provide strong leadership after a period of both economic and political crisis. By incorporating the military and security forces within the make-up of his regime, and by implementing a painfully gradualistic approach to meaningful political reform, he has actually managed to completely contain legal political challenges and fiercely suppress the only real, but illegal, Islamist challenge. He was aided, at least in terms of public support, by the drift into violence on the part of Nahda in 1991. Tunisians have been deeply alarmed by the spiral of violence in neighbouring Algeria and, despite their equally profound reservations over Ben Ali's brutal tactics, have not subsequently been able to accord Nahda the wholehearted support which it might otherwise have claimed.

16 Nelson (1993: 436).
17 A straightforward example of this was the Hamrouche government appointed by Chadli ben Jedid in September 1989. Of twenty-three new ministers, fifteen were technocrats who had never previously held office and all were known supporters of the economic reform strategy. See: Vandewalle (1992: 200). For evidence of the establishment of the Tunisian 'change management team' see: Murphy (1998).

Volker Perthes, in his study of political liberalisation in Syria,[18] has described a related strategy utilised by Hafez al-Assad. A series of carefully timed prisoner releases, which were interpreted by many as purely propagandist acts, served equally to reinforce the status of the president.

"Primarily, the act expressed a certain relaxation of domestic political strain, but it remained very much embedded in the form of an authoritarian presidential monarchy granting private amnesties on occasion – end of Ramadan or the beginning of a new presidential term – and it can hardly be seen as a sign of political change."[19]

The apparent easing of the political arena was a gift bestowed by the president upon his subject, an act of private generosity and one that reasserted the patrimonial role of the leader.

This is not to say that there is no genuine move towards democratisation in the Arab world. Undoubtedly, the language and norms of liberal democratic political behaviour have percolated through Arab civil society during the past two decades. As Brynen, Korany and Noble have pointed out, Arab intellectuals, non-governmental organisations, and media have led the way in creating bottom-up pressures for political reforms which conform to democratic requirements.[20] The Islamist movements which seek to capture the moral high ground of opposition away from the secularists have been forced to articulate their own positions in response to the arguments and demands of democrats. Thus, though they may reject the concept of a democratic political system along Western liberal lines, they have nonetheless been forced to present their own colours on a bat-

18 Perthes (1995: 243–269).
19 Perthes (1995: 252).
20 Brynen/Korany/Noble (1995: 4–7).

tlefield chosen by the secular liberals. While civil society is busy defining and articulating its demands in this way, however, democracy and political reform are a different currency for political elites. They represent not a set of values and norms to which regimes necessarily aspire, but rather tactical weaponry in the battle for power which can be utilised or abandoned as strategic necessity dictates. This is, of course, a generalisation and one which some leaders, perhaps with a little justification, such as King Hussein of Jordan, would ardently deny. The problem remains, however, that even when their own commitment to the values seems genuine, such leaders have proved ultimately unable to relinquish real power in order to advance practical implementation of those values.[21]

A second strategy for re-establishing regime legitimacy, and one which now has the recommendation of international lending agencies, is to create a new balance in public and private provision. Regimes such as those of Mubarak and Ben Ali have realised that, while the head of the opposition remains the intellectual and lower-middle classes, the heart of the opposition lies with the poorest and most economically marginalised of the population. It is here that activists can be recruited and protesters mobilised. Equally, it is these people who suffer proportionately most from economic liberalisation. Thus, although a general policy of austerity is maintained, what social provision remains is targeted closely to reach these sections of the population. Special funds such as the Tunisian National Solidarity Fund are established which combine treasury monies with private contributions and donations extracted from businesses and which are then directed into the pockets of the poorest in the form of food, clothing, educational, rural development and health allowances. In effect, this serves to spread the cost of economic reform

---

21 Hudson argued that this was not simply a case of insincerity on the part of leaders but a result of their own estimation that democratic reform would lead to chaos given what they perceive to be the subversive and ruthless nature of opposition movements in the region. Hudson (1977: 395).

more evenly, with the middle classes taking a heavier burden and with the state's commitment to social justice and provision being seen to be revived, at least to some degree. At the other end of the scale, taxes and tariffs on luxury goods and the kind of consumer items which are most desired by the 'profiteers' of economic reform, can be raised in an effort to reduce the conspicuous consumption that offends lower income groups.

A third strategy, but one which requires tremendously careful balancing, can be identified as ruler-regime differentiation. In some cases, presidential or monarchical rulers have found it necessary to try to disassociate themselves, as heads of state, from the technocrats of government who design and implement the policies of reform. Then, in times of crisis, the head of state can partially reverse policies which have provoked fierce public reactions. Ministers can be sacked or reshuffled, passing the responsibility downwards rather than upwards and serving to reassure populations that they have an ultimate protector in the head of state himself. While the head of state endorses the general process of reform, he acts as a shut-down switch when the reforms go too fast or are too painful for the population to endure. Acting this way serves to legitimise the head of state and reassure the population that, while the policies may in general be necessary, the ruler will guarantee the people's ultimate well-being. This strategy has been to some extent effective in Jordan where bread riots have resulted from sudden subsidy removals. While the state has responded with heavy policing and suppression, the King has been at pains to show that he himself will hold the ministers accountable. The Crown Prince is sent on a speedy fence-mending visit to the area of rioting, consulting widely and demonstrating the determination of the monarchy to be responsive to the complaints and concerns of the people. Habib Bourguiba also tried this strategy in 1984, with less success. By reversing the decisions of his ministers to increase bread prices, he gained temporary popularity with the public but destabilised the entire process of reform at a time when the country was struggling not to descend into crisis.

There can be no doubt that rulers who seek to project themselves as above the nitty gritty of economic reform decisions are aided by the fact that their governments are increasingly composed of technocrats who have no party bases to protect them from demotion and redundancy. However, rulers must be equally aware that they cannot undermine the technocrats too greatly or they risk the credibility of the entire liberalisation process. Ben Ali has taken the opposite strategy, identifying himself wholly with the policy of economic reform and throwing the weight of the presidency behind his ministers. In his case, he is counting on speedy evidence of the successes of reform to legitimise his decisions.

The issue of success is critical to countering accusations that regimes have caved in to a new form of western imperialism. If reform can be shown to bring tangible economic rewards, at least to a significant proportion of the population, then legitimacy may be restored. To this extent, regimes can seek financial assistance from the more developed states but must be careful not to appear to be simply sinking deeper into the spiral of indebtedness that ultimately benefits only the lenders. One example of positive reward is that of the Tunisian association agreement with Europe. In return for Tunisian commitments to free trade, the EU is providing financial assistance for Tunisian firms to meet the deadline of competitivity and sound performance. This process of 'mise a niveau' has benefited individual private firms who can see the benefits to be gained from streamlining their management and production procedures and who welcome EU financial assistance to do so. This type of funding gives businessmen/women and their employees a stake in reform even as it provides help for them to maximise the opportunities which will become available.

At a more general level, structural adjustment programmes are less likely to detract from a regime's legitimacy if the terms are not dictated by international financial institutions. Thus early reform, initiated by the regime itself and designed by nationals familiar with the specificities of their particular country, are more likely to be seen as legitimate than programmes introduced reluctantly and under international pressure at a time of crisis. The latter will inevitably carry conditionalities which heighten the sense of imposition and reduce the credibility of the regime as a defender of national independence.

When it comes to dealing with counterclaims of legitimacy, notably by Islamist opposition, the regime is invariably in a weaker position. Regimes have attempted to bolster their own claims to legitimacy in a number of ways: on the one hand, some have argued that political Islam represents a regressive and reactionary force which will thrust the Arab world back into the dark ages. In contrast, the regimes themselves are modernising and progressive, seeking to confine Islam to the realms of private religious activity in order to defend the rights of non-observers, religious minorities and liberals. Where Islamist movements have operated outside of the legal political environment, or where they have utilised violent or coercive means to enforce their agendas, it has been easier to argue that – whatever the faults of existing regimes may be – it is the Islamists who are intrinsically undemocratic. It is easier in such instances to claim that Islamist violence is destabilising and that the virtue of current regimes lies in their determination to maintain political stability, not least in order that economic reform might proceed unabated. Finally, regimes may seek to re-establish their own, moderate Islamic, but not Islamist, credentials. By offering a watered-down version of Islam, they project themselves as inclusivist, in contrast to the exclusivity of extremist Islamist movements. Of course, regimes are weakened by both their own failures to introduce meaningful political reform, their inability to do so given the potential challenge which could arise from widening the political arena, and by the character of the means that they use to suppress the Islamists. The extensive abuse of human rights and the intrusion of the security/military apparatus into the civil domain both serve to undermine the legitimacy of regimes.

The case of women deserves attention, although there is insufficient space for proper consideration here. Women are often on the front line of economic liberalisation. While they may gain from new income opportunities in a flexible, low-wage labour market, they are nonetheless the most easily exploited labour and the first to feel the impact of reduced government food and welfare subsidies. When the Islamist opposition to economic reform is combined with a message that may appear antithetical to the interests of women accustomed to certain social rights, they can nonetheless be mobilised by a regime in its own defence. In such cases the regime attempts to derive legitimacy from linking the economic opposition of the Islamists to other potentially reactionary elements of their agenda.

Conclusion

The Arab World is not unique in finding that structural adjustment policies have impacted upon society in such a way as to mobilise previously acquiescent populations, providing a focus around which they may articulate demands upon political elites and systems for greater political participation and influence upon economic decision-making. A study of economic reform processes in developing countries around the globe in the 1980s concluded that:

"Public reactions tend to mobilise existing pressure groups, encourage the formation of new ones to oppose the reform, and stimulate organised opposition to the government. Thus, when the response to a policy reform takes place in the public arena, not only are the stakes high for the reform and for those directly involved in taking a leading role in it, but often the stakes are high for the continued viability of the regime itself."[22]

22 Grindle/Thomas (1991: 175).

At the end of the day, it is only the successful transformation and growth of Middle Eastern economies, and a reasonable distribution of the benefits that accrue there from, which will serve to restore the legitimacy deficit of Arab regimes. Even this will not, in the long term, be enough. Civil society is a blossoming flower in the region and the acceleration of trends in the fields of international communication, transnational associations and institutions of global governance can only fuel demands for popular representation and some form, albeit a localised variation, of democracy.

It may be that once economic stability and good growth patterns are restored to the region, regimes will begin to introduce more genuine, rather than simply tactical, political reforms, secure in the knowledge that society can absorb political change without plummeting into Algeria-type chaos. Alternatively, they may count on the satisfaction of material demands on the state as being enough to pre-empt political demands. The risk is that in denying the route of political reform to restore legitimacy, they are failing to address the most basic needs of civil society and are creating the potential for the very instability and chaos which they seek to avoid. Christopher Clapham argued in his classic introduction to Third World politics[23] that the solution to the economic and social failures of developing states was essentially political, lying specifically "[...] in the incorporation of the governing elites into a set of shared values which acknowledge their accountability to the governed". The principal dilemma for the Arab states is that regimes are attempting to correct the economic mismanagement of the past without addressing to the necessary extent the problem of political accountability. Thus, there is little channelling of popular values upwards into policy-making elites and legitimacy remains fragile during a phase of major economic and social transformation.

---

23 Clapham (1985: 185–186).

List of References

Beblawi, Hazem 1987: The Rentier State in the Arab World, in: Beblawi, Hazem/Giacomo Luciani: The Rentier State, London.

Bill, James/Carl Leiden 1984: Middle East Politics, Canada.

Brand, Laurie A. 1992: Economic and Political Liberalization in a Rentier Economy. The Case of the Hashemite Kingdom of Jordan, in: Harik, Ilya and Denis J. Sullivan (eds.): Privatization and Liberalization in the Middle East, Bloomington.

Brumberg, Daniel 1992: Survival Strategies versus Democratic Bargains. The Politics of Economic Reform in Contemporary Egypt, in: Barkey, Henri (ed.): The Politics of Economic Reform in the Middle East, New York.

Brynen, Rex/Bahgat Korany/Paul Noble (eds.) 1995: Political Liberalization and Democratization in the Arab World. Volume 1, Theoretical Perspectives, Boulder.

Clapham, Christopher 1985: Third World Politics. An Introduction, London.

Ehteshami, Anoushiravan/Emma C. Murphy 1996: The Transformation of the Corporatist State in the Middle East, in: Third World Quarterly, 17/4.

Grindle, Merilee/John W. Thomas 1991: Public Choices and Policy Change. The Political Economy of Reform in Developing Countries, Baltimore.

Halliday, Fred 1988: The Iranian Revolution. Uneven Development and Religious Populism, in Halliday, Fred/Hamza Alavi (eds.): State and Ideology in the Middle East and Pakistan, Basingstoke.

Hudson, Michael 1977: Arab Politics. The Search for Legitimacy, New Haven.

Lipset, Seymour Martin 1960: Political Man. The Social Basis of Politics, Garden City, N.J..

Murphy, Emma C. 1998: Economic and Political Change in Tunisia. From Bourguiba to Ben Ali, Basingstoke.

Nelson, Joan 1993: The Politics of Economic Transformation. Is Third World Experience Relevant in Eastern Europe?, in: World Politics, 45/3.

Perthes, Volker 1995: The Private Sector, Economic Liberalization and the Prospects of Democratization. The Case of Syria and Some Other Arab countries, in: Salamé, Ghassan (ed.): Democracy Without Democrats? The Renewal of Politics in the Muslim World, London.

Letwin, Oliver 1988: Privatising the World. A Study of International Privatisation in Theory and Practice, London.

Rustow, Dankwart 1967: A World of Nations. Problems of Political Modernisation,

Rustow, Dankwart 1971: Middle Eastern Political Systems, Englewood Cliffs.

Vandewalle, Dirk 1992: Breaking with Socialism. Economic Liberalization and Privatization in Algeria, in: Harik, Ilya and Denis J. Sullivan (eds.): Privatization and Liberalization in the Middle East, Bloomington.

Political Consciousness and the Crisis of Political Liberalisation in the Arab World

Walid Kazziha

It has been noticed in recent years that the tide of global democratisation which has swept many parts of the world, including most
notably the former republics of the Soviet Union, has stopped short
of penetrating the resistant walls of the Arab World.[1] Despite the
structural political and economic changes which have been introduced in a number of Arab countries, especially after the Gulf War,
the ultimate results of the so-called process of political liberalisation
have been rather disappointing. An increasing number of Arab intellectuals and scholars and their colleagues in the West have come to
realise that their earlier optimism with the establishment of representative institutions and political parties has been greatly exaggerated.
The discussions among them as well as the focus of their political
debates reflect a rapid shift in their political mood.

---

1 This contribution was presented to the workshop *Choosing the Best? Elections in
   the Middle East and North Africa*, Rabat, January 1998.

During the 1970s and 1980s, a good number of them seemed to be encouraged by the decline of the powers of the central state in some Arab countries, and the concessions it made to the advancing private sector. Their hopes were enhanced by the collapse of the Soviet Union, and the declaration by the US during and after the Gulf War that the world, including the Arab World, would be witnessing the dawn of a new world order. Democracy appeared to many Arab intellectuals to be not only a plausible option, but an international imperative. However, when these dreams did not materialise, the discourse gradually shifted to focus on the issue of civil society. For a while, the concept of civil society became a central theme and a major concern in the discussions of Arab and Western thinkers, but soon it gave way in turn to the subject of human rights. A few years from now the debate may probably experience another shift to focus on how to bridge the gap between the intellectuals in the Arab countries and their sultans, a call which has already been advocated by none other than the guru of civil society in Egypt, Saad El-Din Ibrahim. The ultimate objective of such a call would not be to champion the causes of the downtrodden masses, but to secure a position of significance to those Arab intellectuals who have been waiting in the cold for an opportunity to gain acceptability in the corridors of power and wealth.

It is rather disturbing and disheartening for many of those who are concerned with the future fate of the Arabs to watch the withering away of their long-entertained hopes to see some form of political liberalisation emerging in the Middle East. The move from one slogan to another, from democracy to human rights to possibly secure a place under the sun without achieving a substantial measure of political participation opens a wide range of questions concerning the nature of Arab societies. Are these societies capable of hosting democratic forms of government? Or are they facing some transitory obstacles which may in time disappear? The failure to democratise has triggered off a search for answers to understand the phenomenon. Historians and social scientists by the very nature of their disciplines very often deal with a wide range of variables, which eventually interlock in the process of explaining a phenomenon and produce a variety of interpretations. Consequently, attempts at explaining the failure of political liberalisation in the Arab world had fallen under three major categories.

Political Culture

Some social scientists drawing on the views of orientalists came to the conclusion that there were deeply-rooted permanent features, which distinguished the Islamic World from the West. They perceived Islam to be a religion with a soil inhospitable to the evolution and development of political liberalisation. In their view there was first a continuous division in the Muslim World between the men of the sword, those who have power, and the common people. Such a relationship seemed to have existed throughout history and was somehow irreversible, because it was sanctioned by God. According to them Islam was a religion which preached submission and surrender not only to the Creator, but even to the will of unjust rulers.

Once the argument was posed in this rather deterministic fashion, Muslims regardless of time and place were seen as the prisoners of their own convictions and beliefs. Therefore, there was nothing unnatural about the aversion of Muslim countries to democracy. It was a state of affairs which both the rulers and the ruled accepted for a very long time as an integral part of the teachings of their religion and their political experience. Elie Kedourie asserted that "the idea of democracy is quite alien to the mindset of Islam [. . .] there is nothing in the political traditions of the Arab world [. . .] which might make familiar, or indeed intelligible, the organising ideas of constitutional and representative government".[2]

2   Anderson (1995: 87).

Michael Hudson, while not denying the value of the political culture approach found Kedourie's explanation too general and too sweeping. He described it as "reductionist". Instead he proposed that before dismissing political culture altogether empirical studies should be conducted to evaluate its impact on political liberalisation.[3] Lisa Anderson rejected in the same volume the political culture approach and suggested that similar to other political regimes elsewhere in the world: "The nature of the political regimes in the Arab world [...] can best be understood as reflections of the political economy of the countries in question, particularly the character of their integration into the world economy".[4]

The difficulties associated with using Islam as a political culture are numerous, involving a number of unsubstantiated assumptions. First among them is the assumption that Islam offers a unified culture consisting of uniform traditions, habits, and attitudes. Islam is definitely no such thing. Secondly, it is assumed that Muslims are bound by the intellectual and political traditions of that unified culture and, therefore, reflect in their daily lives and behaviour the principles of their religion. Thirdly, unlike other peoples in this world their perceptions, ambitions and dreams are permanently stamped by their religious beliefs and, thus, are not affected by changes in their political, social or economic conditions. They live continuously in the realm of religious doctrines and ideas outside history and above the real world.

For political culture to become a viable nexus of analysis it is necessary to identify it empirically within a historical context. The relevant question thus becomes: if political culture lies at the basis of the Arab rejection of democracy in contemporary times then what are the characteristics of that culture? Is it a hybrid derived from the Muslim experiences in some or all epochs of the past mixed with

3   Ibid.: 61–75
4   Ibid.: 78

innovations from the West? Or is it a synthesis of a variety of cultures? Still it is possible to reject the political culture approach on the basis that it is a symptom of political economy and not a cause. To uncover the real reason for lack of political liberalisation in the Arab World it is necessary for some to adopt a political economy approach. This has become a favourite approach of a majority of scholars in their attempts to unravel the causes of the Arab alienation from democracy.

The Institutionalist Approach

However, before considering the validity of political economy it is worthwhile addressing a related issue which has gained some prominence in recent years, namely civil society. A wave of writings had appeared in the last few years claiming that while democracy was not attainable in the Arab countries, yet some modest forms of political participation were being experienced and could in the long run advance the cause of democracy. Evidence of such progress had been monitored by academics from the West and the Middle East. The prevailing notion of civil society which was adopted as a result had been heavily influenced by the institutional and structural approach.

A consensus emerged among those who discussed the issue to acknowledge the fact that a great number of organisations "[...]" have mushroomed in the last two decades. The number of Arab NGOs is estimated to have grown from less than 20,000 in the mid 1960s to about 70,000 in the late 1980s".[5] Unfortunately on closer examination, the evidence suggested that these associations, despite their great number, had very little direct political impact on society, simply because they were either, ineffective or were coopted by the state. The existence of institutions in themselves was not sufficient to

5   Ibrahim (1995: 41).

produce the desired outcome, unless they were enabled to perform the functions which were expected of them. In the Middle East no such development was evident. State control over the activities of syndicates, professional associations, and even political parties rendered them ineffective or at best a mere extension of state apparatus.

On the other hand the more viable institutions in society which exercised some measure of autonomy such as the tribes, ethnic groups, villages, regions, sects, and others did not lend themselves to any advanced forms of political participation. Therefore, in the context of the Middle East, it is misleading to focus too much hope on the emergence of associations, institutions syndicates, NGOs, political parties, and others for the achievement of substantial progress toward democracy. A case in point were the elections held in Algeria in the mid-1990s. Despite the election of the president in 1995, the legislative elections in June, and in the municipalities and regions in October 1997, Algeria was no closer to democracy than at any other time before.

Political Economy Approach

The political economy approach offers an interesting explanation for the rise and decline of the levels of political participation in the Arab World. Most scholars choose as their starting point to examine the nature of the Arab state which emerged in the post-colonial era, and seemed to undermine in theory and practice the tendencies toward political participation. Although the Arab countries exhibited since then a variety of political systems, yet two models appeared to be more prevalent. A group of major Arab countries which included Egypt, Syria, Iraq, Algeria and others appeared to develop a type of state which was monopolistic in nature. A state which did not satisfy itself with acquiring full control over the political and security institutions of society including the organisation of a one-party system, but sought to appropriate the wealth and the economy too. The corporatist state evolved with a strong centralised government in charge of planning, resource allocation, production and distribution. In return the newly emerging state offered its lower and middle classes numerous social services and subsidies which enabled them to maintain a respectable standard of living, and nurtured among them a feeling of pride and independence vis-à-vis the foreign powers. Political participation during that period was selective and limited, and only sanctioned by the state. Whenever the ruling elite, consisting of army officers, bureaucrats and technocrats, felt that in the course of an internal struggle for power or regional or international conflict there was a need to mobilise the masses, it did so but only for the duration of the crisis. The involvement of the wider public in politics was never sustained to become a permanent feature of the political system, nor was it independently organised lest it might challenge the authority of the state. In theory the idea was sold to the public by claiming that political freedom was meaningless unless preceded by economic justice. Man had first to be liberated from economic exploitation before he could freely make his political choices. Consequently, democracy had to take the back seat on the road to socialism. However, despite this intellectual distortion, the corporatist system struck an honest bargain with its patient audience, economic and social security in return for the surrender of their political rights.

Another group of Arab countries, mainly the oil producing Arab states developed a model which came to be known among scholars as the 'rentier state'. Basically, it was a political system in which a ruling family or coalition of families of tribal background were in control of the political institutions as well as the revenue from oil. While in most of the Gulf countries the social rights of the population were extensive, their political rights were curtailed, and in some cases were almost non-existent. For example, Kuwaitis enjoyed an entirely free education, free health care and practically free housing; and until the late 1980s, all were guaranteed jobs in the public sectors. Furthermore, most of the basic services were generously subsidised by the government from water to electricity to basic foodstuff. On the other hand, the majority of Kuwaitis had to give up a significant part of their political rights. The latest parliament which was elected in October 1996 might be dissolved at the will of the ruler like other parliaments before it, and no guarantee had existed to secure the continuation of parliamentary life. In essence, the rentier state was a political arrangement where the state bribed its citizens to accept the monopolisation of political power by the few at the top of the political and social hierarchy. It was also a state which controlled the bulk of the national revenue, thus, enabling itself to distribute its lucrative financial donations to whoever it chose to favour.

In both models the ability of the state to take control of the sources of national wealth enabled it to introduce some measure of welfare, which appeared to satisfy the basic needs of the peoples. The two models forged an honest bargain with their citizens; the public acquiesced to the accumulation of political power in the hands of the few and tacitly consented to the dominance of the rulers, some of whom quite charismatic, in exchange for their economic and financial comfort.

Retreat of the State

However, this easy and smooth relationship did not last forever. Due to a variety of external and internal economic pressures and difficulties, especially by the late 1980s, the Arab regimes were forced to concede some grounds in the economic sphere to private enterprise. The collapse of the Soviet Union ushered in on a global scale the victory of a free market economy. The corporatist and the rentier states were unable to resist the onslaught, and finally both systems gave in to privatisation, and to economic open door policy. Economic liberalisation became the main slogan of the 1990s, and the welfare state began to experience a steady retreat.

In most of the Arab countries, which had previously adopted the corporatist model, the upper ranks of the state bureaucracy and ruling elite moved quickly to form an alliance with the newly emerging entrepreneurial class and its foreign partners. Without essentially relinquishing its control over the state apparatus it joined forces with the bourgeoisie. It was at this point that some faint impulses in the direction of political participation began to appear. Laws controlling the formation of political parties and regulating the freedom of the press were slightly relaxed, and for a while elements from opposition parties were admitted into the elected bodies. Political liberalisation at this stage was more like a process of opening the garbage lid slightly to spray an odorizer, but not to get rid of the garbage altogether. Similarly, outside pressures, especially after the Gulf War and domestic demands, at a time of declining oil revenues forced the rentier state to make some cosmetic concessions. In some of the Arab oil rich countries the rulers decided to appoint, rather than elect, consultative and legislative institutions.

As the Arab state took serious steps to withdraw from some sectors of the economy, and simultaneously introduced a few guarded measures toward political participation, a great deal of enthusiasm was generated among some intellectuals and observers of the political scene in the region. The discussions appeared to center around the emergence of a new kind of bargain in the Middle East. The old bargain had somewhat been reversed; it is no more welfare in return for the abdication of political rights, but austerity and impoverishment of the majority of people in return for illusions of political representation. If the earlier bargain was an honest one, the new bargain was terribly dishonest.

Nevertheless, the newly-founded optimism was based on some elaborate argument that in the process of entering a free market economy, the dominance of the corporatist and rentier states over society was weakened, and thus it left behind a power vacuum. The retreat of the state was the signal for the advance of civil society as well as the emergence of the Islamists as substitute political forces to fill the vacuum. In an attempt to guard against the Islamic threat the state tended to liberalise politically, and at the same time opened the economy to domestic and foreign capital. It was perhaps in the vacuum theory where most of the illusions about the gradual progress of Middle East societies toward political liberalisation resided. The illusions were deepened further by the assumption that the appearance of independent entrepreneurial classes in the Middle East enhanced the cause of democracy and political liberalisation.

Economic Realities and Political Mirages

Far from it, the newly emerging bourgeois class owed much of its wealth and status to its close alliance with the rulers, and the upper ranks of the state bureaucracy. Many of its members were former government officials and army officers who found it financially more lucrative to resign their posts and enter the world of business. The new alliance between state and business had no interest in introducing reforms for greater political participation, nor allowing opposition political parties to challenge the hegemony of the rulers and the government party. Unlike its counterpart in the West, the Arab bourgeoisie of the 1990s did not want nor wished to become a driving force toward democracy. Arab intellectuals, who in the first instance sang its praise soon realised that their trust had been totally misplaced. The new class had little or no interest in political liberalisation simply because the new economic order from which it benefited had impoverished the middle and lower classes. It had no stake in empowering these classes, lest they might reverse the process of privatisation. Subsequently, its political activities were very selective, mainly concerned with the dismantling of those earlier welfare laws which inhibited the private accumulation of wealth, such as the labour laws. In fact it did not care less for the political participation of the Arab masses.

Secondly to claim that the vacuum created by the withdrawal of the state allowed the Islamic movements to come forward and exercise their influence is highly misleading. The political and social impact of the Islamists and their growing political role in the region preceded the process of state retreat. A closer look at the resurgence of political Islam clearly reveals that it owed its origin to two most important factors. The first can be directly related to the American strategic posture in the Middle East, since the early 1950s, which encouraged Islamic political activism against Soviet penetration of the region. In the course of its confrontation with the Soviet Union, the US sponsored and supported a wide range of Islamic political activities, including the establishment of the Baghdad Pact in 1954, the creation of the Islamic Pact countries in 1964, and the eruption of an Islamic revolution against the Soviet presence in Afghanistan in 1979, which eventually had enormous repercussions on the rise and development of militant Islamic groups in some major Arab countries. Similarly, two of the major regional powers in the Middle East, namely Saudi Arabia and Iran under the Shah encouraged and financed a variety of Islamic political movements in the Arab and Islamic World in an effort to undermine the political influence of the nationalist and socialist regimes in the region.

In the long run it would appear that both the US and its allies in the Middle East lost their control over the Islamic movements which they initiated. However, that did not alter the fact that it was not the vacuum created by the recent retreat of the state as much as the active policies of powerful international and regional players which eventually precipitated the phenomenon of Islamic resurgence and gave it its political space in the Middle East. There is an exaggerated misconception which surrounds the notion of the retreat of the corporatist and rentier states. It is often perceived as a retreat which had taken place on all fronts, and consequently led to the weakening of the powers of the state not only economically but also politically.

There is no doubt that the state in the Arab World had lost some of its control over the economy in recent years, but it is rather inaccurate to think that it had surrendered its political leverages over society too. To perceive the change as being similar to that which had taken place in the West in the 19th century, and describe it as 'no taxation without representation' is a fallacy. In the Middle East there can be 'taxation without representation'. The few cosmetic political reforms which had been introduced in some Arab countries were not meant to respond to a popular demand from the masses or the new Arab bourgeoisie. It was more of a response to please the 'Yankees' from afar. Ironically the Arab world did not register any strong demand for democratisation. No one was knocking at the doors of the state urging it to grant the people their political rights. With the exception of a few voices here and there among the intelligentsia, there was hardly any such call. The state was under no serious pressure to retreat politically and give way to the participation of a wider segment of its public. Politics remained the monopoly of the men of power and wealth. A reorganisation of that monopoly took place to adjust to the changes in the international market and to adapt to the end of the Cold War. The Arab states unloaded some of their economic burdens, but political liberalisation was not a serious item on their agenda.

If neither the Arab state nor its new allies in the world of business opted for wider political representation, why did the middle and lower classes who suffered most from the decline of the welfare state maintain their utter silence on the subject?

The Crisis of Political Liberalisation

This is crucial and legitimate question to ask. In answering it we may uncover the secrets of the deep-rooted crisis of political participation and democracy in the contemporary Middle East.

A correlation has often been made between democracy and the economic standard of living in society, or the level of education, or sometimes the impact of outside powers. However, such generalisations have been challenged. For example some drew the attention to the fact that India had democratised under conditions of poverty. On the other hand the oil rich Arab countries had not done so, despite their higher standards. Wealth, education and external influences might at times facilitate the transformation of societies from authoritarianism to democratic forms of government, but in the final analysis it depends largely on the level of political consciousness which a society enjoys. If there is a greater political awareness among the bulk of the population transformation can be achieved, but if it is low or negligible then the chances of any significant change are minimal.

Political consciousness in the Arab World is mainly derived from two major sources, namely the system of education and the means of mass communication and mass media. Most Arab countries have since the beginning of the century introduced a so-called modern system of education, and with varying degrees abandoned the traditional system which was based on religious institutions and methods of learning. In the post-colonial era numerous schools were opened which covered the various stages of education from elementary levels to universities. However, schools soon became overcrowded and the levels of instruction took a downward dip. Institutes of higher education and universities faced the same fate in most Arab countries with few exceptions. According to a recent report on school children in Egypt, it had been asserted that in the last few decades the systems of education applied in schools had led to the deterioration of the level of intelligence among young Egyptians.[6] Education in modern times is closely related to the financial investments a society makes in that

---

6 Reference to the report was alluded to in Fahmi Howeidi's article in *Al-Ahram* newspaper, 4 November 1997: 11.

field. The meagre budgets for education in most Arab countries cannot be compared to the huge but totally secret expenditures on the presidential or royal families and the armed forces. Over and beyond this, education in itself may or may not lead to a higher level of political awareness. What brings that about is the type and direction of the content of education. Is it the type that prepares and encourages the new generations to exercise their independent judgement and freedom of thought? Does it train them to take individual initiatives to pursue their interests, and nurture in them a sense of community and public service? Is the system of education in the Arab World well disposed and particularly designed to the promotion of the principles of political liberalisation and democracy?

On the contrary, education in the Arab countries is mainly controlled by the governments and as such it promotes values of submission and obedience to authority. It is dedicated to the pursuit of knowledge through memorisation rather than analysis, experimentation and innovation. The Arab world has imported a wide range of institutes of learning from the modern West, but it paid more attention to the form rather than the content.

Therefore, what looks to the outside observer to be educational institutions comparable to those found in the West are merely deformed replicas incapable of performing the functions they normally perform in the West. During the last 50 years or so, the system of education in the region have unfortunately produced one generation after another of young men and women whose political consciousness is narrow, limited and dogmatic, largely manipulated and controlled by the policies of the state, and ill disposed in theory and practice to the notions of political participation. Unlike the experiences of the Western nations, the prevalent systems in the Middle East did not provide a breeding ground for the growth of democracy or the appearance of strong impulses toward democracy.

The anti-democratic trend in the region was reinforced further by the modernisation of the means of mass communication and the mass media at the hands of the state. This took place under the direct auspices of the corporatist and rentier states. However, while in recent years the press may have been partially allowed to express the views of the opposition, yet by and large it remained subject to government control. Perhaps today, more important than the press is the television, which has become the most important single source in the process of formulating the political outlook of the Arab peoples. Apart from being entirely in the hands of the government, it has not been affected in the least by the retreat of the state. Arab governments continue to have full control over their TV networks, and radio broadcasts. The impoverished Arab masses have no access to satellite services and international networks, simply because they cannot afford it nor can they understand foreign languages. Still the TV in the Middle East is the main source of political education for the masses. In the most populated Arab country today, there are some eight TV channels which broadcast daily. These channels fall under the direct administration of the minister of information, who is an ex-military intelligence officer and has been in his past as senior cabinet minister for over twenty years.

Conclusion

The government controlled systems of education and the mass media in the Arab countries promote a political culture which is diametrically opposed to political liberalisation. The introduction of satellite services and the Internet has not touched except a very thin segment of society. It is a segment which is subjected and exposed to an overwhelming barrage of American serials and soap operas with little political value. The Arab state may have relaxed its grip on the economy, but it has not conceded any substantial grounds on the issue of political rights. Whatever steps were taken in any of the Arab countries to introduce some semblance of political participation had been taken by the rulers and could be reversed by them any time. In response to accusation of human rights violations in Jordan, the monarch responded by declaring "It was we who in essence decided that democracy, respect for human rights and general freedom is the course we ought to follow".[7] In the absence of a wide base of political awareness in Arab societies for political liberalisation, the reluctant steps taken by the governments in that area could only be explained in terms of external pressures and possibly the demands of some members of the alienated elites who seek to be integrated in the clubs of power and wealth. However, once the governments respond to these limited pressures and demands they find it unnecessary to make any further concessions and gradually reassert their authority by diluting the so-called democratic measures.

The political economy of Arab societies had undoubtedly created a mechanism which controlled the progress of democracy in the region. The expansion of the role of the state in the post-colonial era led to the establishment of its control over all aspects of the life of civil society. Its functions were not limited to the realms of politics and economics but extended to include culture, education and even the moral values governing the private lives of individuals and communities. The recent rearrangement of the role of the state in the context of a new world order characterised by a free market economy forced the Arab state to surrender to private capital some of its economic leverages. It did not, however, surrender in the process any substantial part of its political or cultural influences over society. Through its continued control of education and the mass media, the Arab state perpetuated a political culture among the bulk of its population, which was neither liberal nor democratic. In doing so it also perpetuated submission to authoritarianism.

In the final analysis a political economy approach and a political culture approach are not mutually exclusive. In the context of the

---

7 *Al-Hayat*, 2 November 1997: 6.

Arab World the separation is fictitious. What the Arabs are experiencing is a synthesis between the two. Where political economy ends political culture picks off; and where the latter ends the former reinforces it.

List of References

Anderson, Lisa 1995: Democracy in the Arab World. A Critique of the Political Culture Approach, in: Brynen, Rex et al. (eds.): Political Liberalisation and Democratisation in the Arab World, Boulder.

Ibrahim, Saad Eddin 1995: Civil Society and Prospects of Democratisation in the Arab World, in: Norton, August (ed): Civil Society in the Middle East, New York.

Power Sharing and Elections
in the Middle East and North Africa

Anoushiravan Ehteshami

Generally speaking, during the Cold War the nature of the political regimes in power in developing countries was not the determining factor in the West's relations with them.[1] Broader strategic considerations seemed to underwrite Western approaches towards key Third World countries and regions. These considerations often included some assessment of the ways in which the Soviet Union's influence in the Third World could be checked, and the extension of Western presence in the same. This Western approach was based on the principle of 'containing' or 'rolling back' international communism. At its worst, it encouraged Western support for some unsavoury Third World dictators (Marcos, Mobutu, Noriega, Batista, Somoza, Park, Pinochet, Suharto), and military-led authoritarian regimes

---

1 This contribution was presented to the workshop *Choosing the Best? Elections in the Middle East and North Africa*, Brussels, January 1998. It provided the basis for the published article in 1999: Is the Middle East Democratizing?, in: British Journal of Middle Eastern Studies, 26/2.

(Argentina, Pakistan, Brazil, Turkey, Nigeria, Sudan). Western policy did little to reward good government, nor did it encourage pluralism. In practical terms, 'being on our side' mattered more than being democratic, accountable, or representative.

The strategy of alliance building, irrespective of regime-type, was also keenly deployed by the Soviet Union, some of whose friends and allies were a mirror image of the pro-Western ones; Assad, Saddam Hussein, Kim Il-Sung, Ghaddafi, Mengistu Haile Mariam are good examples. For the Soviets, in the absence of the 'dictatorship of the proletariat', a coalition of anti-Western, 'socialist-oriented', petite bourgeois and nationalist forces could conceivably make reliable Third World allies in the struggle for supremacy against the West. In practice, this Soviet strategy legitimised Moscow's support for a range of authoritarian regimes, from Afghanistan to Angola.

In the Middle East/North Africa (MENA) region as a whole, however, while authoritarianism ruled the day in the Cold War period, few powerful dictators emerged to dominate this region. The Middle East subsystem was always overshadowed by the rivalrous struggles between a number of fairly evenly matched regional powers, which perhaps helped in checking the power of dominant regional hegemons. Nevertheless, it has been blatantly obvious that the majority of the peoples of this region did not really enjoy anything better than the grace of 'benevolent dictators' and a crop of authoritarian rulers. So much so that by the 1980s it had become clear that the region had begun paying a high price for the years of neglect of the peoples' political rights by its autocrats, not only in purely political terms, but also in terms of social malaise and economic bankruptcy.

Elections in the Cold War years, when they did take place in the Arab world, were, more often than not, a feature of revolutionary-nationalist regimes which were intent on using them as a tool for mobilising support for the ruling regime or party. I have in mind in this regard a cluster of Arab states – Algeria, Egypt, Iraq, Syria and Tunisia – which were characterised by single (or limited) party activity. Rarely in the sixties, seventies or the eighties did elections serve as an independent variable in a representative or participatory political system. While suffrage did remain universal, the course of elections were controlled or manipulated through a number of constitutional, bureaucratic and political channels. Beyond the Arab world, the picture was not much better either. In Iran, elections were never meant to change the political landscape; in Turkey, the army ruled as frequently as the elected political leaders; and in Israel, the prevailing political system allowed for the creation of a sort of one party rule from 1948 until the late 1970s.

Impact of the End of the Cold War

The surge of democracy in Europe and the resurgence of pluralism in parts of Asia, Africa and Latin America followed the end of global power bloc rivalries which had conditioned much of the political process in the Cold War era. The end of the Cold War lifted the restrictions that the two superpower blocs had placed on the political process in the states of their allies. The depolarisation of international relations, furthermore, seems to have provided the basis for the resurgence of the 'domestic setting' in the developing countries in Western foreign policy thinking. Before long, external pressures, and more intrusive involvement by major international agencies (such as the IMF and the World Bank) in the domestic arena of poorer countries, began placing political liberalisation and reform high on the post-Cold War international agenda. The Western message was that political liberalisation and pluralism should go hand-in-hand with economic liberalisation. Multilateral fora, from 'Partnership for Peace' to 'Euro-Med Dialogue', begun echoing the same message in Europe's eastern and southern peripheries.

In the MENA region, it was a combination of external pressures and domestic failures (particularly in the socio-economic realm) which acted as the powerful push factors for the ruling regimes to seriously consider holding regular elections, and to contemplate opening up the political system to more public scrutiny. In the new international environment, Middle Eastern rulers soon learnt, legitimacy was no longer a function of Cold War partnerships, but a commodity whose value could only be realised if they could be seen to be addressing the economic and political needs of their citizens. So, political reform, in its early stages at least, may have been no more than a tactical response to the fiscal crisis of the state, and the desire to please Western audiences.

Looking at the short post-Cold War period across the MENA region, however, we cannot deny that a noticeable degree of political liberalisation has been taking place. This phenomenon might be seen as a hopeful sign that political reform is becoming a strategic option for changing the political landscape in several Middle Eastern countries. But one is still struck by the resilience of the 'fierce state' in the region, particularly in the Arab world, and the general absence of a 'revolutionary' democratic wave which was expected by some to push out of Europe and sweep across the whole region. Here, it is still such terms as 'quasi-democratic' or 'partial democracy' which convey a special meaning about the relationship between the ruler and the ruled, between the state and civil society, and less such phrases as 'democratic transitional'. Indeed, one of the virtues of the end of the Cold War has been the way in which it has exposed the on-going struggle between civil society and the state.

The process of openly contested competitive elections within a democratic and pluralistic political system remains unfulfilled in much of the MENA region. In this, the Middle East is perhaps not a unique region. The uniqueness of this region, however, lies elsewhere; in the resilience of undemocratic behaviour across its wide range of regime types and political systems, rentier or corporatist. From traditional (Jordan, Morocco) and conservative monarchies (the GCC countries) to secularist (Egypt, Iraq, Syria, Tunisia, Turkey) and Islamic (Iran, Sudan) republics, to mixtures of secularist and religious-inspired governments (Libya, Yemen), a satisfactory formula for popular participation in determining the destiny of the state remains unfounded.

The reasons for this, however, might have less to do with culture, than with the nature of the reform process itself. It is becoming amply evident that reform (i.e. change), when it has been introduced into the region, has often been directed from above, and sometimes even from the outside. Thus, typically, the political reform process, which has been sweeping across the MENA region, has stemmed more from the ruling regime's perceived strategy for survival, than from a direct response to any ground swell of protest to its policies. I would argue here that the impact of food and price riots, as a form of protest, in the Middle East has not always been felt in the political realm.

Reform from above, therefore, does not always provide the essential basis for the growth and development of civil society, the ultimate guarantor of pluralism in any political system I would submit. Indeed, civil society could have been lagging behind the regime-introduced reforms so much that its natural growth may have been hampered by the rise of other (perhaps hitherto dormant) social forces in the region. Traditional social forces, like tribalism, have resurfaced in the second half of the nineties to intervene in the electoral process of several Arab countries (Jordan, Kuwait, Yemen), for example. And often on behalf of the rulers.

But other forces, such as ethnicity, regionalism, kinship and sectarianism, have also begun playing a part in the electoral process. The involvement of these forces in the political reform process has, at times, adversely affected the natural growth of other kinds of associations which are essential for the creation and functioning of a healthy civil society. These forces have also tended to encourage the process of fragmentation in several Arab societies. Some of the tensions, which the above alludes to, between elections and power sharing, will be examined in the remainder of this paper.

Elections in the 1990s

Broadly speaking, MENA elections in the 1990s can be examined from five (related) angles. First, their regularity and frequency – for their 'intensity'. Secondly, their type (local, national, presidential, parliamentary, and others). Thirdly, the type of political forces taking part. Fourth, the role of political forces taking part. And, finally, the impact of national elections on (a) the prevailing political system, and (b) the wider arena.

In assessing MENA elections in the 1990s up until 1997, the time of writing of this piece, one is struck by the regularity and frequency with which they have been occurring. As Table (1) demonstrates, elections have become a common feature of political life in the Middle East, a common feature of the political landscape, particularly since representative institutions – elected majlises, consultative shuras, peoples assemblies – have increasingly acquired a life of their own. This is so, I hasten to add, despite the absence of a 'third democratic wave' sweeping through the region.

It is evident that, in total, some 70 elections have taken place in the MENA region from 1989 to 1997, including elections for trades union bodies, chambers of commerce, for mayors and a host of other offices. This is an astonishingly high figure for any region in the international system, let alone compared with the MENA region's own recent past! Indeed, elections are emerging as an indicator of development and progress by the ever-judgmental outside parties, as well as by Middle Eastern rulers themselves.

In fact, several of these elections have been so significant in terms of their fall-out and direct impact on the area that I have chosen to characterise them as 'very significant'. These most obvious of such elections have been: the Algerian municipal and parliamentary elections of 1990/91, the Turkish parliamentary elections of 1995, the Israeli parliamentary elections of 1996, and the Iranian presidential elections of 1997.

*Table 1: Survey of National Elections in the MENA Region,
1989–1997*

Country	89	90	91	92	93	94	95	96	97
Algeria	–	L	M	C	–	–	P	R	M/L
Egypt	–	M	–	–	P	–	M	–	L
Iran	P/R	–	–	M	P	–	–	M	P
Israel	–	–	–	M	P	–	–	M	–
Jordan	M	–	–	L	M	–	L	–	M
Kuwait	–	M	–	M	–	–	–	M	–
Lebanon	–	–	–	M	–	–	–	M	–
Palestine	–	–	–	–	–	–	–	P/M	–
Mauritania	–	–	–	P/M	–	–	M	–	P
Morocco	–	–	–	R	M	–	–	R	M
Tunisia	P/M	L	–	–	–	P/M	L	–	–
Turkey	L	–	M	L	–	L	M	L	–
Syria	–	–	–	–	–	M	–	–	–
Sudan	–	–	–	–	–	–	L	P/M	–
Yemen	–	–	R	–	M	–	–	–	M

Key: P = Presidential, M = Majlis or Parliamentary, L = Local or Municipal, R = Referendum, C = Cancelled.

As is clear from Table 1, in every year since 1989 one type or another national election has taken place in one or more MENA country. Since 1992 in particular, we can see a flood of election activity grip-

ping the region and even sometimes in countries where meaningful
elections had been almost completely absent in previous decades
(Algeria, Jordan, Kuwait, Morocco, Tunisia), ranging from presidential, parliamentary and municipal elections to national referenda and
plebiscites. It is worth noting that election activity is in evidence not
only horizontally (in other words, across the region), but also verti-
cally (in other words, in terms of different types of elections taking
place within the same country). Between 1993 and 1997, for
instance, eight MENA states held at least three types of national elections. In 1996, nine countries had held national elections, and in
1997, seven. Algeria, Iran and Morocco held major elections in both
1996 and 1997. These figures seem to suggest that the era of sus-
pending or postponing elections for political reasons may well have
passed into history; the last instance of cancellation of a major election in the region for political reasons was in 1992, in Algeria. The
consequences of that folly are still reverberating in the western Mediterranean area.

Furthermore, while several MENA countries have held more than
one national election in the post-Cold War period (Iran, Jordan,
Morocco, Tunisia), others have been attempting to modernise their
political systems by overhauling their more traditional forms of
regime-people associations. Omani and Saudi efforts to establish
shuras with some political muscle are cases in point. Other countries,
meanwhile, have desired (and managed) to hold elections even difficult political situations. So, despite tense domestic situations and
civil unrest, Algeria, Sudan, and Yemen have held national elections
in the second half of the 1990s.

While I readily concede that some of these elections may have
been designed as window dressing for the benefit of outside parties,
or that some have been rather cosmetic, having had little impact on
the life of the average citizen, other elections have been quite crucial,
even historic, events. As already stated, note the outcome and dramatic impact of national elections in Algeria, Iran, Israel and Turkey,

for example, on the societies concerned, as well as on the region as a whole.

Today, more than ever before, electoral politics is influencing the lot of ordinary MENA citizens. Perhaps even more significantly, elections are also touching more lives than ever before. The 15 countries (in Table 1) in which elections have been held since 1989 account for the bulk of the MENA region's population, accounting for over 250 million people. Indeed, the most encouraging sign is that it is in some of the region's largest countries that forms of representative government have been taking shape, if not spreading roots. More promising still, several of these elections, though by no means all, are being based on multi-party competition for office.

The election process, as a process, has served many purposes, of course. It has, on the one hand, been skilfully used to legitimise the ruling regime's hold on power (Iran, Jordan, Kuwait, Tunisia). But the process has also served to threaten or undermine the ruling regime's legitimacy, either directly (Algeria in the early 1990s), or indirectly (perhaps in Jordan in the late 1990s with the extensive boycott of the parliamentary elections by majority of the opposition forces).

Table 2: MENA Elections since 1989

Relatively open or politically significant elections	*Politically insignificant elections or no elections*
Algeria	Bahrain
Egypt	Iraq
Iran	Libya
Israel	Oman
Jordan	Qatar

Relatively open or politically significant elections	Politically insignificant elections or no elections
Kuwait	Saudi Arabia
Lebanon	Sudan
Mauritania	Syria
Morocco	United Arab Emirates
Palestinian National Authority	
Tunisia	
Turkey	
Yemen	

As implied already, not all is well in the political reform process in the Middle East however. In several countries, the ruling elite has managed successfully to manipulate the electoral system and/or process to render elections futile in terms of their political impact. In some countries, electoral law has been drafted in such a way as to make open contestation and meaningful political change an impossibility. The electoral process in these instances has been nothing more than another weapon in the armoury of the incumbent rulers. In other cases, constitutions and complex electoral procedures have ended up becoming barriers to participation of 'undesirable' political forces. In these circumstances, the danger always exists for elections to become irrelevant acts, which, in the end, block, instead of facilitating or allowing the circulation of power amongst competing forces. Elections sadly, though numerous, have in fact served to subvert the democratic process, not helped by the boycott of elections carried out by the main opposition forces in several instances in recent years (Jordan, Mauritania, Yemen in their 1997 elections).

A few examples collected at the time of writing will suffice to illustrate the above points: in Egypt, the government-dominated party nominates presidential candidate(s) to be voted upon by the electorate, thus giving the ruling party virtual control of the outcome. Also in Egypt, under the direction of the president, the parliament has passed new martial law legislation (in 1997) which provides the government with quite extraordinary powers; in Morocco, the parliament is elected indirectly, through a (loosely controlled) electoral college and wage earners; in Iran, all candidates standing for elected office must have their credentials checked and vetted by the interior ministry and the Council of Guardians. The vetting procedure has prevented the entry of 'undesirable' trends into the political system; in Kuwait, only a minority of the population is allowed to participate in the elections; in Algeria, the 1996 constitutional amendments allow the president to appoint one third of the deputies to the new upper chamber, where a three-quarter majority will be needed for the passage of bills into law; and, in Jordan and Morocco, the ruling monarchs have retained full influence over the executive branch and continue to play an active role in the political system, going as far as hiring and firing ministers and ministerial appointments.

Also, while the populace may have been allowed to enter the poll booth across the MENA region, if other quite crucial conditions for elections are not satisfied, elections will end up being quite empty gestures. The most important of the necessary conditions for a successful electoral process are: political transparency, the rule of law, constitutional government, freedom to express different opinions, have the right to organise, mobilise, publicise, and congregate, have unhindered access to information, and, ultimately, have confidence in the voting process.

Additionally, a sound economy has always been a prerequisite of the democratisation process in the MENA region. Today, even agencies such as the IMF have come to regard economic prosperity as underpinning political stability. Sadly, economics has been cutting both ways in the MENA region. On the one hand, deep economic crises in the rentier MENA states and their dependants in the rest of the region has pushed them towards broadening their political base. From Oman and Qatar, to Saudi Arabia and the United Arab Emirates, we now see this process in action. It could be argued, with some justification, that economic problems did in fact aid the democratisation process in the first half of 1990s, when several MENA economies were still smarting from the costs of the Kuwait crisis, the relatively low oil prices, large currency devaluations and general economic stagnation.

On the other hand, without a sound and expanding economic base, it is difficult to see how the political reform process can be sustained. A burgeoning economy, furthermore, seems to be seen by MENA political elites – who have already committed themselves to carry through IMF's harsh economic reform package, which often requires an iron political will and not a little dose of authoritarianism – as a reason for not liberalising the political system, as licence not to democratise!

In this context, the issue of power-sharing, which has emerged as a key element of the political reform package, acquires special relevance. In tandem with the growth of the electoral process experiment in the Middle East has come the challenge to several political systems and ruling elites of the Islamist opposition, which is today inspired, organised and committed. The Islamists have created not only the type of organisation which can (and does) violently challenge the ruling regime in several Arab countries, but have typically played an active part in the political space which the Arab ruling regime has chosen to free up, whether in terms of holding elections, reducing censorship, or permitting the formation of charitable or political organisations. With the gradual demise of secularist forces and their credibility as reliable opposition parties, it is the Islamists who seem to form the hard core of the opposition political forces, and the force actively taking part in the political space of many Arab countries.

For these reasons, the role of the Islamists as the only opposition political force of the hour has received much attention in the 1990s. While in some MENA countries the main Islamist challenge to the ruling regime in recent years has come from the armed factions of the Islamist forces – Algeria, Egypt, Libya, Palestine, Saudi Arabia, for example – in others Islamist forces have used the electoral process to gain access, if not aim to take full control, of the levers of power. The strategies of the Refah and Islah parties in Turkey and Yemen respectively, and those of the Islamist fronts in Jordan and Kuwait during elections provide useful examples of the peaceful, electoral, path to power that these Islamist forces adopted. Even the Hezbollah movement in Lebanon has found it prudent in the 1990s to add a political wing to its organisation, and, through it, gain access to the Lebanese centres of power, notably the national parliament.

Neither Islamist trend, violent or peaceful, however, has succeeded in loosening, let alone breaking, the grip of the existing elites on power. In none of the above cases, in other words, can one identify a lasting transfer of power from one type of political leadership to another. The striking reality seems to be that ruling elites have proved more resilient and robust in the defence of their realm than was expected at the beginning of the 1990s. Even in Algeria, where after all the bloody civil war occurred precisely because the Islamists were not allowed to politically cash-in their electoral successes, the military-backed ruling regime has managed to reconstitute itself, reform the constitution, and also hold new elections in which it has managed to secure (some would say engineer) its the dominant political position.

In general terms, there are two reasons for the failure of the Islamist forces to translate their early electoral victories into broader political successes. The first reason has much to do with the conduct of the Islamists themselves. While undoubtedly the Islamists carry some moral weight in their battles with their ruling regimes, on several occasions they have failed to adjust their message and their policies to the aspirations of the Arab masses and to the political mood of the electorate. The result of such mistakes has been quite costly in electoral and political terms, where they have ended up loosing ground (Jordan, Kuwait and Yemen) and splintering into fractions (Algeria, Egypt, Palestine). Furthermore, it is now undeniable that the indiscriminate use of force by the radical Islamist groups in the Arab world has been badly damaging to their popularity amongst the masses, and their credibility with the middle classes.

The second reason for the Islamists' failure to secure a firmer grip on power has to do with the responses of the ruling Arab elites themselves to the Islamist challenge. The Arab governments' willingness to use force against the violent Islamic groups has succeeded in checking the Islamists' organisational growth in several countries (Algeria, Egypt, PNA, Tunisia, Syria). Secondly, ruling regimes in the Middle East have shown a greater degree of agility, flexibility and creativity than in the past when confronting their Islamist opponents. They have shown the ability to select their tools carefully when dealing with the Islamist groups, and to track the problem along several tracks simultaneously. Some countries have encouraged the growth of non-Islamist forces (Algeria, Jordan, Tunisia, Turkey) as an antidote to the Islamists, while others have manipulated the constitution and/or the electoral systems in order to stunt the institutional growth of the Islamist forces. All governments, in the meanwhile, have sought quicker and more lasting solutions to their country's endemic socio-economic problems as a means of undermining the popularity of the Islamist opposition, though not always very successfully it has to be said.

It is interesting to note, however, that not in one single case in the Arab world has power actually been shared between ruling regimes or elites and the opposition. In Algeria, Egypt, and Tunisia, the ruling elite might have adapted, and the regime might have evolved, but it has still managed to exclude the Islamist opposition from power; in Jordan, Kuwait, Turkey, and Yemen, the Islamists have had a taste of power, but – and without meaning to write their obituaries – their successes have proved to be short-lived. In all these countries, Islamist electoral power has been checked.

Conclusions

Let me not end my contribution on a survey of the on-going struggles between the Islamist forces and the state in the Arab world, but rather on a reflection on possible future twists in the relationship between the state and civil society, as mediated by the electoral process. And here, I am particularly interested in the case of Iran, where not only an Islamic state has been in existence since 1979, but one whose rulers has turned the holding of national elections into an art form. In Iran today, one can almost detect an opposite trend to what has been going on in the Arab world in the 1990s. Elections have become a hallmark of the Iranian Islamic system, no doubt, with over a dozen national elections held in the country in less than twenty years. In the 1990s, however, presidential and parliamentary elections have acquired a greater level of importance, largely because of the impact that they have been having on the balance of power amongst Iran's faction-ridden power elite.

An important aspect of the operation of the political process in post-Khomeini Iran has been its gradual but steady shift towards less Islamisation (dare one say secularisation!) of the electoral and political processes, and the rapid growth of civil society. The May 1997 presidential elections highlighted the trend rather well, and the people's deep-felt desire for more openness and pluralism. As it happened, the popular candidate, who scored an overwhelming and historically unprecedented victory in this election, was also the one who had promised Iranian people more political, cultural and social liberties, the rule of law, and the right to organise and to have freedom of thought. Hojjatoleslam Khatami's victory at this juncture then was perhaps no accident. Although President Khatami himself is a relatively senior cleric, and quite loyal to the Islamic system founded by Ayatollah Khomeini, he nonetheless has stood for such blatantly "liberal" values and political measures that he has even surprised the West. But the real vibrations of his views and public policies, which are no greater than what the people of Iran themselves voted for, are being felt across the Arab world, where his government's policies and some of President Khatami's speeches have rocked the Arab Islamist fronts to their foundations. In Iran, some Islamists have gone as far as arguing, we are seeing political Islam in retreat. If political Islam is losing ground in Iran, some Arab Islamists have begun asking, what chance does it have to succeed in Arab lands?

So, if we were to extrapolate from the Iranian case, could we not argue that over time the tide of Islamism in the Arab world might also ebb? And if this were to happen, could we not look forward to an era of open politics where neither ruling regime nor active opposition could claim to have a monopoly on the truth as well as power? Is not this what power-sharing is all about! Looking beyond the struggle between ruling MENA regimes and the opposition Islamist forces, we can say that the first few years of the political reform process in the 1990s were rather experimental, based on trial and error, until a stable and workable system could be found which facilitated power-sharing but not necessarily power transference. Ruling elites and Islamists may now be entering a new phase of interaction, which will necessarily be conditioned by a more daring civil society – those other social forces, associations and movements which have poured into every opening in the political space in the 1990s. Civil society is now a considerable force to be reckoned with, despite its continuing timidity in several MENA countries. Its mediating power is to have a moderating impact.

Finally, citizen and ruler alike have now learnt that sudden political pluralism and ill-planned democratisation can bring as much harm to a fragile social system as benefit. Such has been the perception of the dangers of instability spilling over into other countries, and such has been the impact of the Algerian crisis on our thinking, that Western leaders now often speak of the need above all to preserve stability in the area, and more softly of the need to democratise. The review of the nineties is causing subtle shifts in outlook, amongst both the ruler, the ruled, as well as among outside parties. Therefore, we could be approaching the moment for reaching a new political contract between the ruler and the ruled in the MENA region, and one which is based on serving more than one section's interests in society. Whether such a new contract will necessarily have to have an Islamist face still remains to be seen.

The Authors

Joseph Alpher is former Director of the Jaffee Center for Strategic Studies, Tel Aviv University and former Director of the American Jewish Committee's Israel/Middle East Office, Jerusalem.

Abdel Monem Said Aly is Director of the Centre for Political and Strategic Studies, Al Ahram Foundation, Cairo.

Sven Behrendt is Middle East Senior Research Fellow of the Bertelsmann Group on Policy Research of the Center for Applied Policy Research, Ludwig-Maximilians-University, Munich.

Barry Buzan is Professor of International Studies at the University of Westminster, London.

Anoushiravan Ehteshami is Professor of International Relations and Director of the Centre for Middle Eastern and Islamic Studies, University of Durham, United Kingdom.

Christian-Peter Hanelt is Director of the Division Middle East at the Bertelsmann Foundation, Gütersloh, Germany.

Rosemary Hollis is Head of the Middle East Programme of the Royal Institute of International Affairs, London.

Walid Kazziha is Professor of Political Sciences at the American University of Cairo.

Phebe Marr is former Senior Fellow of the National Defense University, Institute for International Strategic Studies, Washington DC

Jörg Monar is Director of the Centre for European Polititcs and Institutions at the University of Leicester.

Emma Murphy is Lecturer at the Center for Middle Eastern and Islamic Studies of the University of Durham, United Kingdom.

Joel Peters is Senior Lecturer, Department of Politics and Government, Ben Gurion University of the Negev, Israel.

Eberhard Rhein is Political Adviser to the European Policy Centre, Brussles and former Director, Mediterranean and Middle Eastern Affairs, European Commission, Brussels.

Riad al-Khouri is Director of the Middle East Business Association, Amman.

Trevor Taylor is Professor of International Relations at Cranfield University, United Kingdom.

Ole Wæver is Professor of International Relations at the Institute of Political Science at the University of Copenhagen.

Werner Weidenfeld is Member of the Board of the Bertelsmann Foundation and Director of the Center for Applied Policy Research, Ludwig-Maximilians-University, Munich.

Person Index

Subject Index